Beyond Machismo

Chicana Matters Series
Deena J. González and Antonia Castañeda, series editors

Chicana Matters Series focuses on one of the largest population groups in the United States today, documenting the lives, values, philosophies, and artistry of contemporary Chicanas. Books in this series may be richly diverse, reflecting the experiences of Chicanas themselves, and incorporating a broad spectrum of topics and fields of inquiry. Cumulatively, the books represent the leading knowledge and scholarship in a significant and growing field of research and, along with the literary works, art, and activism of Chicanas, underscore their significance in the history and culture of the United States.

Beyond Machismo

Intersectional Latino Masculinities

AÍDA HURTADO AND MRINAL SINHA

University of Texas Press ⌁ *Austin*

All illustrations courtesy of the authors

Excerpt from "Now Let Us Shift . . . The Path of Conocimiento . . . Inner Work, Public Acts," by Gloria Anzaldúa, in *This Bridge We Call Home: Radical Visions for Transformation*, edited by Gloria E. Anzaldúa and AnaLouise Keating, © 2002 by Gloria E. Anzaldúa and AnaLouise Keating. Reproduced by permission of Taylor and Francis Group, LLC, a division of Informa plc.

Requests for permission to reproduce material from this work should be sent to:
  Permissions
  University of Texas Press
  P.O. Box 7819
  Austin, TX 78713-7819
  utpress.utexas.edu/index.php/rp-form

♾ The paper used in this book meets the minimum requirements of ANSI/NISO Z39.48-1992 (R1997) (Permanence of Paper).

Library of Congress Cataloging-in-Publication Data
Hurtado, Aída, author.
  Beyond machismo : intersectional Latino masculinities / Aída Hurtado and Mrinal Sinha. — First edition.
     pages   cm — (Chicana matters series)
  Includes bibliographical references and index.
  ISBN 978-1-4773-0876-9 (cloth : alk. paper) —
  ISBN 978-1-4773-0877-6 (pbk. : alk. paper) —
  ISBN 978-1-4773-0878-3 (library e-book) —
  ISBN 978-1-4773-0879-0 (nonlibrary e-book)
1. Men—Latin America—Identity.   2. Machismo—Latin America.
3. Masculinity—Social aspects—Latin America.   4. Men—Latin America—
Social conditions.   5. Men—Latin America—Economic conditions.   6. Men—
Education—Latin America.   7. Feminism—United States.   8. Mexican American
women—Ethnic identity.   I. Sinha, Mrinal, author.   II. Title.   III. Series:
Chicana matters series.
  HQ1090.7.L29H87   2016
  305.31098—dc23   2015029050

DEDICATION

Para Daniel Márquez

Y Para

Isaac Torres
Que descansen en paz

Y Para

José G. Hurtado
Who lived to see a new path

Y Para

Don Luis Leal
Caballero, scholar, mentor, an exemplar
of a new Chicano masculinity

Contents

Tables

Preface

One of the most persistent social narratives in our society is the notion of machismo, with its inherent sexism, as a defining feature of all Latino cultures. According to this master narrative (Stewart and Romero 1999) machismo continues to exist in Latino communities in the United States, which are generally perceived as homogeneous in nature, with little internal diversity regardless of differing geographical location, national origin, or educational levels. Many times Latino cultural practices are used as the measure of the liberal sexual and gender attitudes of other nation-states, including the United States. This perception of the Latino population is a powerful representation, not only in the US media but in academic writing as well.

This book challenges the prevailing notions of Latino machismo, sexism, and homogeneity by presenting the narratives of young, educated Latinos living in the United States and by demonstrating how a combination of education, life experiences, and exposure to feminist ideas has contributed to changes in norms, values, and perceptions, not only for our respondents but for their communities as well. The young, educated Latino men presented in this book have grown up in a world in which feminism is a viable framework for understanding culture and gender relations that affords them the opportunity to reconfigure what it means to be a man. The respondents in our study spoke eloquently about the privileges they had as men, as well as their vulnerabilities as they contended with issues of race, ethnicity, sexuality, and class. The respondents also represent the next generation of Latino leaders as all of them at the time of the interviews were attending or had attended institutions of higher education. This book, therefore, sets forth the possibility of feminist masculinities emerging in this generation of Latinos.[1] Furthermore, the analyses presented here, including the writings of Chicana feminists, document the effects feminist movements have had on changing gender norms and privileges that may potentially lead to a men's movement that critically examines and redefines masculinities.

The second contribution of the book is the application of a Chicana feminist Intersectional Theory to the study of Latino masculinities. This approach allows for the simultaneous examination of the advantages Latino men have because of the privileges accorded to masculinities *and* the disadvantages they are subject to because of derogated categories such as class, sexuality, ethnicity, and race. Chicana feminist writings elucidate the process our respondents have undergone that has resulted in a deeper understanding of feminist issues.

A third contribution of this book is a focus on successful, educated Latinos instead of the more frequently examined focus on young Latinos who have not succeeded in the educational system. This emphasis on success rather than failure allows the reader to go beyond the usual narratives describing Latino men as well as other men of Color. Therefore, the lens shifts from Latinos as a social problem to Latinos as contributors to US society.

Another intention of the book is to highlight the nature of cultural change achieved through education. Our respondents eloquently recounted how their perceptions, ideas, and values were transformed through education. But education alone does not explain their transformation on feminist issues; they also attributed these changes to witnessing the hardships experienced by the women in their lives (especially their mothers) and to the Chicana feminist frameworks they were exposed to in their journey through higher education.

Traditionally, scholarly feminist analyses have focused primarily on white men's gender consciousness. Absent are studies that examine Latino men's views on feminisms. This book's theoretical framework facilitates the integration of three areas of research: the interdisciplinary study of masculinities, including the extensive literature using the concept of machismo as an organizing concept; the theoretical and empirical work on Intersectionality as embodied in Social Identities and extended through Anzaldúa's Borderlands Theory; and the writings of Chicana feminists, specifically, the theoretical writings on mestiza consciousness and the writings on the process of conocimiento for personal and political transformations. Together these research areas provide the evidence and direction for identifying new Latino masculinities.

Overview

Chicana feminisms are characterized by "finding absences and exclusions and arguing from that standpoint" (Hurtado 1998b, 135).[2] Arredondo et al. (2003, 2) claim that "Chicana feminist writings move discourse beyond binaries and toward intersectionality and hybridity." Their work is "grounded in our understanding of power as relational" and "working toward an explanatory matrix that confronts the shifting boundaries of discourse and captures ties to lived experiences" (2). The Chicana feminist project aligns itself with Anzaldúa's notion of "Chicanas' bodies as bocacalles. Literally, bocacalle translates as an intersection where two streets cross one another" (Arredondo et al. 2003, 2). Because Chicana feminists speak and live in complex social realities that are constantly crossing borders—physical and metaphorical—they situate their writing in multiple constituencies. Working within this standpoint can be arduous, entailing consideration of multiple debates and critiques. Chicanas strategically engage and move fluidly among different social formations, always risking the consequences of not aligning themselves absolutely with any of them (Arredondo et al. 2003).

This articulation of Chicana feminists' standpoints aptly captures the structure and content of *Beyond Machismo*. The lack of scholarly attention to the complexity of Latino men's experiences qualifies as an "exclusion" to be addressed. Furthermore, in her groundbreaking anthology *Making Face, Making Soul/Haciendo Caras* (1990, xvii–xviii), Gloria Anzaldúa organizes writings by women of Color that reflect what she calls "our fragmented and interrupted dialogue which is said to be discontinued and incomplete discourse" and asks readers to participate "in the making of meaning . . . to connect the dots, the fragments." The analyses in this book are based on three original studies, which we use to follow Anzaldúa's articulation of the purpose of the Chicana feminist project to "connect the dots" and create a "dialogue" that is either "discontinued" or "incomplete" among Latinos, Latinas, and white men. The respondents in all three studies help us understand their experiences at the intersections of their various Social Identities and illuminate (by connecting the dots between their Intersectional Identities and the usefulness of a Chicana feminist intersectional framework) the potential emergence of new Latino masculinities.

The three studies are described in detail in Chapter 1 and were conducted by the authors: the Latino Masculinities Study (LMS), the Chicana Feminisms Study (CFS), and the Brown and White Masculinities

Study (BWMS). Although we use all three studies in this book, the core arguments come from the Latino Masculinities Study. This study was conducted among Latino men and was designed to mirror the Chicana Feminisms Study (presented in *Voicing Chicana Feminisms: Young Women Speak Out on Sexuality and Identity* [Hurtado 2003b]), which was conducted among Latinas of Mexican descent. Both of these studies are based on in-depth qualitative interviews with over 100 respondents of Latino ancestry between the ages of twenty and thirty who had education beyond high school and who hailed from different locations across the United States. In the LMS, the respondents were considered Latino if they had at least one parent of Latin American ancestry. In the CFS, only respondents who had at least one parent of Mexican ancestry were interviewed.

The similarities in research design between the LMS and the CFS allow for important theoretical and empirical comparisons. Although our primary focus is on young Latinos, we take advantage of the research design and the comparability of the data from the two studies. The structure of this book and of *Voicing Chicana Feminisms* permits scholars and educators to use both books in tandem, as two sides of one coin. What do young Latinos and Chicanas think about their lives in the context of their communities, gender socialization, views on feminism, and commitment to social change? How do these young people's intersectional positionings as embodied in their Social Identities of race, class, ethnicity, sexuality, and gender influence their views and behaviors? The reading of *Beyond Machismo* and *Voicing Chicana Feminisms* (Hurtado 2003b) is designed to communicate, dialogue, and theorize about and, ultimately, to bridge the experiences of Latinos and Chicanas through the lens of their multiple and, many times, stigmatized Social Identities.

The third source of data is the Brown and White Masculinities Study, a comparison questionnaire study of Latino and white college-educated men and their views on feminisms. In this questionnaire study we examined men's attitudes toward feminism and political commitments to gender equality quantitatively. Following Arredondo et al. (2003), we consider the three studies (LMS, CFS, BWMS) used in this book as our core empirical glorieta (roundabout) to open up avenidas (avenues) in each chapter to explore different aspects of Latinos' masculinities.

In *Beyond Machismo* we combine methodologies, data sources, and findings from multidisciplinary writings to gain a better understanding of a long-overlooked segment of the Latino male population and to broaden the readers' perspective of Latino men's views on gender relations. We see education and other processes as potential means of fostering a commitment to gender equality and new definitions of Latino masculinities. By documenting these changes, we hope that Latinos will be viewed as complex human beings and that the general perception of them inside and outside the academy will move beyond machismo.

A Word about Our Dedication

We begin this book with a dedication to Daniel Márquez, Isaac Torres, José G. Hurtado, and Don Luis Leal.[3] Don Luis was an internationally recognized scholar who made his last academic home at the University of California, Santa Barbara, in the Department of Chicana and Chicano Studies. Don Luis, as everyone affectionately referred to him, lived a long, healthy, productive, intellectually engaged life and passed away in 2010 at the age of 101. He was also known for his kindness, sense of humor, and mentoring of young men. He represented a masculinity that we are very much in need of, and this book honors that history on which we should build.

José, Aída's only brother, served five years in prison for possessing and selling drugs. After his release, he came to live with Aída and her family and received a bachelor's degree as a reentry student in community studies at the University of California, Santa Cruz. Two years later, he received his master's degree in social work from San José State University.

Unlike Don Luis and José, Daniel and Isaac died young and were unable to fulfill their gifts. Daniel died in a drive-by shooting on August 22, 2005. He was twenty-seven years old and the brother of a respondent in *Voicing Chicana Feminisms*. He was killed less than four miles from the University of California, Santa Cruz campus, the university from which his sister graduated with a bachelor's degree in psychology, where Aída Hurtado built her academic career in psychology, and where Mrinal Sinha completed his doctoral degree in psychology.

Isaac grew up in Newark, New Jersey. He too was connected to the academy. His sister Mellie Torres writes eloquently about the relationship she had with her brother and his tragic death (Torres 2009). Aída Hurtado advised Mellie Torres on her dissertation, and Mellie assisted her on a book covering the topic of Latino men and boys (Noguera, Hurtado, and Fergus 2012). Mellie Torres's dissertation also focuses on young Latinos and their educational vulnerabilities. She received her doctoral degree in education in 2012 from New York University.

Daniel and Isaac had several Intersectional Identities in common with

José: Latino, working class, men, and heterosexual. They also had sisters who considered themselves feminists and were educationally successful: Aída Hurtado and Mellie Torres are professors, and Sandra Marquez is a social worker. The same family and environment that created the educationally successful women also created the circumstances that led to Daniel's and Isaac's deaths and José's incarceration. We propose that Intersectionality connected to Social Identity Theory (SIT) as developed by Chicana feminists and other feminists of Color, facilitates an understanding of José's successful reintegration into and contributions to society. We also trust that Intersectionality Theory will facilitate an understanding of how the systems delineated as successful in José's reintegration failed to help Daniel and Isaac. In fact, Daniel was killed in the same community that saved José from reincarceration.

It is obvious that the presence of a feminist community, supportive familial relationships, and a commitment to feminism are important elements but not sufficient for the successful engagement of young Latinos. Also needed are individuals involved in the day-to-day application of this framework to the intricate dance of survival—the application of mestiza consciousness, the process of conocimiento, the network of caring, the importance of feminist nonprofits in alliance with men's organizations, the inclusion of women in the process of redefining masculinities, the reconstitution of culture and language as a healing practice, and the recentering of treatment for addiction on indigenous practice rather than on Western medical modes of recovery. All have to be coordinated and balanced to produce a successful outcome similar to José's.

Why should we commit such tremendous resources to save one life? Shouldn't individuals be responsible for their own recovery? Shouldn't they pull themselves up by their own proverbial bootstraps? Why should feminists be responsible, again, for the recovery and healing of men— even if those men are family members? Isn't the cost to women high and at the expense of their own development? These questions generate much debate and have no clear-cut answers. We offer one answer, which is in line with a Chicana feminist consciousness: by saving one life we break the cycle of violence, despair, and loss. Another answer lies in Chicana feminist writings, as noted by Jennifer Browdy de Hernández, who wrote the following in a blog post:

> I would say that spiritual activism is any form of engagement with the world undertaken out of love, compassion and the desire to collaborate with others in a common project of highlighting the interconnection of

all beings on our planet, and perhaps in our universe as well. "Love thy neighbor as thyself" and other conventional formulations along these lines contain the essential kernel of spiritual insight, which is that we are all sparks of a divine flame and the positive forces in our world pull us toward unity and harmony and the apprehension of our interbeing.

What makes Gloria Anzaldúa such a wonderful model for spiritual activism and the process of conocimiento (coming to awareness, and then taking action on that new awareness) is that she somehow manages to balance the spiritual and the material, the intellectual and the emotional, the theoretical and the pragmatic. These are the strands she is weaving together so brilliantly in her texts and in her lifework, and we women of the world must take note, and gird ourselves to continue her important project in her absence. (http://womenscrossroads.blogspot .com/2006/01/gloria-anzaldua-personal-is-political.html)

We believe that Chicana feminisms' answer to the question, "Why care?" is that by saving the Josés of the world, we ultimately save ourselves and those we love.

Acknowledgments

We are grateful to our undergraduate research assistants: Luis Acosta, Nancy Aguilar, Olga Aguilar, Angélica Amaral, Perla Cucue, Edyn Fion, Shane Fisher, Adrian Flores, Alejandra González, Dora González, Mariaelana González, Nadia Grosfoguel, Lea Grossman, Leidy Hernández, Corrine Lee, Jacqueline Lima, Patricia López, Geovana Mendoza, América Portillo, Myra Rodríguez, Jasmine Rojas-Bell, Christina Santana, Janelle Silva, Lisette Silva, Carlia Suba, Chanel Treviño-Hurtado, Patricia Valencia, and Jessica Vásquez.

In addition we thank the group of graduate students who met with us on a regular basis to discuss the ideas in this book: Karina Cervántez, Ruby Hernández, Michael Eccleston, Jessica Lopez Lyman, and William Calvo.

We also acknowledge the invaluable input of various colleagues: Dolores Inés Casillas, Norma Cantú, Gerardo Aldana, Chela Sandoval, Ellie Hernández, Victor Rios, Patricia Quijada, Laura Rendón, Rosie Cabrera, Ciel Benedetto, Patricia Gurin, Mike Rotkin, Nane Alejándrez, Luis de Jesús Acosta, and Luis Vega. As always, Kim Loretucci makes our writing better with her magic pen.

A special acknowledgment to Professor Julie Figueroa, who introduced the topic of young Latinos in the academy and the vulnerabilities they face (2002). Her work inspired the beginning of this research project.

A special thanks to Professors Deena J. González and Antonia Castañeda, series editors for the Chicana Matters Series. Their unconditional support made writing this book a pleasure. Also, special thanks to all of the staff at UT Press. We are especially indebted to senior editor Kerry Webb and to editorial assistant Angelica Lopez for their expert guidance in bringing this project to fruition.

Aída Hurtado acknowledges her new campus community at the University of California, Santa Barbara. She thanks colleagues, staff, and graduate students at her new academic home in the Department of Chicana and Chicano Studies, all of whom make her happy to come to work in a department that she loves. She also acknowledges the support of Melvin L. Oliver, SAGE Sara Miller McCune Dean of Social Sciences and Executive Dean of the College of Letters and Sciences. He welcomed her to campus and has always acknowledged her contributions. Thank you to Chancellor Henry T. Yang for his unconditional support for the ethnic studies departments and for always taking the time to write personal notes thanking us for our accomplishments.

In addition, Aída Hurtado acknowledges the financial and spiritual support of the Luis Leal Endowed Chair. Professor Luis Leal left behind a vision of ethical and substantive scholarship, compassionate leadership, and, above all, a commitment to future generations of Chicana/o students and scholars. Professor Hurtado is deeply honored to hold the endowed chair whose namesake is one of the most revered names in the academy in the United States and beyond.

As always, we also thank our families, who are with us through thick and thin: Craig Haney, Arcelia Hurtado, José G. Hurtado, María Hurtado, Lynne Haney, Erin Haney, Matt Haney, Chanel Treviño-Hurtado, Tristan Tapokai, Joaquín Guadalupe Hurtado Solís, Sisto Guadalupe Hurtado Solís, Monu Priyadarshini Sinha, Kunal Sinha, and Urvashi Sinha. We are deeply grateful to our fathers, Guadalupe Hurtado and Upendra Nath Sinha, for being the pioneers of new masculinities, and to our mothers, Magdalena Hurtado and Mrinalini Sinha, who were the unnamed feminists who carried all these changes forward.

Introduction

Arredondo et al. (2003, 2–3) propose that one of the best

> metaphor[s] for capturing the multiple engagements by Chicana femi-
> nists is of women living and working in an intellectual *glorieta* (a round-
> about), a space that centers on the Chicana experience and is a stand-
> point from which we engage in dialogue with different audiences and
> participants. The *avenidas* that we face in a glorieta allow Chicana femi-
> nists to make assessments of power in relation to our varied locations.
> Like a Mexico City glorieta, the dialogue is fast-paced, fluid, and flex-
> ible, at times unnerving; it forces intellectual dexterity. Such agility is
> foundational to the Chicana feminist political project, which intervenes
> in important ways to raise consciousness and further the struggle for
> decolonization against multiple oppressions.

In this book we use three studies that focus on a different bocacalle, or intersection (using Arredondo et al.'s metaphor), creating a new avenida out of the glorieta with the goal of deconstructing the oppressive aspects of masculinity to permit new ways of being a Latino man and thereby, ultimately, "further[ing] the struggle for decolonization against mul-tiple oppressions" (Arredondo et al. 2003, 3). We trust that each avenida we propose will also generate dialogue and advance the study of Latino masculinities.

A Word on Race and Ethnic Labels and the Use of Spanish

Before we provide an overview of the book and the different intersections examined in each of the chapters, we want to clarify the use of ethnic/race labels and the use of Spanish.

Race

In *Beyond Machismo* we use the phrase *people of Color* to refer to Chicanos/as, Latino/as, Asians, Native Americans, and Blacks, all of whom are racialized groups in US society. Therefore, we capitalize *Color* because it refers to specific ethnic groups. We also capitalize *Black* following the argument that it refers not merely to skin pigmentation but also to a "heritage, an experience, a cultural and personal identity, the meaning of which becomes specifically stigmatic and/or glorious and/or ordinary under specific social conditions. It is socially created as, and at least in the American context no less specifically meaningful or definitive than, any linguistic, tribal, or religious ethnicity, all of which are conventionally recognized by capitalization" (MacKinnon 1982, 516). The term *white* is lowercased because it refers not to one ethnic group or to specified ethnic groups but to many. One of the three studies used in this book is the Brown and White Masculinities Study (BWMS), and in that study we followed this capitalization convention.

Ethnicity

Different groups of people whose origins are from Latin America and who reside in the United States have many labels available to them to identify their ethnicity. Some labels refer to the specific country of origin (e.g., Mexican, Salvadorian, and Nicaraguan). Other labels correspond to US geographic location and emphasize regionally specific identities and cultural practices, for example, *Tejano* (Texan) and *Californiano* (Californian). In some cases, labels serve political functions and can be indicative of views regarding cultural assimilation. Examples of such labels include *Chicana/o* for those of Mexican descent and *Boricua* for Puerto Ricans. Both terms communicate cultural pride and awareness regarding the hybridity of cultural practices and language use in these US communities. Other labels, for example, *Latino/a*, emphasize the importance of expressing cultural and political solidarity with other Latin American national groups. History, however, is central to all of these choices.

Ethnic labeling for Latinos/as is linked to each group's historical trajectory (Hurtado and Roa 2005). Of special significance is the history of colonization suffered by various groups of Color. As Comas-Díaz (2000, 1319–1320) states, "As conquered enemies, Native Americans, African Americans, Latinos, and Asian Americans have been subjected to repression by the U.S. government, which has designated them as savages, slaves, and colonized entities." For Puerto Ricans, the relationship between Puerto Rico as a protectorate of the United States with no official representation in the US government also influences the group's ethnic identification. Mostly because of economic necessity, large numbers of island residents, who are legally US citizens, have historically migrated from Puerto Rico, mainly to New York City. The migration from their home country, where they are national citizens, to the mainland, where they have the status of "labor migrants," disrupts cultural patterns and social norms developed in their native country as well as their ethnic identification (Hurtado and Cervántez 2009, 178–179). For example, when many Puerto Ricans arrive in the United States and become politicized about their colonized status, they use the ethnic label *Boricua*, derived from the Taíno word *Boriken*, to illustrate their recognition of the island's indigenous Taíno heritage (Minority Rights Group International 2005).

For people of Mexican descent, the colonization of the Southwest territories that belonged to Mexico at the end of the Mexican-American War in 1848 was a pivotal moment in creating the group's inferior status in the United States. With the signing of the Treaty of Guadalupe Hidalgo to end the war, Mexico lost almost half of its territory, including what is now California, New Mexico, Arizona, Nevada, Utah, and parts of Wyoming and Colorado. Mexican nationals lost their Mexican citizenship and became culturally and linguistically conquered in their own land (Flores-Ortiz 2004).

Alvarez (1973) delineates four historical periods and generational modes of dealing with their history of colonization that are tied to the ways people of Mexican descent define themselves. The Creation Generation (1848–1900), in light of its loss of Mexican citizenship and homeland through conquest, struggled to maintain a sense of self as Mexican. Members of the Migrant Generation (1900–1942) fled Mexico's economic problems and related political upheavals. They also identified primarily as Mexican as they joined older generations in what was previously Mexican territory. Therefore, for the Creation Generation and the Migrant Generation, being Mexican remained the most salient ethnic identification.

The Mexican-American Generation (1942–1966) was more concerned with dual identifications. The participation of people of Mexican descent in World War II precipitated a strengthened loyalty to the United States, as did the newfound prosperity brought about by the economic expansion that accompanied and followed the war. It became a cultural practice to add the term *American* to the term *Mexican* to define one's identity.

The Chicano Generation (1966–present) is the most economically stable, affluent, and educated group of people of Mexican descent. This generation developed a critique of their parents' loyalty to the United States and created a new identity that was neither Mexican nor accepting of being a hyphenated American. Calling themselves Chicanos and Chicanas was to claim the commingling of US and Mexican culture, language, and social norms to create a new US-based identity—neither fully Mexican nor fully of the United States (Gurin, Hurtado, and Peng 1994). The Chicano movement for civil rights in the 1960s adopted as its cornerstone the right to assert Chicano/a identity and to be of the United States without abandoning Mexican origins. A Chicano/a identity does not accept cultural and linguistic assimilation into the US mainstream as the only avenue for claiming full US citizenship.

This complex history dovetails with the Chicana feminist literature (Hurtado 2003b) that proclaims the label *Chicana* as a political move to highlight an in-between existence in multiple social, economic, and cultural systems. The ethnic label *Chicana* has come to signify the celebration of hybridity and a political assertion through the restitution of self, a self constructed in the interstices of two countries, cultures, and languages (Hurtado 2003b). In the Chicana Feminisms Study, the second of the three studies used in this book, *Chicana* was defined as someone with at least one parent of Mexican descent (Hurtado 2003b). *Chicana* was used because the theoretical framework for the study was explicitly situated in the historical context that produced the Chicana feminist literature that self-consciously labeled itself *Chicana*. Chicana feminisms is a field of study positioned in the Mexican American experience of the US colonization of the Mexican Southwest territories. Consequently, even if not all of the respondents in the CFS claimed the ethnic label *Chicana*, inadvertently, through their lives, they were claiming the intellectual, cultural, and political spaces created by Chicana feminist scholarship (Hurtado 2003b).

The ethnic label *Hispanic*, on the other hand, is a panethnic label for all people of Latin American ancestry residing in the United States. It is viewed by many as emphasizing a European heritage while ignoring the population's indigenous and African roots. Unlike other ethnic labels, *Hispanic* originated in the US government rather than emerging organically from different US Latino/a communities (Hurtado and Gurin 2004).[1] Identification as Hispanic has been associated with individuals aspiring to upward mobility and has been argued to imply acceptance of the stratification system (Hurtado and Gurin 1987). The ethnic label *Hispanic* holds currency on the East Coast and, more recently, in Texas. For these reasons, we use the term *Hispanic* only when citing reports that use this ethnic label in their discussion of Latina/o issues.

In contrast to *Hispanic*, *Latino* and *Latina* are panethnic labels that are commonly understood as claiming solidarity with anyone of Latin American heritage. In the third study used in this book, the Latino Masculinities Study (LMS), we defined *Latino* as any respondent with at least one parent of Latin American ancestry.

In many ways, the panethnic labels *Latino/a* and *Hispanic* are meta-identities; they are used for the political, social, and economic recognition of various Latin American ancestry groups. As meta-identities there are no Hispanic or Latino/a cultural groups, as Hurtado, Cervántez, and Eccleston (2009, 293) note: "These panethnic labels, however, are not yet tied to a new ethnic group that has indeed emerged from the intermarriage and co-mingling of different Latino/a cultures and language. In many ways, Latino/a panethnicity is a meta-identity that is deployed for political, social, and economic recognition of a variety of Latino/a groups, with the largest group being Mexican ancestry, followed by Puerto Ricans and Cuban Americans. Other Central American groups, like Guatemalans and Salvadorians, are smaller in number."

Regardless of the internal diversity of these different groups, the political and social realities they face have much in common, making the labels *Latino/a* and *Hispanic* real in their consequences. Further, the similarities in language and culture across Latin American countries are such that the panethnic labels are based on commonalities sufficiently powerful to warrant their use (Hurtado, Cervántez, and Eccleston 2009).

The ethnic labels of other Latino groups such as Cubans and Central Americans reflect an immigrant experience because they were not colonized through war or conquest. Most members of these groups prefer their national identities when naming themselves and choose a panethnic label such as *Hispanic* or *Latino/a*, depending on the region of the country.

The use of ethnic labels also varies based on social context and is related to language competence (Hurtado and Arce 1987). For example, when interacting with older family members such as grandparents, a US-born man of Mexican descent may communicate primarily in Spanish and identify as Mexicano while simultaneously identifying as Chicano when interacting in English with his Mexican-descent peers at the university. The same person, when interacting with members of out-groups, for example, whites, may identify as Latino in order to avoid confusion with those who lack familiarity with the meanings embedded in the label *Chicano*. The context-specific choices of ethnic labeling highlight the heterogeneity in Latina/o communities and the diversity in their deployment. Because ethnic labels have historically, regionally, and culturally specific dimensions, the meaning imputed to the labels can vary based on who is involved in the interaction, the language being spoken, and geographical location.

It is important to note that the way we use ethnic labels in this book is consistent with Spanish-language conventions. Gender is indicated in many of these labels by the vowel at the end of the word. Labels ending in *a* indicate female, whereas labels ending in *o* indicate male. Similarly to English-language conventions, in Spanish the generic is usually male. In an effort to avoid sexism in language use, many scholars use Chican*os/as* or Chican*as/os*. Some writers elect to use the female (e.g., Latin*a*) as a generic to raise gender consciousness. Others switch randomly between female and male to equalize language use (Hurtado 2003b). Here, we use the term *Chicano* to refer to men (in conjunction with the theoretical underpinnings described above). We use *Latinos/as* as a more inclusive term that includes Mexican-origin as well as other people of Latin American descent.

Spanish Use

We are intentional in the ways we use Spanish and English in this book. We do not italicize Spanish words because Spanish is not a foreign language in the context of the history of colonization of Mexican Americans in what is now the US Southwest. We have chosen to follow Dolores Inés Casillas's (2014) admonition to respect the integrity of Spanish use in the United States by equating its use with English, which is obviously not italicized: "I have chosen not to signal to the reader by way of italics when Spanish is written, since, in my opinion, this supports U.S.-based class, racial, and linguistic hierarchies, particularly in regard to Spanish. The visually marked difference to reflect the shift from English to Spanish interrupts the flow of the text. It assumes that readers are monolingual in English. It differentiates the Spanish while affirming English as the norm. I privilege the bilingual reader by refusing to italicize the Spanish" (2014, xiii).

We turn now to summarizing the chapters and elaborating on the different aspects of Intersectionality Theory covered in each chapter.

Overview of *Beyond Machismo* and the Intersections Examined

We begin in chapter 1 by providing a detailed description of each of the three studies: the Latino Masculinities Study, the Chicana Feminisms Study, and the Brown and White Masculinities Study. Paramount in our theoretical emphasis on intersectionality is the description of the research design, the sociodemographic characteristics of the three samples of respondents, and the main focus in each study.

In chapter 2 we review the most recent developments in Intersectionality Theory and the influence of Chicana feminist writings on this framework, thereby providing a theoretical foundation for subsequent chapters. Additionally, we offer our expanded interpretation of Intersectionality, which we link with Borderland Theory as proposed by Gloria Anzaldúa and developed in Chicana feminist writings. We bridge Borderland Theory and Intersectionality through the social-psychological framework found in Social Identity Theory as proposed by British social psychologist Henri Tajfel and his colleagues. We conclude by illustrating how our theoretical expansion of Intersectionality Theory facilitates the examination of Latinos' views on feminism and the potential deconstruction of the oppressive aspects of masculinities. Our theoretical lens also permits the examination of political collaborations across difference to create progressive alliances that will initiate more equitable social and political arrangements than those that currently exist.

Chapter 3 explores a subsample of respondents from the Latino Masculinities Study who self-identified as feminist and who declared their class background while growing up as working class or poor. We focus on these qualitative data from LMS respondents' answers to the open-ended question, "What does the word 'manhood' mean to you?" Answering the question required respondents to take into account how their race, sexuality, ethnicity, and social class intersected with their concept of manhood. The respondents spoke eloquently and freely about their definitions of manhood and how all their Social Identities influenced them. Rather than mentioning each Social Identity separately, they defined manhood in relational terms and embedded it in rich, textured narratives that, depending on the topic, made one or another social identity intersection salient. This chapter focuses on gender, social class, race, and ethnicity and whether individuals ascribing to this constellation of Intersectional Identities go beyond machismo in defining manhood for themselves and for the men they admire.

In chapter 4 we use qualitative data from the LMS and the CFS doctoral students who were part of the larger samples. We take advantage of the flexibility facilitated by Intersectionality to examine similarities and differences between Intersectional Identity Constellations, as well as the flexibility of subsamples by using two studies designed to mirror each other. Our purpose was to focus on the highest achieving Latino men and women in both studies to explore the intersectional context (or background) of their gender socialization and its effects on educational achievement. By holding constant two social identities—ethnicity (all respondents were Latino/a) and race (all respondents were racially mestizo)—we were able to focus on the intersectional node of gender (young men versus young women) and on the differences in parental messages about educational achievement given to doctoral students and whether this affected their educational pathways.

In chapter 5 we address the following questions using quantitative questionnaire data derived from the Brown and White Masculinities Study: (1) What are the components that underlie Latino and white men's attitudes toward gender and feminism? (2) How do the structure and content of these components differ across ethnicity, race, and class lines? (3) How does using the theoretical paradigm of Intersectionality as proposed by Chicana feminists help explain potential commonalities and differences in the component structure and content of Latino and white men's views on gender and feminisms?

In the BWMS we used attitudinal statements requiring responses from *strongly agree* to *strongly disagree* to ask college-educated Latino and white male respondents their views on gender norms and feminisms. These quantitative data were investigated using factor analysis to determine whether Latino and white men held different gender and feminist attitudes. In this chapter we look at the Intersectional Identity Constellation of gender, race, and ethnicity by focusing on Latino and white men's views on feminisms and, given all men's access to patriarchal privilege, the similarities. We delineate in this chapter the dimensions Latino men have in common with white men and highlight how Latino men's experience of a "lesser" masculinity (Connell 1995) affects their beliefs about gender inequality.

In chapter 6, we use qualitative data from the LMS to explore respondents' definitions of feminisms and their commitments to political action in behalf of gender issues. We selected a subsample of the respondents who identified as feminists and who stated that they considered themselves as working class or poor while growing up. We examine the answers to the questions posed to the respondents in the LMS: "Do you consider yourself a feminist?" and "If so, why?" In answering these two questions, respondents revealed the complexity of their life histories as a consequence of their intersectional existence. First, we provide a qualitative analysis of the respondents' definitions of feminisms followed by their reasons for considering themselves feminists. We also identify some possible influences on Latino men's commitment to feminist ideas. We conclude with the respondents' views on forming political collaborations with women to work in behalf of Latino and women's issues in the future.

By applying Borderlands Theory to this particular Intersectional Identity Constellation, we find that many Latinos manage the disjuncture created by their Intersectional Social Identities (say, ethnicity—being Latino) and gender (being male) in creative and politically progressive ways. In many instances, respondents gained a deeper understanding of social reality, which led to a commitment to social justice. We address the question of how oppression at the intersections of race, ethnicity, social class, and sexuality contributes to the deconstruction of Latino masculinities and potentially develops a feminist consciousness. We have found that an intersectional analysis permits the possibility of *Latino feminist masculinities* that can form alliances with feminism to fight sexism and homophobia, and even to subvert the privileges of patriarchy.

In chapter 7, we provide a case study of José Hurtado, a Latino man, and his journey to reintegrate into his family and society after incarceration. Anzaldúa's process of conocimiento helped interrupt masculinist socialization by teaching, from an intersectional viewpoint, alternative modes of behavior through family, friendships, and community. Conocimiento applies an intersectional perspective on gender socialization by addressing stigmatized Social Identities and helping individuals reach a new level of consciousness to avert masculinist negative adaptations.

We conclude by highlighting the application of Chicana Intersectionality to propose a plan of action for developing a critical men's movement that may result in reconfiguring masculinities and, potentially, dismantling the most egregious aspects of patriarchy. As the African American feminist writer bell hooks (2000) alerts us, "feminism is for everybody," not just for women. That "everybody" includes Latino men.

CHAPTER 1

Beyond Machismo: The Research Context

In the popular imaginary, the word *machismo* has become the social signifier of all that is male chauvinism. The use of a Spanish word has cast an entire hemisphere as the epitome of male patriarchal privilege and small-mindedness. In view of such intense cultural overlay, it may seem nonsensical to pursue the study of Latino men's views on gender. Such a study may seem on its face to propose a ridiculous divergence from the popular views of Latino masculinities. The overemphasis on machismo—or male domination of women (and some men)—is not only a popular bias but one to which even scholarly analysis has succumbed. A thorough review of the scholarly literature on Latino masculinities, both in the United States (e.g., Mirandé 1997) and in Latin America (e.g., Gutmann 2003), reveals that few concepts beyond machismo have been adequately explored. Recognizing this void, we have developed three studies to explore many other areas of Latino masculinities.

Masculinity Studies

The field of masculinity studies is no exception in exploring Latinos' views of manhood primarily through the concept of machismo (Bilmes 1992; Strong, McQuillen, and Hughey 1994; Tombs 2002). Indeed, with few exceptions (Almaguer 2004; Baca Zinn 1982), the concentration has been on delineating the negative (Bilmes 1992; Strong, McQuillen, and Hughey 1994; Tombs 2002) or the positive (Mirandé 1997) aspects of machismo. As proposed by Chicana feminist writers (Baca Zinn 1982; Hurtado 2003b) Latinos, like other men, are complex individuals embracing much more than their gender; each Latino belongs to other social formations embodied in his Social Identities.

In the United States, the number of masculinity studies on men of Color is not extensive. Although Black masculinities have received in-depth analysis in a few studies, most of this scholarly attention has not been developed within an elaborate theoretical framework. The majority of these studies have been characterized by a framework that implies "either/or thinking" (P. Collins 1991, 376–377). These projects have focused exclusively on the subordination experienced by Black men due to race or class (and, infrequently, sexuality) or to their gender-based privilege. Men of Color have been cast either as victims or as victimizers, with little attention to the space in between or what Emma Pérez terms "third space" existence (1999, 33). Because only minimal research has examined Latinos, they have yet to enter this intellectual dialogue (Noguera, Hurtado, and Fergus 2012).

As a whole, the field of masculinity studies has lagged behind feminist theorizing. Latino men occupy a contradictory position within a system of privilege, one that offers them advantages but concurrently disadvantages those belonging to devalued social categories, that is, men who come from working-class backgrounds, who are immigrants, who speak Spanish, who often look racially nonwhite, who have a Latino background, and who may be gay—all statuses that contribute to experiencing racism, ethnocentrism, classism, and heterosexism. Although men as a group are privileged by patriarchal structures, all men do not share in the privileges equally (Connell 1995). In some cases, the disadvantages increase because of the convergence of these categorical assignments.

A number of studies have explored the racial disadvantage experienced by African American men (Franklin 1987; Majors and Billson 1992) and boys (Ferguson 2000), the class-based oppression felt by white men (Archer, Pratt, and Phillips 2001; Fine et al. 1997; Pyke 1996), and the heterosexism imposed on white men (Anderson 2005; Nardi 2000). However, few investigators have examined the ways in which queer sexualities converge with masculinities, race, and ethnicity, particularly among gay Latino men (Almaguer 2004; L. Cantú 2000, 2004).

Examining the views of gay Latino men toward gender is especially important, given the manner in which culturally dominant forms of masculinities function in the United States. Because of their sexuality, gay men are many times explicitly excluded from the category of "real" men. This point is exemplified in the assertion that gay men represent the repository of all that is feminine within the gender order (Connell 1995). In other words, gay men are subordinated to heterosexual men and relegated to an inferior social position because of their sexuality; race, ethnicity, and social class can further complicate this ranking. Therefore, it is imperative to examine how queer sexualities interact with race and ethnicity to influence views of manhood (and gender) as well as other social inequalities based on multiple stigmatized Social Identities.

Latino Men and Feminist Consciousness

The experience of multiple oppressions, which varies based on social context, may, in theory, facilitate the development of a consciousness about the denigrated position of a Latino/a group affiliation in society. In essence, masculinities are constructed in complex ways at the intersections of race, ethnicity, social class, and sexuality. When some of these Social Identities are derogated, they may interact with various forms of masculinities in ways that make gender-based privilege problematic. In other words, Latinos' experience of oppression due to race, class, and sexuality may provide insights into and empathy regarding the nature of women's oppression and can have profound consequences for the development of a feminist consciousness in men.

Although men cannot experience women's patriarchal oppression firsthand, imagination, as described by Adu-Poku (2001, 163), makes it possible for some men to gain an understanding of women's standing within the gender order. Stoetzler and Yuval-Davis (2002) argue that, much like knowledge, imagination is socially situated based on one's location in the social hierarchy. Latino men's material experience of oppression based on race and class can have a profound role in shaping their imagination, particularly in relation to women's oppression. For example, because Latino men are disproportionately overrepresented in the lower economic strata of society (Hoynes, Page, and Stevens 2005), many are raised in working-class neighborhoods where violence is prevalent as a result of limited economic opportunities (Canada 1995; Greene, Haney, and Hurtado 2000; Wacquant 2001). Latino men may have sisters who live in the same environment and who may have experienced disadvantages such as sexual harassment and violence at the hands of men. Observing their sisters' experience of patriarchy may mobilize their imagination and create empathy.

Empathy is especially likely when coupled with feelings of love and compassion based on familial ties. According to Tajfel (1981), empathy for women's experience can create a "conflict of values" when dominant group members, in this case Latino men, perceive their higher position in the social hierarchy as illegitimate. This conflict of values can propel privileged individuals to "exit" the dominant group and join subordinate ones in the struggle for social justice (Tajfel 1981). Hurtado and Gurin (2004, 63) conceptualize this social and political process as "renunciation of privilege." However, material experiences in many cases require what Adu-Poku (2001, 159) calls "a transformative process" in order for feminist consciousness to develop. Exposure to critical thinking through education can be one mechanism facilitating this transformative process, a process identified in empirical examinations as facilitating the development of men's feminist consciousness.

Education has been conceptualized as a factor leading to the questioning of societal arrangements, gender, and power. In the case of Latino men, education can have profound implications for reevaluating and interpreting experiences, both past and present. It can facilitate awareness of how power defines relationships with others, especially when those relationships cross lines of difference based on race, ethnicity, gender, social class, and sexuality. An awareness of the arbitrary nature of power can lead to evaluating the legitimacy of subordinate social positions or to questioning the legitimacy of one's own privileged status. For Latino men, this amounts to perceiving previously unconscious male privilege and the deconstruction of machismo as a culturally specific form of hegemonic masculinity. The impetus for the questioning and deconstruction of machismo (and other hegemonic forms of masculinities) can be traced back to experiences which are systematically denied to certain groups of people (such as relationships and dialogue with others belonging to stigmatized groups and formal education) (Gurin, Nagda, and Zúñiga 2013). Our goal in this book is to make these experiences visible and, ultimately, utilitarian, thereby perpetuating the deconstruction of all forms of domination.

Overview of Studies Used

Chicana feminists have written prolifically about the development of feminist consciousness among Chicanas and other Latinas (Hurtado 2003b, 2009). These writers have delineated the importance of material experiences organized around multiple axes of oppression (e.g., race, class, ethnicity, gender, sexuality, physical ableness), in-group solidarity among Chicanas and Latinas, and exposure to the transformative power of higher education (Hurtado 2003b). However, few empirical studies have examined the development of feminist consciousness among men (Christian 1994; Vicario 2003), and even fewer among men of Color (White 2008).

The impact of academic feminist theory has not "hit the streets" in any significant way among Chicanas; however, the same can be said for Latino men. Access to higher education, though, is one of several avenues that can allow women and men to engage in dialogue and become informed by feminist discourses. Exposure to scholarship in feminist and ethnic studies increases the likelihood of having firsthand knowledge of feminist writings (Hurtado 2003b) and decreases the likelihood of relying on the (mis) perceptions and feminist stereotypes in the popular media (Griffin 1989). With the new perspectives provided by higher education, young educated men who identify as Latino are more likely to be exposed to, and even better equipped to articulate, feminist viewpoints.

The Chicana Feminisms Study (CFS) and the Latino Masculinities Study (LMS) were designed to assess young Chicanas' and Latinos' views on gender relations and feminisms. Both studies fill the void in the literature about how educated Latinos and Latinas are changing the landscape of gender relations in their communities and beyond.

We turn now to a description of the three studies used in this book: the Latino Masculinities Study, the Chicana Feminisms Study, and the Brown and White Masculinities Study.

The Latino Masculinities Study

We use multiple sources of empirical data for our analysis and conclusions about new Latino masculinities. However, our primary source is the LMS, which was designed to mirror the CFS, highlighted in *Voicing Chicana Feminisms* (Hurtado 2003b). In the LMS we asked Latino men the same questions (with a few exceptions) that were asked of Chicanas in the CFS. In both studies we questioned respondents extensively on the socialization practices of their families, their significant Social Identities (including social class while growing up, gender, race, sexuality, and ethnicity), their views on feminism, the attributions contributing to their educational success, and their commitment to work on behalf of feminist issues and other political causes. In the CFS, Hurtado interviewed 101 Chicanas, defined as women who had at least one parent of Mexican descent (Hurtado 2003b, 22). The respondents were between the ages of twenty and thirty, with some education beyond high school. The study was situated in the framework provided by the Chicana feminist literature.

For the LMS we used the same sampling rationale as in the CFS by drawing from a population that had experienced higher education and had explicitly identified themselves as Latino. As with the CFS, the sample was nationally nonrepresentative, in this case consisting of 105 Latinos interviewed in the West and Southwest (Arizona, California, Colorado, New Mexico, and Texas), the Midwest (Illinois and Michigan), and the East (Massachusetts, New York City, and Washington, DC) (see table 1.1).

Respondents' Backgrounds

Our sample of 105 respondents was relatively young, with ages ranging from nineteen to thirty-three, with an average age of twenty-four. The majority of respondents were attending institutions of higher education (78 percent, 82 respondents) at the time of the interview. Most of the students were undergraduates (54 percent, 57 respondents), either in community colleges (10 percent, 11 respondents) or in four-year universities (44 percent, 46 total); the remainder (24 percent, 25 respondents) were enrolled in graduate (20 percent, 21 respondents) and professional schools (4 percent, 4 respondents), including doctoral programs (none of the respondents had completed their doctoral degrees at the time of the interview). Respondents were attending a wide range of institutions, including community colleges, state schools, and private universities (see table 1.2). Most respondents were single (94 percent, 99 respondents); only 5 respondents were married (3 of whom had children), and one respondent was single and had a child.

The sample was largely of Mexican descent (72 percent, 76 respondents), while the remaining respondents were primarily of Puerto Rican (4 percent, 4 respondents), Central American (2 percent, 2 respondents), or South American descent (7 percent, 7 respondents). The remainder was of mixed ethnicity (15 percent, 16 respondents), with no single ethnicity prevailing. The most common combinations were Mexican and white ancestry, which was reported by 19 percent (3 respondents) of the respondents, and Puerto Rican with another ancestry, which was reported by 31 percent (5 respondents) of the respondents (table 1.3). Most respondents were born in the United States (87 percent, 91 respondents), and those who had immigrated (13 percent, 14 respondents) had done so before the age of 11. These immigrants came from Mexico, El Salvador, Colombia, Bolivia, and Peru.

Almost half of the respondents identified themselves as being poor (24 percent, 25 respondents) or from a working-class background (25 per-

Table 1.1. Location of Latino Masculinities Study interviews

Interview location	Number of respondents (N = 105)
Arizona	
Phoenix	2
Scottsdale	2
California	
Berkeley	1
Davenport	1
Marina	11
Oakland	1
Palo Alto	1
Salinas	1
San Francisco	3
San Jose	2
Santa Cruz	9
Colorado	
Boulder	3
Illinois	
Chicago	11
Mundelein	1
Wheeling	2
Massachusetts	
Boston	4
Cambridge	2
Michigan	
Ann Arbor	8
New Mexico	
Albuquerque	9
New York	
New York City	7
Texas	
San Antonio	17
Washington, DC	7

Table 1.2. Educational institutional affiliations of Latino Masculinities Study respondents

Institution	Number of respondents (N = 105)
Arizona State University	
Undergraduate	4
Boston College	
Undergraduate	2
Cabrillo Community College (CA)	
Undergraduate	2
California State University, Monterey Bay	
Undergraduate	8
City University of New York	
Master's program in urban planning	1
College of Mount Saint Vincent (NY)	
Undergraduate	1
DePaul University (IL)	
Master's program in sociology	1
Undergraduate	1
George Washington University (DC)	
Master's program in education administration	1
Undergraduate	2
Georgetown University (DC)	
Master's program in communication, culture, and technology	1
La Guardia Community College (NY)	
Undergraduate	1
Massachusetts Institute of Technology	
Undergraduate	4
Northwestern University (IL)	
Undergraduate	2
Palo Alto Community College (TX)	
Undergraduate	1
Roosevelt University (IL)	
Undergraduate	1
San Antonio Community College (TX)	
Undergraduate	4
San Francisco State University (CA)	
Master's program in ethnic studies	1
San Jose City Community College (CA)	
Undergraduate	2
Stanford University (CA)	
Doctoral program in comparative literature	1

Table 1.2. *Continued*

Institution	Number of respondents (N = 105)
Triton Community College (IL)	
Undergraduate	1
University of California, Berkeley	
Doctoral program in zoology	1
Doctoral program in comparative literature	2
Doctoral program in chemistry	1
University of California, Santa Cruz	
Doctoral program in psychology	1
Doctoral program in sociology	2
Doctoral program in engineering	1
Undergraduate	3
University of Chicago	
Medical school	1
Doctoral program in anthropology	1
Master's program in public policy	1
Undergraduate	1
University of Colorado, Boulder	
Undergraduate	3
University of Illinois, Chicago	
Undergraduate	1
University of Michigan	
Medical School	1
Doctoral program in sociology	1
Law school	1
Master's program in architecture	1
Master's program in public health	1
Undergraduate	3
University of New Mexico	
Law school	1
Master's program in Latin American studies	1
Master's program in community and regional planning	1
Undergraduate	5
University of Texas, Austin	
Undergraduate	2
University of Texas, San Antonio	
Undergraduate	3
Not enrolled in school at time of interview	23

Table 1.3. Ethnicity of Latino Masculinities Study respondents

Ethnicity (by descent)	Number of respondents (N = 105)
Mexican	76
Puerto Rican	4
Salvadorian	2
Peruvian	2
Colombian	2
Bolivian	2
Ecuadorian	1
Mixed (father/mother)	
Mexican/Armenian	1
Filipino/Mexican	1
Nicaraguan/Chinese	1
White/Mexican	1
Mexican/Salvadorian	1
Mexican/white	2
Cuban/white	1
Dominican/Cuban	1
Puerto Rican/Dominican	1
Ecuadorian/Puerto Rican	1
Peruvian/Puerto Rican	1
Chilean/Puerto Rican	1
Dominican/Ecuadorian	1
Puerto Rican/Canadian	1
Jewish/Mexican	1

cent, 26 respondents). The rest of the respondents identified themselves as coming from the lower (10 percent, 11 respondents), middle (34 percent, 36 respondents), or upper-middle class (7 percent, 7 respondents). None identified themselves as upper class or rich (see table 1.4).

Most of the respondents grew up in households with both parents present (86 percent, 90 respondents), but some grew up in households in which only the mother was present (10 percent, 11 respondents; see table 1.5). Grandparents raised 3 of our respondents, and an aunt raised one.

The educational level of the two-parent households was as follows: 40 percent (36) of the fathers and 36 percent (32) of the mothers had less than a high school education; 18 percent (16) of the fathers and 24 percent (22) of the mothers had completed high school; and 14 percent (13) of the fathers and 18 percent (16) of the mothers had attended some college (several earned an associate's degree but did not complete a bachelor's). Nineteen percent of the parents had earned a bachelor's degree (9 percent [8] of the fathers and 10 percent [9] of the mothers), and 17 percent (15) of the fathers and 12 percent (11) of the mothers had graduate or professional degrees (see table 1.6). Of the eleven households in which only mothers were present, 3 of the mothers had less than a high school education, one had completed high school, 2 had attended some college but did not complete a bachelor's degree, 3 had a bachelor's degree, one had a professional degree, and one had a law degree.

For respondents growing up in two-parent households (90), parents' workforce participation rates were high (see table 1.7). Seventy-one percent (64) of the fathers and 83 percent (75) of the mothers worked outside the home. The remaining mothers stayed at home (7) or stayed at home

Table 1.4. Social-class identification of Latino Masculinities Study respondents

Social-class identification	Number of respondents (N = 105)
Poor	25
Working class	26
Lower middle class	11
Middle class	36
Upper middle class	7

Table 1.5. Household composition during childhood, Latino Masculinities Study respondents

Household type	Number of respondents (N = 105)
Two-parent	90
Mother-headed	11
Nonparent family member-headed	4

Table 1.6. Parents' educational level, two-parent households, Latino Masculinities Study respondents

Education level	Number of fathers (N = 90)	Number of mothers (N = 90)
Less than high school	36	32
Completed high school	16	22
Some college, no degree	12	12
Associate's degree	1	4
Bachelor's degree	8	9
Master's degree	8	7
Doctoral degree	4	1
Professional degree	2	3
Law degree	1	0
No data	2	0

Table 1.7. Parents' work status, two-parent households, Latino Masculinities Study respondents

Work status	Number of fathers (N = 90)	Number of mothers (N = 90)
Worked outside the home	64	75
Stayed home, worked on the side	0	4
Stayed home	3	7
Retired	12	3
Disabled/health issues	2	0
Deceased	9	1

and worked on the side (4); several had retired (3), and one had passed away. Some fathers did not work because they had retired (12), and 2 had a disability/health issue (see table 1.7). Of the fathers present while the respondents were growing up, 10 percent (9) were deceased at the time the respondents were interviewed, a relatively high number for respondents in their twenties and early thirties.

In the households in which only the mother was present, workforce participation was also high. Nine worked outside the home, one was deceased at the time of the interviews, and one did not work because of health issues (see table 1.8).

Regardless of household composition, the majority of parents worked in either unskilled or skilled jobs. In two-parent households, 46 percent (41) of the fathers and 61 percent (55) of the mothers held jobs that included factory worker, farmworker, construction worker, sales representative, cashier, and secretary. Eighteen percent (16) of the fathers and 19 percent (17) of the mothers who were active in the labor market worked in professional settings. They held jobs such as K–12 teachers, professors, physical therapists, and bank administrators. Finally, 3 percent (3) of the mothers and 8 percent (7) of the fathers ran their own business (see table 1.9).

Table 1.8. Mother's work status, mother-headed households, Latino Masculinities Study respondents

Work status	Number of mothers (N = 11)
Worked outside the home	9
Disabled/health issues	1
Deceased	1

Table 1.9. Parents' occupation, two-parent households, Latino Masculinities Study respondents

Occupation	Number of fathers (N = 90)	Number of mothers (N = 90)
Unskilled (e.g., factory worker, laborer, truck driver, farmworker)	31	30
Skilled (e.g., postal worker, receptionist, mechanic)	10	25
Professional (e.g., teacher, social worker, professor)	16	17
Business owner (e.g., painting, landscaping, car repair)	7	3
Retired	12	3
Unemployed	5	11
Deceased	9	1

Table 1.10. Mother's occupation, mother-headed households, Latino Masculinities Study respondents

Occupation	Number of mothers (N = 11)
Unskilled (e.g., factory worker, laborer, truck driver, farmworker)	3
Skilled (e.g., postal worker, receptionist, mechanic)	3
Professional (e.g., teacher, social worker, professor)	2
Business owner (e.g., painting, landscaping, car repair)	1
Unemployed	1
Deceased	1

In mother-headed households, over half (55 percent, 6 mothers) held jobs such as restaurant worker, food vendor, nurse's assistant, teacher's aide, and travel agent (see table 1.10). One single mother worked as a correctional counselor and another held the post of vice president of student affairs at a university. One mother owned a beauty salon.

Overall, the sample in the Latino Masculinities Study was fairly diverse and demographically similar to that of the Chicana Feminisms Study.

The Chicana Feminisms Study

Our second major source of data is the Chicana Feminisms Study. As table 1.11 illustrates, both the CFS and the LMS had approximately the same number of respondents (CFS, 101; LMS, 105), the interviews were conducted in the same states and in similar locations, and the age range and average age of respondents were approximately the same (see table 1.12).

Respondents in both studies also had similar social-class identifications. Fifty CFS respondents and 51 LMS respondents self-identified as poor or working class while they were growing up; 46 CFS respondents and 47 LMS respondents identified as lower middle or middle class (see table 1.13).[1]

The only significant difference between the two studies is the more inclusive definition of LMS respondents' ethnicity. In the CFS group, the respondents were required to have at least one parent of Mexican descent. No such restriction was placed on potential respondents in the LMS group; individuals were eligible to participate if they had at least one

Table 1.11. Interview locations, Chicana Feminisms Study and Latino Masculinities Study

Location	Number of CFS respondents (N = 101)	Number of LMS respondents (N = 105)
Arizona		
Scottsdale	0	2
Phoenix	0	2
Tempe	8	0
California		
Berkeley	0	1
Davenport	0	1
Marina	0	11
Los Angeles	2	0
Oakland	7	1
Palo Alto	2	1
Salinas	0	1
San Diego	1	0
San Francisco	0	3
San Jose	0	2
Santa Cruz	8	9
Watsonville	3	0
Colorado		
Boulder	0	3
Colorado Springs	6	0
Illinois		
Chicago	13	11
Mundelein	0	1
Wheeling	0	2
Massachusetts		
Boston	0	4
Cambridge	7	2
Michigan		
Ann Arbor	6	8
New Mexico		
Albuquerque	9	9
New York		
New York City	7	7
Texas		
Austin	1	0
Edinburg	8	0
McAllen	1	0
San Antonio	8	17
Washington, DC	4	7

Table 1.12. Respondents' ages, Chicana Feminisms Study and Latino Masculinities Study

	CFS respondents	LMS respondents
Age range	19–32[a]	19–33[b]
Average age	24	24

[a]Two CFS respondents were nineteen, one respondent was thirty-one, and one was thirty-two.
[b]Four LMS respondents were nineteen, one respondent was thirty-one, one was thirty-two, and one was thirty-three.

Table 1.13. Respondents' social-class identification, Chicana Feminisms Study and Latino Masculinities Study

Social-class identification	Number of CFS respondents (N = 101)	Number of LMS respondents (N = 105)
Poor	18	25
Working class	32	26
Lower middle class	16	11
Middle class	30	36
Upper middle class	4	7
Rich	1	0

parent of Latino ancestry, regardless of the country of origin. However, in the final samples of both studies, there were a number of mixed-ancestry respondents, many of whom came from Latin American countries besides Mexico (see table 1.14)

The main rationale for restricting CFS participation was the theoretical framing of the study within Chicana feminist writings. At their core these writings address the historical experience of colonization of Mexicans at the hands of the US government through the Treaty of Guadalupe Hidalgo, which ended the Mexican-American War in 1848. The creation of Chicanas and Chicanos as a colonized group redefined a nationality— Mexican—into a group with no legal, political, social, or economic standing. Chicana feminist writings analyze the effects of colonization on gender relations in Chicano/a communities and make specific proposals for the liberation of women within Chicano/a communities.

Non-Mexican Latinos, with the exception of Puerto Ricans, whose island became a US protectorate after the Spanish-American War in 1898, have not undergone a similar experience of colonization in the United States; theirs is a history of immigration rather than colonization. Consequently, there is no comparable literature on masculinities (or on any other topic) that has the same theoretical and philosophical underpinnings as the literature on Chicana feminisms.

Given these significant differences, it did not seem viable to restrict the study of Latino masculinities to only people of Mexican descent. Instead, all Latinos residing in the United States were included as long as potential

Table 1.14. Mixed-heritage respondents, Chicana Feminisms Study and Latino Masculinities Study

Parents' ethnic background (father/mother)	Number of CFS respondents (N = 14)	Number of LMS respondents (N = 16)
Chilean/Puerto Rican	0	1
Colombian/Mexican	1	0
Cuban/white	0	1
Dominican/Cuban	0	1
Dominican/Ecuadorian	0	1
Ecuadorian/Puerto Rican	0	1
Filipino/Mexican	0	1
Jewish/Mexican	0	1
Mexican/Armenian	1	1
Mexican/Indian	1	0
Mexican/Mexican and white	1	0
Mexican/Mexican and Jewish	1	0
Mexican/Salvadorian	0	1
Mexican/white	6	2
Nicaraguan/Chinese	0	1
Peruvian/Puerto Rican	0	1
Puerto Rican/Canadian	0	1
Puerto Rican/Dominican	0	1
Puerto Rican/Mexican	1	0
White/Mexican	2	1

respondents had at least one parent of Latino/a ancestry. Furthermore, the concept of machismo has also been applied to all Latinos, not just to people of Mexican descent.

Brown and White Masculinities Study

Our third source of data is the Brown and White Masculinities Study. The purpose of this study was to examine Latino and white men's views on gender issues and feminisms. In this study, 150 Latino men and 151 white men with education beyond high school were given a self-administered questionnaire.[2] Of the 150 Latino respondents, ages ranged from 18 to 37 years, with an average age of 26. Seventy percent of Latino respondents (105) were undergraduates, and 15 percent (23) were graduate students. Most of the Latino respondents were recruited from Northern California four-year institutions (61 percent, 92 respondents). The remaining respondents were recruited from colleges in the Southwest, the Midwest, and the East Coast of the United States.

White respondents' ages ranged from 18 to 36 years, with an average age of 24. Most of the white respondents were undergraduate students (95 percent, 143 respondents); only one was attending graduate school. All white respondents were recruited from Northern California.

With these three studies as the empirical base, we examine through Intersectionality Theory respondents' views on gender, feminisms, and definitions of manhood.

CHAPTER 2

Chicana Intersectional Understandings: Theorizing Social Identities and the Construction of Privilege and Oppression

We open our discussion of Intersectionality and its importance for understanding Latino feminist masculinities by quoting one of our respondents from the Latino Masculinities Study. Issaac was a biracial (Nicaraguan and Chinese) twenty-five-year-old who had completed his master's degree in education from Columbia University and was working as an elementary school teacher in New York City. When asked whether he considered himself a feminist, Issaac responded as follows:

> I think feminism and more particularly women of Color feminism, Black feminist thought, and now emerging Chicana feminist thought has made the most sense for me than any other perspective because I know we haven't talked about this too much but I'm biracial in the sense that both of my parents are from Nicaragua and my grandfather is from China. And so my mom grew up in a Chinese community in Nicaragua. To be biracial in terms of Asian Latino for me . . . I was always looking for a space to really make sense of my life from. And so more often than not I would come back to feminist thought; like kind of an intersectionality of where my different threads meet and make up, you know, like Gloria Anzaldúa, in nepantla,[1] you know, like the Venn diagram, the borderland. And so for me . . . not only my sexuality but my sense of race and identity, [I] find myself in the borderlands and the advantages and disadvantages of being in the borderlands or coming from the borderlands or living within the borderlands. So in that sense yeah, feminism really kind of shapes a lot of my worldview and how I relate with others and think about things and the reflections that I make on whatever kind of life experiences I've had.

Issaac encapsulates the core of Intersectionality and informally combines it with Anzaldúa's Borderlands Theory. He also illustrates the usefulness of Intersectionality in understanding human existence in the interstices of different social categories—biraciality, immigrant family, working class, and first to finish college in his family. He needed a framework to fully understand his "in-between" social existence. His daily life is a struggle to inform those around him about his group memberships: "Growing up in a Chicano, Mexican, immigrant community, I was seen as chino [Chinese], you know, and it's like we'd play basketball and they'd say all these things about me, you know, chino and like da da da da. I'm like, I'm understanding everything you say 'cause I don't speak Chinese, I'm a Spanish speaker who happens to be Chinese." We can understand Issaac and he can articulate his beliefs because of the apertures of theory and discourse provided by Intersectionality. His deep understanding of the contingency of social categorization is not an accident; to the contrary, it is the work of Chicana feminists and other feminists of Color who have pushed us to think beyond binaries and do justice to "third space" existence.

The consideration of gender and race and how these categories intersect is critical to understanding social conditions. In this chapter, we review the theory of Intersectionality and elaborate it with the social-psychological framework of Social Identity Theory to frame our analyses of the condition of young Latino men and their constructions of masculinities. We readily acknowledge that patriarchy grants degrees of privilege to various masculinities, including those that are racialized. Feminist frameworks, especially those proposed by Chicana scholars, view privilege and subordination as fluid social and psychological processes that allow us to examine racialized, ethnicized masculinities as another site for liberation and transformation.

We begin with a brief historical overview of the origins of Intersectionality and its development in response to the lack of analysis in white feminist theorizing in the 1980s about the diversity of women in the United States and worldwide. We continue by integrating Intersectionality with Social Identity Theory, SIT, (Tajfel 1981) to propose the concept of *Intersectional Identities* as embodied in the Social Identities constituted by the master statuses of sexuality, gender, class, race, ethnicity, and physical ableness. We continue by using Borderlands Theory (BT), as written by Gloria Anzaldúa (1987) and expanded upon by Chicana feminist writers, to understand the social-psychological functioning of individuals with Intersectional Identities as they cross social, psychological, and economic borders to develop a multilayered understanding of social reality. By applying Intersectionality to Latino masculinities, one can examine intersections of disadvantage, say, being gay and of Color, or intersections of both disadvantage and privilege, say, being male and Latino. Intersectionality also permits the study of privilege when Social Identities that confer unearned benefits are problematized.

Historical Overview of Intersectionality

The understanding that women around the world are subjected to multiple sources of oppression was first documented by activists addressing the practical issues and needs of poor and racialized women (P. Collins 2000; A. Y. Davis, personal communication, February 3, 2007). Obviously, the feminisms developed by such influential figures as Betty Friedan and Gloria Steinem in the 1960s could not be applied without modification to women in Africa, for example, who suffered from starvation as well as rape and other gender-specific oppressions resulting from political upheavals, historical circumstances, and economic and cultural oppression (White 2008). This was also true among African American women in the United States, whose disadvantages had as much to do with their race as with their gender (P. Collins 2000).

Writing in the 1980s and 1990s, Kimberlé Crenshaw identified the inadequacy in the legal system of examining gender oppression in isolation (that is, without consideration of other sources of subordination). Crenshaw's pioneering work on Intersectionality (1989, 1995) eloquently exposed the insufficiencies of the legal system for handling the multiple sources of discrimination experienced by African American women. Crenshaw systematically demonstrated that, for example, in the case of employment discrimination, African American women were forced to bring suit either as women or as Blacks. The courts would not accept their claims solely on the basis of identifying as Black women because that would create another protected category, with the potential of endless cumulative oppressions. As stated by the courts and as quoted in Crenshaw (1989, 142), "The legislative history surrounding Title VII does not indicate that the goal of the statute was to create a new classification of 'black women' who would have greater standing than, for example, a black male. The prospect of the creation of new classes of protected minorities, governed only by the mathematical principles of permutation and combination, clearly raises the prospect of opening the hackneyed Pandora's box."

Crenshaw also applied her incisive analysis of Intersectionality to rape, where she found that the law's archaic assumptions of (white) women's purity had historically led to tougher punishment of Black men than white men in the case of interracial rape and to fewer prosecutions in the case of rape of Black women by any man. She continued by applying Intersectionality to domestic violence and found that the excessive punishment handed down by the criminal justice system to Black men led Black women to fear and refrain from reporting physical abuse by men in their communities.

When Crenshaw (1995) explored the notion of political Intersectionality, she found that Black women felt forced to choose between joining political movements to end racism and joining feminist movements to end sexism. These women found it difficult to be allied with both movements simultaneously. In the early writings on Intersectionality, Crenshaw's work did not explicitly examine other social categories that oppress women, such as class and sexuality, but her work in the areas of race and gender established the conceptual framework for considering multiple sources of oppression within feminist analysis.

While Crenshaw's initial analysis focused on the hidden legal injuries of Intersectional subordination, following the decade of Crenshaw's initial writings, Patricia Hill Collins (2000) focused on the nonlegal, societal structures that colluded to create the same phenomenon. As originally defined by Collins (2000, 299), "intersectionality is an analysis claiming that systems of race, social class, gender, sexuality, ethnicity, nation, and age form mutually constructing features of social organization, which shape Black women's experiences and, in turn, are shaped by Black women." Central to Collins's analysis is the premise that societal structures are formed and sustained to exert power over people of Color in general and African Americans in particular. As she (2000, 82) views the matter,

> The very notion of the intersections of race, class, and gender as an area worthy of study emerged from the recognition of practitioners of each distinctive theoretical tradition that inequality could not be explained, let alone challenged, via a race-only, or gender-only framework. No one had all the answers and no one was going to get all the answers without attention to two things. First, the notion of interlocking oppressions refers to the macro-level connections linking systems of oppression such as race, class, and gender. This is a model describing the structures that create social positions. Second, the notion of intersectionality describes micro-level processes—namely, how each individual group occupies a social

position within interlocking structures of oppression described by the metaphor of intersectionality. Together they shape oppression.

Central to Collins's analysis is the notion that the media generate "controlling images" that lead to the objectification and commodification of Black bodies (2004, 51), thereby justifying many kinds of oppression, since these images contribute to Blacks not being perceived as fully human. These controlling images, which Collins considers much more powerful and complex than simple stereotypes, have their origins in the institution of slavery. Historically, to justify the buying and selling of human beings, images were developed to enforce institutional control and oppression. According to Collins (2004, 55), "the objectification of people of African descent as chattel, the commodification of objectified Black bodies as property, and the exploitation of Black people as property and as workers are all closely linked." Controlling images are gender-specific and often complement each other. For example, the controlling image of the "bitch" is used to defeminize and demonize Black women, whereas the controlling images of the Black male as criminal and athlete help justify the incarceration of Black men and the devaluation of their intellectual capacities (versus their athletic prowess). Controlling images, according to Collins' analysis, do not apply solely to Blacks but to all people of Color through a racialization process: the darker the individual (regardless of race), the more these controlling images are applied by various societal institutions. Controlling images are particularly relevant to Intersectionality as they serve to disempower groups of women in different ways depending on the context.

Intersectionality has been applied to the understanding of categorical differences between women in different nation-states. For example, Rosa-Linda Fregoso problematizes the human rights paradigm applied by "First World Feminists" to women worldwide (2003, 23): "Claiming a singular transnational identity for women ignores the profound differences among women across the globe, but especially within specific localities. . . . Although First World Feminists have contributed significantly to 'the theoretical and practical revision of international rights law,' especially in their redefinition of women's rights as human rights, the challenge today involves framing women's international human rights within very complex and specific cultural contexts." By applying Intersectionality to her analysis, Fregoso avoids homogenizing all Mexican women; thus, she can probe why young, working-class, dark-skinned Mexican women rather than wealthy light-skinned Mexican women were the victims of "feminicide" in the border city of Ciudad Juárez (across from El Paso, Texas). The murders began in 1993 and continue to the present. For Fregoso, Intersectionality provides a theoretical bridge for identifying variations based on class and race among different Mexican women, which can give rise to a more penetrating analysis, including why the murders continue and remain unsolved, than the one provided by human rights discourse alone.

Intersectionality has historically been applied to intersections of subordination. Recently, however, it is being used to study contradictory intersections, for example, when one social category (say, male gender) confers privilege and the other (say, nonwhiteness) is the basis for subordination. In this vein, Intersectionality is beginning to be used to analyze the position of men of Color in general and to study the experiences of Latino men in particular (Hurtado and Sinha 2008). One of the most in-depth applications of Intersectionality to gender and race is the pathbreaking work of Aaronette White (2008), who uses Intersectionality to analyze the lives of twenty African American men who identify as feminist. We also expand the use of Intersectionality to analyze the experiences of privilege and oppression of Latino men by connecting Intersectionality to these men's significant Social Identities.

Intersectionality and Social Identity Theory

Hurtado (1996, 1997, 2003b) links the theories of Social Identity as first proposed by Henri Tajfel (1981) to Intersectionality and Borderlands Theory. To understand these linkages, it is necessary to elucidate several theoretical distinctions that aid in understanding the processes that individuals undergo in constructing their Social Identities. The foremost distinction, as held by most social psychologists, is between personal and Social Identity, which together form a person's integrated sense of self (Baumeister 1998). Tajfel (1981) posits that personal identity is that aspect of self composed of psychological traits and dispositions that give rise to personal uniqueness. In contrast, Social Identity is defined as "that part of an individual's self-concept which derives from his knowledge of his membership of a social group (or groups) together with the value and emotional significance attached to that membership" (Tajfel 1972, 292). Social psychologists argue that although personal identity and Social Identity are not entirely independent of each other, neither are they one and the same (Tajfel 1981).

Tajfel's proposed theoretical distinction is very helpful in avoiding dispositionalism, that is, the tendency in the field of psychology to over-attribute all behavior to individual characteristics (mostly encased in the concept of personality or in such personality traits as self-esteem) and to underestimate the influence on behavior of social context and structural variables (Haney and Zimbardo 2009). Personal identity is derived from intrapsychic influences, many of which are socialized within family units (however those are defined) (Hurtado 1997, 309). From this perspective, human beings have a great deal in common precisely because their personal identities comprise universal processes such as loving, mating, and doing productive work. However, these universal components of self are filtered through language, culture, historical moment, social structures, and social context (Reicher 2004). For example, children in all societies are considered to belong to their biological parents, not to neighbors, aunts, uncles, or other relatives. There are, though, infinite variations in the constellations considered appropriate for raising children—from an entire village, to a nuclear family, to foster care.

Tajfel (1981) considers personal identities as less socially salient than Social Identities and therefore more fluid than Social Identities because they are less socially monitored. A person is permitted, without a perception of incoherence, to be happy and effervescent one day and gloomy and depressed another. Furthermore, those emotional variations require social interaction for the evaluation to take place. In contrast, an individual's gender, race, ethnicity, and socioeconomic class are relevant in most social contexts with little if any social interaction. As such, the presentation of self is regulated through these group belongings in most social contexts such that coherence is a necessary prerequisite for social functioning. For example, an individual categorized as a man cannot dress as a woman one day and as a man the next without social (and sometimes violent) consequences. According to Tajfel (1981, 325–326), personal identity is for the most part a private sense of "me-ness" that is not necessarily negotiated or challenged in every social interaction. For instance, people generally consider themselves kind and open-minded; until someone or some incident challenges this self-assessment, there is no reason to doubt this judgment. In the ordinary course of social events, the unchallenged personal self-assessment does not motivate the person to reevaluate the personal self. Tajfel's theory of self addresses *intergroup relations*, not *intrapsychic influences* that may lead to changes in personal identity.

As stated earlier, *Social Identity* is that aspect of self derived from the knowledge of being part of social categories and groups, together with the value and emotional significance attached to those group formations. Tajfel argues that the creation of Social Identities is the consequence of three social-psychological processes. The first is *social categorization*. Nationality, language, race and ethnicity, skin color, and other social or physical characteristics that are meaningful socially, and many times politically meaningful in particular social contexts, can be the basis for social categorization and thus the foundation for the creation of Social Identities. For example, Alice Warren Colón (2003, 668) writes about the differences in the assignment to the race category "Black" of Puerto Ricans in the United States versus those in Puerto Rico:

> The dichotomous racialization that is imposed by dominant (white) sectors in the United States on African Americans, as well as on colonized populations and "unassimilated" migrants contrasts with the hierarchy of racial mixture in Puerto Rico. On the Island, race ranges along a continuum from white to Black, running through a variety of categories related to the presence of particular phenotypical traits, such as mulatto, *trigueño* (lighter skinned or as a euphemism for Black), or *grifo* (tight, curly hair). . . . It is also more evidently a social definition, based on behavior as well as on physical characteristics, so that moving from a lower to a higher social status could allow for a person's whitening.

As a result of these differences in race assignment, from a continuum in Puerto Rico to a dichotomous assignment in the United States, Puerto Ricans migrating to the US mainland from the island have to readjust their self-perceptions around issues of race—from a phenotypic description (e.g., morenito, "a bit dark") to the racial category "Black." Tajfel (1981) would call the change in "race" assignment joining a stigmatized social category tied historically to the institution of slavery and thus also tied to negative political and social connotations.

Another process underlying the construction of Social Identities is *social comparison*. In this process, the meaning of an individual's group affiliations, a group's status, its degree of affluence, or other characteristics achieve significance *in relation to* perceived differences and their value connotations from other social formations in the environment. For example, in a qualitative study of educated Chicanas, Hurtado (2003b) found that respondents considered themselves "middle class" when they lived in predominantly working-class communities. Upon entering institutions of higher education attended largely by middle- and upper-class white students, the participants shifted their comparison from neighborhood to college peers and reassessed their class identification, most often from middle class to poor or working class.

The third process for developing a Social Identity involves *psychological work*, both cognitive and emotional, which is prompted by what Tajfel (1981) claims is a universal motive: the achievement of a positive sense of self. When different values are attached to different group affiliations, individuals have to do psychological work to come to terms with their Social Identities. As Tajfel posits, individuals strive to be different from other groups, but the difference has to be positive. The social groups and Social Identities that present the greatest obstacles to a positive sense of self are those that are disparaged (including "invisible" identities, such as sexual orientation), those that have to be negotiated frequently because of their visibility (physical attributes, such as dark skin color), those that have become politicized by social movements, and so on. Moreover, these Social Identities become especially powerful psychologically; they are easily accessible and dwelt on, likely to be salient across situations, and likely to function as schemas, frameworks, or social scripts (Gurin, Hurtado, and Peng 1994; Hurtado and Gurin 2004). For example, a poor, gay, Latino adolescent with a physical disability is more likely to reflect seriously on his Social Identities than is a middle-class, white, heterosexual adolescent with no physical impediments.

Unproblematic group memberships—that is, ones that are socially valued, accorded privilege, or indistinguishable to others—may not even become Social Identities. For instance, until the emergence of whiteness studies, being racially white and male was not considered a problematic category and is still not widely thought of as a Social Identity (Fine et al. 2004; Hurtado and Stewart 2004; Phinney 1996). Although there may be different groups of whites (e.g., varying by class—poor whites versus middle-class whites), the privileges accrued because of the racial benefits of whiteness are not easily articulated by its possessors, regardless of class, because white race privilege is considered the norm in the United States (McIntosh 1989).

Intersectionality and Master Statuses

In addition to linking Social Identity Theory (Tajfel 1981) to Intersectionality, Hurtado (2003b, 2010) contends that from a social-psychological point of view, Intersectionality refers to the particular constellation of

Social Identities that is the primary basis for power distribution *and* stigmatization and subordination, that is, class, race, sexuality, gender, ethnicity, and physical ableness. These same social categories are based on what sociologists call *master statuses* (Hughes 1945) and are the basis for significant Social Identities because individuals must psychologically negotiate their potentially stigmatizing effects. Conversely, if these master statuses confer privilege, and that privilege becomes problematized, then individuals holding such privilege must negotiate the psychological effects of devalued group memberships. In the United States, as in many other countries, master statuses are used to make value judgments about group memberships and to allocate political, social, and economic power (Reicher 2004). Furthermore, all measures of inequality, such as education, income, and accumulated wealth, are affected by these master statuses. Tajfel's (1981) theory of Social Identity, which has been elaborated upon by others (Gurin, Hurtado, and Peng 1994; Hogg and Reid 2006; Hurtado 1997; Reicher and Hopkins 2001), provides a framework for understanding both unproblematic and stigmatized group affiliations, especially those based on master statuses.

Given the powerful effects of master statuses for Social Identity formation (Reicher 2004), it becomes important to distinguish Social Identities based on master statuses from other social categories. Individuals can construct multiple group identities that are not based on master statuses, and multiple identities do not necessarily refer to master statuses. According to Tajfel, *nonstigmatized social memberships* are part of an individual's *multiple identities*. For example, a person may identify with a political party (Democrat or Republican), a geographical area (California or Texas), and a profession (architect or teacher). These multiple group memberships are significant to people and have social consequences, but, from a Tajfelian perspective, they do not constitute an individual's Social Identity—primarily because they have no consistent stigmatizing effects. They are not used systematically to assign political, social, and economic power; membership can be changed; and membership does not intersect in significant ways to produce any of the delineated consequences ascribed to Social Identities (Turner and Onorato 1999).

A second concept currently in vogue is the use of diversity to describe the process of inclusion based on multiple group identities. There is a difference between master statuses and diversity, as exemplified in the use of the latter to adjudicate "fair representation" in various social spheres based on a multitude of axes of difference ranging from geography, to age, to interests, and so on (Russo and Vaz 2001). The definition of diversity is left up to those in charge of fulfilling it.² In turn, master statuses, as embodied in stigmatized Social Identities, are used to justify the distribution of power, historical exclusion, and cultural, ethnic, political, and economic colonization. For this reason, we do not use the terms *diversity* or *multiple identities* as proxies for Intersectionality. Instead, we propose the concept of *Intersectional Identities* to refer to Social Identities embodied in master statuses that constitute Intersectionality; when these statuses intersect, they result in specific political, social, and economic consequences.

The Social Self and Intersectional Identity Constellations

Social Identities are tied to significant group memberships, which together form a constellation that constitutes a whole and integrated sense of the Social Self (Turner and Onorato 1999). Even if an individual belongs to several significant social categories or master statuses (say, being a woman, Chicana, and poor), these group belongings do not operate psychologically and socially as separate categories but as an integrated sense of the Social Self (Turner and Onorato 1999). Thus, individuals' Social Identity constellations compose their overall Social Identity because human beings experience themselves as whole, not as independent social categories. Thus, when individuals are asked, "What is most important to you, being a woman or being Chicana?" most have difficulty creating a hierarchy because they experience these Social Identities as integrated social categories. If pressed, individuals can indeed rank their social categories, but this ranking is cognitively created, not one that is naturally occurring in the social world.

Although individuals may not necessarily rank their Social Identities, the salience of different affiliations varies according to social context (see fig. 2.1); that is, which stigmatized Social Identities gain significance is largely context-dependent. As Reicher and Hopkins (2001, 385–386) indicate, "The particular social identity that is salient in a given context will determine who is seen and treated as similar and who is rejected as an alien." Indeed, Turner and Onorato (1999) argue that the meaning of particular social categories can be fully understood only in context because the meaning will change if the circumstances vary. When stigmatized Social Identities intersect in particular contexts, they become intersectional identities (see gray areas in fig. 2.1).

The graphic in figure 2.1 can therefore be conceptualized as a fluid,

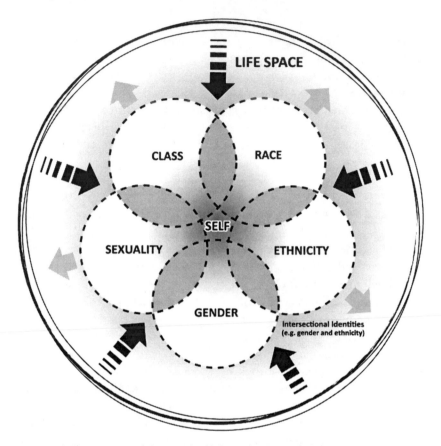

Figure 2.1. The creation of the social self through Intersectionality

amorphous amoeba that changes shape as it moves through its surroundings, making one (or more) Social Identities especially salient depending on the context. Each social category is porous, overlapping others, with boundaries that are not rigid or fixed. We propose that from a social-psychological point of view, Intersectionality refers to this particular constellation of Social Identities, which are the primary basis for stigmatization and for allocation of privilege. Because personal identity is not entirely independent of Social Identities, individuals cannot completely override the negative and oppressive effects of their stigmatized Social Identities on their personal identity. For example, a poor African American lesbian with a physical disability will be treated in many social contexts according to her *visible stigmatized Social Identities* rather than her *personal identity*, which quite possibly may include being a kind, gentle, and intelligent human being. Intersectionality as embodied in stigmatized Social Identities allows for an agile analysis of the different social contexts in which certain stigmatized Social Identities are more salient and likely to be used to impose oppression (Hurtado and Cervantez 2009). This framework also facilitates the examination of the social process of external Intersectional Social Identity assignations by others versus the private self-perceptions of an individual's personal identity.

Intersectional Identities, Social and Political Spaces, and Temporality

Stigmatized Social Identities intersect and form alternating constellations in various social spaces. Consequently, the significance and relationship between these Social Identities (such as class, race, ethnicity, and sexuality) vary from social sphere to social sphere and across time. In some circumstances, one particular group membership or set of memberships may be more salient than others; when functioning within a group that is homogeneous with regard to its significant Social Identities, that particular Social Identity (or Identities) may be much less relevant than it would be in a situation where many groups interact with each other. For example, a high school student may not think about being Chicano when interacting with family members but may be acutely aware of this identity when called on to answer a question in a classroom where he is the only person of Mexican descent (see fig. 2.2). In addition, a person may define a particular group membership differently at one time than at another. For example, a young person growing up in a predominantly Chicano/a neighborhood may take his or her ethnicity for granted. Attending a university and taking courses on Chicano/a history and culture may provide the impetus for this person to reassess his or her ethnicity and its importance in constructing his or her Social Identities (Hurtado and Gurin 2004).

As mentioned earlier, Intersectionality can also illuminate contradictory intersections of subordination and privilege, for example, being male and Latino. Because master statuses can confer privilege, personal identity also benefits from the freedom of stigma if an individual's master statuses protect her or him from subordination. Intersectionality can also be applied to the study of the benefits and consequences of privilege when master statuses are aligned to benefit individuals. The application of Intersectionality to the problematics of privilege, however, has yet to be fully developed. In sum, the concept of Intersectional Social Identities

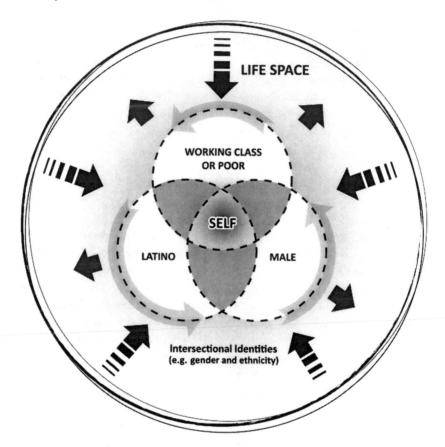

Figure 2.2. The Intersectional Identity Constellation based on the master statuses of gender, class, and ethnicity

allows the examination of this complexity in various social spheres, in different life cycles, and across historical moments.

Intersectional Social Identities, Identification, and Consciousness

While Tajfel's Social Identity Theory provides a sophisticated framework for understanding individual responses to desirable and undesirable group affiliations, Patricia Gurin and her colleagues (1980) provide a different theoretical bridge between group affiliations and awareness of the values attached to the groups' status by making a distinction between identification and consciousness. According to their perspective, most people are aware of their Social Identities when they are tied to master statuses. For example, individuals can almost universally articulate if they are female or male, Chicano or white, poor, middle class, or wealthy, or physically challenged or not. But Gurin and colleagues believe that individuals are less likely to be aware of how the entire group of individuals in that category rank in relation to other social formations in the same life space (Lewin 1948);[3] that is, individuals may be highly identified with particular social formations and be aware of whether that affiliation is desirable or not, but they may not be at all conscious of the status of their entire stratum. According to Gurin and colleagues (1980, 30), "Identification and consciousness both denote cognitions: the former about a person's relation to others within a stratum, the latter about a stratum's position within a society. Identification refers to the awareness of having ideas, feelings, and interests similar to others who share the same stratum characteristics. Consciousness refers to a set of political beliefs and action orientations arising out of this awareness of similarity."

Through identification, then, individuals see themselves belonging to certain social formations, for example, ethnic, gender, and class groups. Through consciousness, they become aware that the social formations they belong to hold a certain status (either powerful or not powerful) in society, and they can decide (or possibly feel compelled) to take action to change this status, not just for their own benefit but for that of others in the group as well. Thus, having a characteristic that could potentially become a Social Identity, such as being a woman, does not necessarily mean that the individual develops such a Social Identity; some consciousness of what that particular category signifies socially and politically is necessary for identity constructions to become *conscious* and result in political mobilization. We contend that Gloria Anzaldúa's Borderlands Theory helps explain a particular type of consciousness, as defined by Gurin and colleagues, in which border crossings or multiple social subjectivities (Hurtado 2005) contribute to political understandings of various social formations' status and thus influence individuals' Intersectional Social Identities.

Intersectionality and Borderlands Theory

Since the late 1980s, Chicana feminist scholars have been at the forefront of Intersectionality by proposing feminisms that take into account culture, class, sexuality, race, ethnicity, and, most recently, masculine gender

(Flores 2000; Hurtado and Sinha 2008; Vásquez 2003). A pivotal theoretical addition to Chicana feminisms has been the work of Gloria Anzaldúa—writer, public intellectual, and one of the first Chicanas to publicly claim her lesbianism (Moraga and Anzaldúa 1981). Anzaldúa wrote extensively on Borderlands Theory, as scholars in the humanities call it, before her untimely passing at the age of sixty-one. Borderlands Theory expands on W. E. B. Du Bois's (1903) idea of double consciousness, applying it to the experiences of Chicanas growing up in South Texas on the border between the United States and Mexico (Martinez 2005). According to Anzaldúa (1987), the border between these two countries is a metaphor for all types of crossings—between geopolitical boundaries, sexual transgressions, and social dislocations, and the crossings necessary to exist in multiple linguistic and cultural contexts. She locates the geographical border between the United States and Mexico as the source of her theorizing, as Hurtado (2003b, 18) summarizes: "The history of conquest, which basically layered another country over a preexisting nation, gave Chicana feminisms the knowledge of the temporality of nation-states. . . . The political line dividing the United States from Mexico did not correspond to the experiential existence on the border. Chicana feminists declare the border as the geographical location (lugar) that created the aperture for theorizing about subordination from an ethnically specific Chicana/mestiza consciousness."

According to Anzaldúa (1987), living in the borderlands creates a third space between cultures and social systems that leads to coherence by embracing ambiguity and holding contradictory perceptions without conflict. La frontera (the border) is also the geographical area most susceptible to hybridity, being neither fully of Mexico nor fully of the United States. As Anzaldúa claims, la frontera is where you "put chile in the borscht/eat whole-wheat tortillas/speak Tex-Mex with a Brooklyn accent" (1987, 195). The word *borderlands* denotes that space in which antithetical elements mix, not to obliterate each other nor to be subsumed by a larger whole, but to combine in unique and unexpected ways (Hurtado 2003b).

Living between two countries, two social systems, two languages, two cultures results in understanding experientially the contingent nature of social arrangements (Martinez 2005). Anzaldúa (1987) asserts that living in the borderlands produces special knowledge from being within a system while also retaining the knowledge of an outsider who comes from outside the system. This "outsider within" status produces a layered complexity within Chicanas' sense of self that is captured in Anzaldúa's concept of mestiza consciousness, as summarized by Hurtado (2003b, 18):

It was at the border that Chicanas/*mestizas* learned the socially constructed nature of all categories. By standing on the US side of the river
they saw Mexico and they saw home; by standing on the Mexican side
of the border they saw the United States and they saw home. Yet they
were not really accepted on either side. Their ability to "see" the arbitrary nature of all categories but still take a stand challenges Chicana
feminisms to exclude while including, to reject while accepting, and to
struggle while negotiating. . . . The basic concept involves the ability to
hold multiple social perspectives while simultaneously maintaining a
center that revolves around concrete material forms of oppression.

Although Anzaldúa developed Borderlands Theory by examining her
experiences as the daughter of farmworkers living in extreme poverty
in South Texas, the theory also applies to all types of social, economic,
sexual, and political dislocations. Her insights help us understand and
theorize about the experiences of individuals who are exposed to contradictory social systems and develop what she terms la facultad (the ability
or gift)—the notion that individuals (primarily women) who are exposed
to multiple social worlds, as defined by cultures, languages, social classes,
sexualities, nation-states, and colonization, develop the agility to navigate and challenge linear conceptions of social reality. Other writers have
called this ability "differential consciousness" (Sandoval 2000), perception
of "multiple realities" (Alarcón 1990), "multiple subjectivities" (Hurtado
2003a), and a state of "concientización" (Castillo 1994).[4]

Anzaldúa presages Intersectionality Theory by attributing Chicanas'
subordination not only to patriarchy, but also to the intersection of multiple systems of oppression. Within Borderlands Theory, oppressions are
not ranked nor are they conceptualized as static; rather, they are recognized as fluid systems that take on different forms and nuances depending
on the context. Borderlands Theory allows for the expression of multiple
oppressions and forms of resistance that are not easily accessible through
traditional methods of analysis and measurement. This theoretical approach has produced rich and unique analyses in various academic fields,
including the social sciences (Hurtado 2003a), literature (Saldívar-Hull
2000), history (Pérez 1999), education (Delgado Bernal 1998), and political theory (Barvosa 2008, 2011; Barvosa-Carter 2007).

Another application of Borderlands Theory is found in the analysis of
Intersectionality through the concept of Social Identities. The fluidity
and context-dependent nature of Social Identities result in "social travel"
between social systems, cultural symbols, and cognitive understandings,

ultimately creating a nonnormative consciousness of the arbitrary nature of social reality. Following the logic inherent in Borderlands Theory, stigmatized Social Identities based on master statuses are not additive: they do not result in increased oppression with an increased number of stigmatized group memberships. Instead, individuals' group memberships are conceptualized as intersecting in a variety of ways, depending on the social context (Hurtado and Gurin 2004).

Borderlands Theory is particularly important for social action and coalition building. There are no absolute "sides" in conflict; instead, there are contingent adversaries whose perceptions can be understood by examining (and empathizing with) their subjectivities. Furthermore, no one is exempt from contributing to oppression in limited contexts (Pérez 1999). Self-reflexivity and seeing through the "eyes of others" become more important to gaining a deeper consciousness than staying within one's social milieu. As explained by Anzaldúa (1987, 78–79),

> It is not enough to stand on the opposite river bank, shouting questions, challenging patriarchal, white conventions. A counterstance locks one into a duel of oppressor and oppressed; locked in mortal combat, like the cop and the criminal, both are reduced to a common denominator of violence. The counterstance refutes the dominant culture's views and beliefs, and, for this, it is proudly defiant . . . but it is not a way of life. At some point, on our way to a new consciousness, we will have to leave the opposite bank, the split between the two mortal combatants somehow healed so that we are on both shores at once and, at once, see through serpent and eagle eyes. . . . The possibilities are numerous once we decide to act and not react.

The development of a mestiza (hybrid) *consciousness* that simultaneously embraces and rejects contradictory realities to avoid excluding what it critically assesses is the result of individuals living in many liminal spaces (Lugones 2003). A mestiza consciousness permits individuals to perceive multiple realities at once (Barvosa-Carter 2007). Anzaldúa's work integrates indigenous Aztec beliefs and epistemologies that circumvent linear, positivist thinking, which does not allow for hybridity, contradiction, and, ultimately, liberation from existing social arrangements (Hurtado 2003b; Martinez 2005). As Martinez (2005, 559–560) states,

> The "borderlands" signify Anzaldúa's family history of oppression, her memory of brutal backbreaking work, and her knowledge of border his-

tory. The "borderlands" are the site of her worst struggles with racism, sexism, classism and heterosexism: "*[La] mestiza* undergoes a struggle of flesh, a struggle of borders, an inner war. . . . The coming together of two self-consistent but habitually incompatible frames of reference causes *un choque*, a cultural collision" (Anzaldúa 1987, 28). Yet, this crossroads is also the site of her greatest strength. This "floundering in uncharted seas," this "swamping of her psychological borders" (79) creates the other ways of coping and seeing the world. It forces the *mestiza* consciousness into existence in a psychic birthing and synthesis to become a reflection of the "borderlands" themselves—a juncture, a crossroads, and a consciousness of multiple voices and paradigms.

Through Borderlands Theory, Anzaldúa (1987, 2002) provides the experiential documentation for Tajfel's (1981) Social Identity Theory. Tajfel does not address extensively what it means for individuals, let alone women, to carry the burden of stigma when they have no control over how others categorize them into social groups. Furthermore, he does not explore how individuals cope with the incongruence between their private self-perceptions (say, as competent, intelligent, logical) and others' negative perceptions shaped by stigmatized Social Identities. Anzaldúa's theory proposes that one possibility among many is to use the contradiction to one's advantage, rising above the negative assignation to develop a complex view of the Social Self, or what Gurin and colleagues (1980) call a *consciousness* about one's Intersectional Identities. One potential type of consciousness, according to Borderlands Theory, is a mestiza consciousness. In many ways, Anzaldúa's work exemplifies the poetics of political resistance and rescues Chicanas (and other Latinas) from potential stigma derived from their derogated Social Identities (Bost 2005; Tajfel 1981).

The Role of History and Colonization in Creating Intersectional Identities

As Reicher (2004) indicates, it is important to historicize the origins of particular social categorizations to fully understand their meanings. The master statuses in the creation of Intersectional Social Identities primarily apply to groups that have been colonized (Pérez 1999; Comas-Díaz 2000). For Chicanas/os the colonization of the Southwest territories that belonged to Mexico at the end of the Mexican-American War in 1848 became a pivotal moment in Mexican nationals losing their Mexican citizenship and becoming culturally and linguistically conquered on their own land (Flores-Ortiz 2004). For Puerto Ricans, the relationship between Puerto Rico as a protectorate of the United States with no official representation in the US government has also influenced the group's Social Identity formations. Puerto Rican migration in large numbers from the island mainly to New York City has disrupted Puerto Rican cultural patterns and social norms developed in their native country. In particular, Puerto Rican men migrating from the island to the mainland find it difficult to perform their manhood in the United States. The challenging adjustment to their newfound situation in the United States frequently leads to family discord and even domestic upheaval (Weis et al. 2002).

Other groups of Latinas/os (e.g., Salvadorians, Guatemalans, and Colombians) who have emigrated from their home countries because of economic pressures or political persecution have a different set of influences that affect their definition of what constitutes their Social Identities. Many Latinos are forced to leave families behind and readjust their beliefs about gender relations as they struggle economically in the United States (Zavella 2011). Their varied national histories, however, do not deter them from having certain common concerns and shared experiences based on master statuses that influence the development of their Intersectional Identities.

Comas-Díaz argues that given the structural discrimination that many people of Color suffer in the United States (and in the world), we cannot ignore the "group trauma" produced by such treatment. The experience of racism and discrimination, according to Comas-Díaz (2000, 1320), leads to the Stockholm syndrome:

> People of color are often exposed to imperialism and intellectual domination at the expense of their cultural values. . . . Furthermore, they are subjected to the cultural Stockholm syndrome, a condition in which members of an oppressed group accept the dominant cultural values, including the stereotypes of their own group. . . . The cultural Stockholm syndrome involves being taken hostage by other people's cultures and perceptions of themselves, while coming to internalize and believe them. Hence, politically repressing people of color can lead to terrorism, maintaining the privileges of the dominant group, and silencing cries for racial social justice.

Comas-Díaz argues that, "similar to other survivors of torture, people of color need to learn to reject the feelings of inferiority instilled in them" by the historical experience of colonization and its concomitant "political repression" (2000, 1322). As part of this work, oppressed people need to reject the negative attributions imputed to their identities and communities and instead "develop solidarity with other oppressed groups, thus restoring their sense of continuity with their collective identity, both local and global" (1322). To do coalitional work, "ethnic minorities need to confront and overcome ingrained feelings of division and suspicion instilled by their ancestral history of threatened survival" (1322).

Comas-Díaz (2000, 1320), as well as other scholars (e.g., Flores-Ortiz 2004; Vásquez 2006), argues for an ethnopolitical approach in designing social interventions to restore Chicanas/os' and Latinas/os' identity after they have suffered the effects of "oppression, racism, terrorism, and political repression." According to Comas-Díaz, "Acknowledging racial, ethnic, and political realities as they interact with socioeconomic, historical, psychological, and environmental factors, this approach expands the individual focus to a collective one, one that is national as well as international. An ethnopolitical model can serve as the basis for psychologists to aid people who have suffered racism, discrimination, and repression" (1320).

The ethnopolitical approach "names the terror [of oppression], developing a language that gives voice to the silenced traumatized self" (Comas-Díaz 2000, 1320). This broader conceptualization of identity dovetails almost seamlessly with the perspective of Intersectionality developed in this book. This view takes into account the history as well as the sociopolitical context in which Chicanas/os and Latinas/os exist in the United States (and all of Latin America), leading to a diverse set of therapeutic and social interventions, and, in fact, redirecting therapy from the individual to the social and collective (Comas-Díaz 2000; Flores-Ortiz 2004; Vásquez 2002). To alleviate the pervasive identity conflicts created by colonization in the forms of "identity conflicts," "shame," "rage," pressure to "assimilate" and abandon one's native culture and language, "identity ambivalence," and "alienation" (Comas-Díaz 2000, 1320), Chicana and Latina feminist writers advocate using a variety of social interventions. As Comas-Díaz (2000, 1322) summarizes, "Ethnic and indigenous psychologies provide a culturally relevant lens validating both the importance of racial and ethnic meanings and the historical and political contexts of oppression. Because working with victims of political repression forces individuals to confront questions of meaning, the spiritual beliefs of people of color are rescued and affirmed as examples of indigenous psychological approaches. . . . Psychologists can help trauma sufferers find

something of value in the traumatic experience through a renewed awareness of their strengths."

Comas-Díaz, Lykes, and Alarcón (1998) propose that for some individuals, indigenous approaches to psychic healing help them remember
and "retell their cultural memories," which aids in "identity construction"
(as cited in Comas-Díaz 2000, 1322). For individuals who lack exposure to
their indigenous origins, interventions may include the act of discovery
and recuperation of culture, language, and history. Indigenous approaches
may also be better suited to poor and working-class individuals whose life
experiences may have been especially brutal because of poverty.

Intersectionality and the Chicana
Feminist Analysis of Masculinities

In *The Color of Privilege*, Hurtado (1996) proposes that white women derive a degree of structural and emotional privilege from their familial relationships to white patriarchy in the United States. As daughters, mothers,
sisters, spouses, cousins, and aunts of white men, white women inherit a
relational power that informs their perspectives on gender relations and
thus their feminisms. Conversely, women of Color cannot biologically
provide the pure white offspring necessary for white patriarchy to reproduce itself. This distance and barred biological access to white patriarchy
result in an aperture to a different feminist platform that is at times at odds
with white feminisms. For example, the recent increases in the incarceration of men of Color, especially of boys and young men, has created a new
concern among feminists of Color. For many, it is not an uncommon experience to have a brother, father, uncle, cousin, or other male relative in
the criminal justice system. Consequently, many feminists of Color find
themselves relating to the oppression of incarcerated men from their communities. Differences in incarceration rates for men of Color and white
men, as well as the former's underachievement in the academy, has made
these men's inclusion in a feminist movement a central issue, one that has
not been embraced by white feminists of any age. However, feminists of
Color do not adhere to the notion of the "plight of the Black male [or
male of Color]" (White 2008); they have, instead, opened the analysis to
concentrate on patriarchy as the central problematic in the current incarceration trends. According to White (2008, 19), the study of masculinities of Color adds "complexity to more traditional approaches to social

phenomena that focus only on race, class, or gender, by broadening our understanding of how mechanisms of institutional power mesh with personal expressions of power."

The movement to include young Latino men in the Chicana feminist project has its earliest origins in the feminist theorizing of the 1980s, when a subgroup of feminist writers raised the critique that the diversity of women's experiences, both within the United States and internationally, was not being fully addressed within the boundaries of traditional feminism (Russo and Vaz 2001). Their arguments centered on cultural variations in definitions of gender relations and differences within cultures as determined by class, ethnicities, power, and other socially relevant factors (Zambrana 2011). If the ultimate goal of feminist theorizing and political mobilization is to deconstruct and abolish patriarchy, then the multiple manifestations of patriarchy as they vary but persist across cultures should be addressed in all feminist production (Hurtado 2003a). In other words, multiple masculinities (Coltrane 1994; Connell 1987, 1995; Pyke 1996) and femininities (Pyke and Johnson 2003) are filtered through different cultural manifestations of patriarchies (Baca Zinn and Dill 1996). Chicana feminist theory (as well as other feminisms) was developed in response to this compelling critique and has become a vibrant and prolific field within the larger field of feminist theorizing.

When the diversity of women's lived experiences is included in the definitions of feminisms, it becomes apparent that there is not just one definition of womanhood but, rather, many variations determined by culture and language, sexuality, and social class within cultures (Baca Zinn and Dill 1994). Thus, Chicana feminists' views of culture and language are multidimensional and layered and adhere to a paradigm that privileges lived experience as the basis for embodying culture and language. When examining Chicana culture from this perspective, special attention must be directed to region and national origin, class background, gender, and sexuality—similarly to the axes of difference embodied in Intersectionality (Zambrana 2011). It is understood that in all cultures social context is determinative in accurately assessing behavior. Furthermore, language also has variations, notably in speech style and degrees of mastery. Not all Chicanas speak Spanish, Spanish-English bilingualism being a matter of degree as well as of familiarity with different speech styles (Hurtado and Vega 2004). Chicana feminisms do not adhere to a linear acculturation model in which individuals move from being Spanish-dominant and culturally Chicano/a to becoming English-dominant and Americanized.

Instead, there are many potential cultural adaptations influenced by context and exposure to the culture and language of origin (Gurin, Hurtado, and Peng 1994).

Chicana feminisms, as a field of study, do not uncritically accept Chicano/Mexican culture in its theorizing and offer powerful critiques of the sexist elements found in their communities' cultural practices (Anzaldúa 1987; Hurtado 2003a, 2003b). Simultaneously, there is an emphasis on selectively honoring aspects of Chicano/Latina cultures—such as caring for family members, sharing resources with extended family, and having parents who support educational success, particularly for their daughters—that have strengthened these communities to withstand oppression (N. Cantú 2008; Hurtado, Hurtado, and Hurtado 2007).

Examining culture within a structure of patriarchy results in a more complicated analysis of masculinities and its relationship to feminisms than is ordinarily found in white feminist writings. Instead of perceiving Chicano/Latino men solely as males and thus as beneficiaries of patriarchy, the Chicana feminist project in their analyses of oppression also considers Chicano/Latino men's vulnerabilities. For example, Hurtado and Sinha (2006a) find that Latino families privilege sons by requiring fewer household chores and by giving them greater freedom and fewer rules than are required of their daughters. These young men, however, are also more likely to be harassed by police, to be less close to their parents, and to have fewer close friends than their sisters—all of which leads to less academic success.

The multiple feminisms recognized by Chicana/Latina feminists imply that there must also be multiple masculinities. To be sure, not all womanhoods are equally valued (Hurtado 1999), which is also the case with non-hegemonic masculinities (Hurtado and Sinha 2008). Of course, the systems of patriarchal privilege reward all masculinities at some level (just as all womanhoods/femininities are ultimately a source of restriction, even if it is through seduction [Hurtado 1996; Rubin, Nemeroff, and Russo 2004]). Nonetheless, Chicana feminisms embrace the deconstruction of masculinities and the examination of gender relations within Chicana/Latino communities as an integral part of the Chicana feminist project (Hurtado 2003a; Hurtado and Sinha 2008).

Men are obviously gendered subjects, not only for the purpose of conferring patriarchal privileges, but also for negotiating all power relations, including subordination. A Chicana feminist analysis of masculinities facilitates the application of Intersectionality to men in general and to Latino men in particular. This is a very important development because Intersectionality examines the unified categories of "man" and "patriarchy," systematically unpacking the privileges and vulnerabilities ascribed to the categories and systems of privilege. Intersectionality enables the exploration of the crossroads created by master statuses, cracking open the internal variations of "man" based on significant Social Identities. No longer is it possible to use the social signifier "man" to denote *all* male social formations; rather, "poor man" signifies a different kind of patriarchy than does "rich man," and, even more layered, "poor Black man" begins to unpack the variations in patriarchal privilege and subordination.

In the chapters that follow we use Intersectionality, Social Identity Theory, and Borderlands Theory as influenced by Chicana feminist writings to delineate and understand Latino feminist masculinities.

CHAPTER 3

Toward New Masculinities: A Chicana Feminist Intersectional Analysis of Latinos' Definitions of Manhoods

In Jimmy Santiago Baca's memoir, *A Place to Stand* (2001), the author relates the painful childhood memory of visiting his father in jail. Five-year-old Jimmy does not understand why his father is in this place of chaos and restriction and why his father cannot leave with him and his mother at the end of the visit. Baca is caught in a world of emotion and pain that haunts him for the rest of his life. Even in adulthood, he is unable to articulate the pain of leaving his father behind in a cage.

Baca lacks words both literally and metaphorically because in his world, men do not talk about emotions, and because he is illiterate until his early twenties, when he learns to read and write during his own incarceration. Even after he becomes a writer, his discourse about pain, love, and emotion remains limited because of the restrictions dictated by what it means to him to be a man. These restrictions limit his interactions with and expressions of love toward his brother, his mother, and the rest of his family. Not until he writes his memoir do those he loves learn what he felt as a child, as a young man, and as a mature writer. Through self-education by reading books and in practicing the use of words, Baca acquired the discourse and vocabulary that enabled him to articulate what it means to "be a man."

Jimmy Baca is like many of the young Latinos we interviewed for the Latino Masculinities Study. They too had limited terms for defining manhood until, through education, reading, and relationships with women and, in a few cases, with other men, they discovered the power of words. These resources provided them with the opportunity to explore their feelings through written language and conversation. Here we examine the respondents' answers to the question, "What does the word 'manhood' mean to you?" With the answers to this question, a world of doubt, pride, apprehension, fear, love, and potential change opens up as these young men tell us what they see as their gendered positionings in the world.

In this chapter, we examine the Intersectional Identities of the sub-sample of respondents who identified as feminist and who declared their class background while growing up as working class or poor. As one of our intentions in this book is to explore the possibility of dismantling machismo and of constructing new masculinities, the intersection of pro-gressive feminist identification and economic deprivation in young, edu-cated Latino men is a possible identification node where the disruption of previous definitions of manhood is likely to occur. We begin our analy-sis by reviewing the research on machismo to identify the components that scholars use to delineate the contours of machista behaviors and be-liefs. We then turn to our interviews from the Latino Masculinities Study (LMS) to answer the following questions: (1) How do educated, young Latino men who identify as feminist and grew up as working class or poor define manhood? (2) Do their definitions of manhood include the differ-ent dimensions of machismo identified in the scholarly literature? (3) If not, what other dimensions are present in their definitions? (4) Whom do they admire as men, and what are the characteristics that they find admi-rable? (5) Do these characteristics include machista elements as outlined in the scholarly literature? We conclude by exploring the possibility that young Latino men are constructing new masculinities that go beyond machismo.

The Predominance of Machismo and Its Definitions

According to the Mexican philosopher Octavio Paz (1961, 31), who wrote the classic treatise on machismo, Mexican masculinity dictates that a man be "a hermetic being, closed up in himself. . . . Manliness is judged ac-cording to one's invulnerability to enemy arms or the impacts of the out-side world." Machistas, according to Paz, "must never show weakness nor emotion because such blunders could crack the machismo mask, an opening which enemies would exploit. To the extent that a man opens up and shows emotion or weakness, he becomes less of a man" (as cited in Strong et al. 1994, 19). Paz identifies a second dimension of machismo: "the adroit wielding of power, usually physical in nature, to dominate women" (Strong et al. 1994, 20) and sometimes other men. Machismo involves men displaying a hypermasculinity that thrives on power and domination and that is threatened by weakness (Mirandé 1997). Within the paradigm of machismo, women—conceived as the opposite of men—are disdained, considered weak, and subjected to domination and abuse. Similarly, weak heterosexual men and homosexuals are perceived as being more like women than men, as parodies of what men should be, and are therefore also subject to abuse. As a result, machistas harbor feelings of extreme homophobia with an underlying tendency toward physical domination and abuse of those who fail to live within the parameters of their perspective of Mexican masculinity.

The third dimension of machismo is a disdain of intellectual endeavors, because the acquisition of knowledge negates the physicality of domination. Also the sensitivity required for intellectual work violates the emotional distance required for a machista masculinity. The "denigration of intellectual activities" (Panitz et al. 1983, 35) then becomes another core value of machismo. This three-pronged definition has shaped the perception of Mexican and Latino manhoods, curtailing the examination of other significant Social Identities that Latinos may hold important.

Intersectionality and Masculinity

Intersectionality Theory has not been extensively applied to the study of the experiences of Latino men (Noguera, Hurtado, and Fergus 2012), which leaves unexplained the consequences of their contradictory position as men existing within a system of privilege that offers advantages. As Latinos, however, they also experience the disadvantages of those belonging to devalued social categories, that is, men who come from a working-class background, who are immigrants, who speak Spanish, who often look racially nonwhite, who have a Latino background, and who may be gay. The experience of multiple oppressions in the form of racism, ethnocentrism, classism, and heterosexism may create a space "in-between" (Anzaldúa 1987; Pérez 1999), thereby facilitating the development of a consciousness about the denigrated position of Latinos'/as' group affiliations. According to Intersectionality, Latinos in the United States are more likely to see social injustice based not solely on any one category—their class, their race, their ethnicity, their sexuality—but on all of these categories simultaneously. The experience of Intersectionality therefore also leads to a multilayered, complicated sense of self (Hurtado 2003c).

Intersectionality also provides the theoretical aperture for considering within-group variation. By providing an analytical tool that explicates differences within the social category "man," it permits the examination of other disparaged Social Identities' influence on the experiences of gender. Such variation in men's experiences contributes to more nuanced understandings of how different groups of men view and respond to hegemonic conceptions of masculinities at the same time that it provides insights into potential resistance to hegemonic definitions of gender. As we proposed in the introduction and in chapter 2, Intersectionality can be examined analytically by focusing on the intersection of more than one Social Identity, in this case, the intersection of ethnicity (Latino), gender (male), class (poor or working class), and the effects that this constellation of Intersectional Identities have on the respondents' definitions of manhood.

Looking at the Data

For this analysis we look at interviews from the 36 of the 105 LMS respondents who considered themselves feminist *and* who identified their class background while they were growing up as either poor or working class. From the perspective of Intersectionality, these are the respondents who should be more sensitive to the disadvantages of machismo precisely because they have an Intersectional Identity constellation that should make them more aware of its negative aspects. Gurin and her colleagues (1980) predicted that a subsample's self-identification with a working-class background and Latino ethnicity should form an Intersectional Identity node that could manifest itself in greater consciousness around gender issues, including a feminist identification. Therefore, we have placed the respondents' definitions of manhood under the microscope of empirical scrutiny to determine whether they have indeed rejected the majority of, if not all, aspects of machismo and hegemonic masculinities.

Respondents' Backgrounds

Because one of the goals of the larger LMS was to explore Latino definitions of feminisms (Hurtado and Sinha 2006b; Sinha 2007), respondents could choose to identify as feminist according to their subjective understanding of the term. Further, they were asked to identify the economic background of their families while they were growing up.

The age range of the 36 respondents was between nineteen and thirty-three, with an average age of twenty-five for the subsample. Thirty of the respondents were born in the United States; 6 were born in Latin America (Colombia, El Salvador, and Mexico) and arrived in the United States before age eleven. Seven of the respondents had a bachelor's degree, one had earned a master's degree, 4 were enrolled in a master's degree program, 6 were doctoral students, one was a medical student, and 16 were undergraduates. One respondent had attended a community college, but was not enrolled in school at the time of the interview. The 36 respondents attended twenty different institutions of higher education across the United States, ranging from a community college (e.g., La Guardia Community College) and state colleges (e.g., California State University, Monterey Bay) to large universities (e.g., University of Michigan). Thirty-three of the respondents identified as heterosexual and 3 identified as gay. Thirty-four respondents were single, one was married without children, and one was married and had a child.

Data Analysis

The transcripts of the interviews with the 36 respondents who self-identified as feminists were coded and data analysis was conducted on responses to the question, "What does the word 'manhood' mean to you?" The first thematic coding was based on the three dimensions identified by scholars and researchers as composing the core aspects of machismo: domination of women; denial of emotion; and denigration of intellectual activity. We first coded to see if the three dimensions were mentioned by the respondents. We then conducted a second thematic qualitative analysis of the respondents' answers,[1] which was intended to identify the core characteristics of the respondents' definitions of manhood that were independent of the definition of machismo found in the research literature.

We coded the first three mentions by each respondent when answering the question, "What does the word 'manhood' mean to you?" Few respondents offered more than three mentions; therefore, we were able to account for the full range of responses in the sample.[2] Overall intercoder reliability was 79 percent.[3] Respondents could opt to use their real names or pseudonyms. The majority chose to use their full names, others elected to use only their first names, while a few chose to use a first-name pseudonym or a first- and last-name pseudonym.[4]

To gain further insight into the respondents' definitions of manhood, the initial question ("What does the word 'manhood' mean to you?") was followed by two additional questions: "Who do you admire as a man?" and "Why do you admire him?" The responses to both of these questions were coded following the process delineated above—first, for inclusion of the dimensions of machismo and, second, for the thematic analysis of aspects of manhood that the respondents found admirable.

Respondents' Social Identifications

Consistent with Intersectionality as proposed in chapter 2, all 36 respondents identified their significant Social Identities (Gurin et al. 1980), which included gender, ethnicity, race, sexuality, and class background, and exhibited consciousness through awareness of the valuations placed on their Social Identities within society at large. All identified as men of Latino ethnicity (with slight variations in ethnic labels based on national origin and social context). All of the respondents were aware that their skin color and facial features signaled either their mestizo background (mixed race) or their European lineage, and all of them identified their sexuality either as heterosexual (33 respondents) or as gay (3 respondents).

To determine the salience of the respondents' Intersectional Identities, we conducted a content analysis of the gender issues section of the interviews, which contained eleven open- and closed-ended questions. We asked respondents about their views on feminisms, manhood, and male privilege. We also asked if there was a feminist and/or strong women and men in their family, if they could provide examples of men they admired (as well as the reasons for admiring them), and if they considered themselves to be "men of Color." We counted each time they referenced their race, ethnicity, class, or sexuality. The frequencies presented below are based on the responses to the interview questions.

Table 3.1 presents the results of the content analysis of respondents' identification with their significant social groups. All 36 respondents referenced their race from one to fourteen times (median number of responses was four). They talked extensively about being racialized by their families, communities, and society in general based on their phenotype, that is, whether they were light- or dark-skinned and whether their facial features looked "indigenous" or "European" to others. If respondents

Table 3.1. Respondents' identification with significant social groups

Social identity	Number of respondents	Range (no. of mentions)	Median (middle number of mentions)
Race	36	1–14	4
Ethnicity	32	1–15	6
Social class	22	1–11	2
Sexuality	8	1–9	2

were fair-skinned, they mentioned being misidentified as non-Latino by both other Latinos and non-Latinos.

Further, a few respondents discussed the ways in which their race had affected their higher education experiences. This was particularly salient for respondents who had attended private educational institutions because, many times, they were one of the few working-class students of Color in their classes and at graduation ceremonies.

In some cases, respondents wove references to race throughout their discussions of male privilege. These responses illustrate the way race interacts with gender to complicate the experience of male privilege. Some respondents felt that their race prevented them from gaining access to patriarchal privilege in the same way that white men could. Albert Domínguez III, who was twenty-seven years old and working as a program coordinator at George Washington University, provides an illustrative example:

> Let's not forget we're Latinos. I am not a white male . . . if I was a white man I could say "Hey, I have certain privileges" in terms of society, I could get into or a certain door you can open a little bit easier . . . I am a Latino male . . . let me give you a better example of what I am trying to say. It's as if you are Black, you're Jewish and you're gay . . . that's the ultimate minority right there, right? So I feel like to a certain extent I am a male but I am a Latino male so if I was just a male . . . being of a different ethnicity or a different nationality there may be a little bit of extra perks.

Albert's narrative illustrates an awareness of the stigma attached to his racial and ethnic identity and an understanding of how this stigma intersects with and limits his access to male privilege. In reflecting on his male privilege, he repeatedly emphasized that he was a "Latino male." In narrating his gender identity, he also mentioned his racial and ethnic identities, and did so repeatedly in the same passage. Albert also demonstrated an understanding of the way various disparaged Social Identities (e.g., being Black, Jewish, or gay) could work in combination to limit men's opportunities. Overall, respondents were, like Albert, aware of their subordinate status in society based on their racial and ethnic categorization, which they viewed as influencing their experience as men.

Thirty-two of the thirty-six respondents mentioned their ethnicity in their narratives from one to fifteen times (median number of mentions was six). Respondents referred to their ethnicity by indicating the use of Spanish in the home, by discussing various Latino cultural practices, and by relating parents' immigration experiences. Jorge Morales, a twenty-seven-year-old doctoral student in comparative literature at the University of California, Berkeley, emphasized the role of Latino culture in the way that masculinity was constructed: "I guess it depends on what kind of manhood you're talking about, whether it's manhood as constructed in American culture or as it's constructed in Mexican culture. I think they're very different constructions."

Twenty-two respondents referenced social class in their narratives from one to eleven times (median number of responses was two). These respondents discussed their parents' level of education and working-class occupations and the economic hardships they experienced while growing up. José "Nike" Martínez, who was twenty-two years old and had graduated from California State University, Monterey Bay with a degree in computer science, was unemployed and looking for work at the time of the interview. He described the struggles his father experienced while raising their family:

> He went to like the second or third grade and then he had to drop out of school to support his family. Once he gained his own family, which is us, he immigrated to the United States in search of work . . . back in Mexico, we had it really hard . . . it's just hard to make a living over there . . . he's pretty much worked all his life, he's worked in the fields, like lettuce and strawberries . . . and I've seen him get up every day at like three or four in the morning and come back at like five or six in the evening and every day doing this backbreaking job all sunburned . . . that's all he's done all his life, is work in the fields . . . he's done that for us.

José's narrative describes the reasons he admired his father as a man, alluding to the way that ethnicity and class had interacted in his life to influence his views of what it meant to be a good father (and, ultimately, what it meant to be a man). José inserted class and ethnicity in his discussion of the physical hardships his father endured for the sake of the family. He referenced his own social class (exemplified in his father's limited education, occupation, and long work hours) and ethnicity multiple times. José's narrative, like that of many of the other respondents, illustrates the way his ethnicity, as manifested in his Mexican immigrant background, is inextricably tied to his class background and shapes his views on gender.

Only eight respondents referenced sexuality, from one to nine times (median number of responses was two). Two respondents discussed the fact that they were gay, some talked about their heterosexuality in unproblematic ways (e.g., their relationships with girlfriends or partners), while others confronted the unearned privileges heterosexuality bestowed on them and complicated their definitions of manhood. At the same time, the exaggerated heterosexuality (machismo) attributed to Latinos was a form of racialized stigma.

In discussing his sexuality, Issaac, a twenty-five-year-old elementary school teacher who had earned a master's degree from Columbia University, stated that he had to "fight more stereotypes because" he was not a "macho male of Color." He thought that "in people's minds" the prototypical "Latino male is Ricky Martin or Antonio Banderas," both of whom were represented in the media as a "suave model."[5] Issaac felt this way of thinking was a "paradigm [that] still exists" and one that his version of heterosexuality did not "fit into."

These results suggest that respondents were aware that they belonged to various social categories and, further, that some of these categories were perceived as problematic by society at large. As proposed in chapter 2, problematic Social Identities are reflected upon more often than are Social Identities that confer privilege and require negotiation. It is noteworthy that the majority of our respondents were heterosexual (i.e., this was a dominant social category) and that membership in this group was mentioned the fewest times.

Respondents' Definitions of Manhood

Table 3.2 presents the results to the open-ended question, "What does the word 'manhood' mean to you?" which was coded based on the three dimensions in the definition of machismo: domination of women; emotional distance/reserve; and denigration of intellectual activities. None of the respondents mentioned these three dimensions as a component of their definitions of manhood; that is, these feminist-identified Latino men

Table 3.2. Responses to "What does the word 'manhood' mean to you?"

Dimension of machismo	Number of responses (N respondents = 36)
1. Domination of women	0
2. Emotional distance/reserve	0
3. Denigration of intellectual activities	0

Table 3.3. Themes in respondents' definitions of manhood

I. Relational engagements

Manhood is a developmental process that is reached when a person is responsible for raising a family; commitment to putting family first.

Manhood is relational, as in belonging to a culture, a community, a family (e.g., able to stand in a "circle of men that is constituted by extended family").

II. Positive ethical positionings

Manhood should be equated with womanhood, humanhood, peoplehood.

Manhood is exhibiting ethical characteristics: respect for others, living up to one's word, not cheating, being a responsible person.

Manhood means being comfortable with oneself, being independent, approaching life more confidently.

Manhood entails succeeding educationally (e.g., "putting yourself through school").

III. Rejection of hegemonic masculinity

Manhood is not definable at the present moment because the concept of manhood needs to look beyond biology; requires a more inclusive definition that includes women (if they are responsible for the family) and gay individuals.

Manhood rejects the hegemonic definitions of manhood and its negative manifestations (e.g., "use tools, fix cars," "tough burly guy makes you more of a boy than a man"); rejects dimensions of machismo (e.g., father never exhibited violence against mother); possesses positive attributes instead of negative ones (e.g., not rude, not aggressive, not insulting to others and their beliefs, more collaborative, supportive, less selfish, open to new ideas, able to express emotion).

Manhood is the same as patriarchy and is therefore undesirable (e.g., "patriarchy is bullshit," "manhood is false," "manhood means undeserved privilege and everyone suffers because of men's privileges").

from a working-class or poor background had Intersectional understandings that led to the rejection of machismo.

If Not Machismo, Then What Is Manhood?

If not through the concept of machismo, how did the respondents define manhood? Table 3.3 outlines the three major coding themes that emerged from their definitions and the dimensions (or subthemes) within each general theme: (1) relational engagements of manhood; (2) positive ethical positionings; and (3) rejection of hegemonic masculinity. Table 3.4 pre-

Table 3.4. Themes mentioned by respondents in definitions of manhood

Theme	Number of responses (N respondents = 36)	Range (number of mentions)	Mode (most frequent number of mentions)
Relational engagements	18	1–22	1
Positive ethical positionings	22	1–35	1
Rejection of hegemonic masculinity	14	1–20	1

sents the coding results. The relational engagements theme includes dimensions that emphasize relationships with family, community, and other groups of people as part of the definition of manhood. The positive ethical positionings theme includes dimensions that emphasize taking an ethical stand and exhibiting values such as respect, truthfulness, self-respect, confidence in one's decisions and in one's identity as a man, and pursuit of education to become a better person. The rejection of hegemonic masculinity theme includes dimensions that explicitly critique the dominant definitions of manhood, such as equating it with biological sex instead of valuing an individual's personhood regardless of gender; rejecting dominance and patriarchy; and openly emphasizing positive characteristics to counteract the negative aspects of masculinity. In defining what manhood meant to them, the respondents did not address their individual Social Identities separately; instead, their responses were based on clusters of Intersectional Identities that included gender, ethnicity, race, class, and sexuality.

Relational Engagements as Part of Manhood

Eighteen respondents mentioned relational engagements as part of their definitions of manhood. The mention of this theme ranged from one to twenty-two times (modal number of responses was one). Respondents provided elaborate explanations of manhood as a developmental process that unfolds as individuals mature. The end point of the process is reached when an individual is married and begins raising children. As Andrés Elenes, a twenty-six-year-old senior at MIT majoring in managerial science, indicated, "The word manhood, it's when your mind matures enough that you start thinking as a grown adult. . . . It's a person who from now on, instead of thinking about himself, is someone who starts thinking about repercussions about his actions for his family and for [his] community." Andrés's emphasis on manhood as a developmental process that culminates in a commitment to the family and community is consistent with the definition provided for middle- and working-class African American men (Hammond and Mattis 2005).

A second component of this theme is the notion that manhood can be understood only in relation to cultural and community practices within families and groups of individuals. As Alberto Barragán, a twenty-seven-year-old medical student at the University of Michigan, stated,

> Manhood to me is a culture . . . the ring of men at our family functions—manhood is being able to stand in that ring. And when you stand in that ring that means that you have a job . . . adolescents are able to stand in the ring even though they are low-ranking members. You're a full member of that ring when you're married and have children. . . . Like I said, the men [in my family] tend to be quiet and passive. You don't brag about things. Manhood means being able to stand in that ring and talk and be respected, have an opinion . . . my father having all of his children in college is an incredible booster in the manhood ring.

Alberto's response demonstrates the influence that the interaction between ethnicity and gender had on his definition of masculinity. His emphasis on manhood as constructed in the context of a "culture" and among the "ring of men" at family functions highlights the relational and culturally specific nature of such definitions and echoes the words of respondent Jorge Morales, quoted earlier, that is, that constructions of manhood vary from one culture to another.

Positive Ethical Positionings

Twenty-two respondents mentioned definitions of manhood based on positive ethical positionings in their responses, ranging from one to thirty-five times (modal number of responses was one), making this the most frequently mentioned of all three themes. From this perspective, manhood entails being ethical, standing behind one's word, not cheating or being untruthful, being a good human being, and respecting others. For example, Hugo Hernández, a twenty-one-year-old junior at the University of Arizona, stated that "manhood would be to work hard to respect people." Furthermore, he believed manhood was a commitment to viewing everyone as equals, honoring people as people, and emphasizing their "humanhood." Issaac, the twenty-five-year-old elementary school teacher quoted above discussing his sexuality, eloquently stated his views on the definition of manhood:

> It's coming into one's own about being open to change and to new ideas but also staying strong to principles or values that you have set out for yourself . . . like Gandhi says, "Being the peace that you wish to see"; it's like being the man that you wish to see in others . . . walking through the world in a way that is open but strong. In that sense, it's not only men; all people should be [that way]; kind of like a peoplehood, where we all learn to be strong but also collaborative and open to help and conversation, being open to dialogue about those things but also holding strong to whatever it is you bring to the table in whatever conversations you engage in; knowing who you are. . . . To me that's coming into one's own about being a man or womanhood or peoplehood or personhood, I guess that's how I define it.

Issaac's views about manhood highlight his feminist orientation insofar as the ethical characteristics he describes directly contradict aspects of hegemonic masculinity. He emphasized "being open to change and to new ideas" and identified this openness not only as a positive quality that men should strive for, but also as one that all people, regardless of gender, should try to attain. Issaac's response resonates with the ideas found in earlier scholarly works discussing feminist men (Christian 1994; Vicario 2003; White 2008) in that he emphasized a version of masculinity predicated on a selfhood that stresses the importance of connections (as opposed to isolation), especially collaboration and receiving help from others.

Respondents also felt that part of being an ethical person entailed being comfortable with one's independence and approaching life more confidently. Jesse Obas, who was thirty years old and working for the Educational Partnership Center at the University of California, Santa Cruz, said,

> Manhood is when you are comfortable with your identity. I'm not saying complacent or that's all you want to achieve, I'm not saying it's the pinnacle of your manliness, but . . . for the longest time I was uncomfortable with who I was as a man and who I was as a person. . . . I feel like right now I'm probably the closest I've ever been to the man, the person,

the Chicano, the Filipino, that I've ever been . . . encompassing all those identities. . . . I think that's what manhood is.

Jesse's response directly connects his definition of manhood as an acceptance of his various Social Identities, such as being (bi)racial and, ultimately, a person of Color. He was also able to have a critical view and articulation of his multiple subjectivities, exhibiting a nascent mestiza consciousness as articulated by Anzaldúa (1987).

Rejection of Hegemonic Masculinity

Fourteen respondents provided definitions of manhood that rejected aspects of hegemonic masculinity, ranging from one to twenty responses (modal number of responses was one). These respondents felt that definitions of manhood were in flux because of the intense questioning of gender and sexual roles. As a result, definitions needed to extend beyond biology and the objectification of women as the basis for manhood. Respondents were concerned that biological definitions excluded other people from the rubric of manhood if they did not meet the "physical" requisites. Some were concerned about excluding women who had the responsibilities usually assigned to men, such as being the main breadwinner in their families, or excluding gay men because of their sexuality. Respondents mentioned female single heads of households who fulfilled the responsibilities of both mother and father but received little credit for their hard work in maintaining a family. They advocated for the definitions of manhood to include anyone who took on the responsibility for and care of a family, be they man or woman.

Douglas Arévalo, a thirty-one-year-old student majoring in math and sciences at La Guardia Community College, insightfully noted that he had difficulty defining manhood because a single mother had raised him: "Manhood, I don't know. . . . How do you define a man? . . . The breadwinner of the house? It's very hard, especially nowadays because the breadwinner in my house wasn't my stepfather; it was my mother who was doing the running around — always doing that. I guess a man is just whoever can take the responsibilities for running a household, so it doesn't matter whether you're a woman or who [it is]!" From Douglas's perspective, his mother had lived up to the challenge of caring for the family instead of running from the responsibility. She, in his estimation, had been more of a "man" than his stepfather because it was she who had honored the commitment to raise and support her family financially.

Jesse Obas also indicated that "manhood . . . doesn't mean hetero-sexual, educated man . . . it could also mean gay, white or whatever." Other respondents rejected particular sexual behaviors associated with hegemonic masculinity. Ryan Ramírez, a twenty-year-old sophomore majoring in philosophy at the University of Colorado, Boulder, provides an illustrative example: "There's always that whole thing when you are younger . . . the whole virginity thing, you know, if you don't sleep with someone by the time you're this age, then you're not a man and I'm like, well whatever. . . . I consider myself a man because I've done things." Ryan explicitly rejected the notion that in order to achieve manhood, one had to engage in sexual intercourse with a woman—a rejection of heteronorma-tivity. Instead, he considered himself a man because he had "done things," alluding to the fact that he had overcome economic obstacles to succeed educationally. Ryan traveled from Denver to Boulder alone, enrolled in courses, and was working his way through school independent of financial support from his mother because she was the single head of the household and had to take care of his sisters. His narrative is illustrative of the ways that respondents refused to objectify women in defining masculinity. In-stead, Ryan's definition of manhood emphasizes his educational accom-plishments, especially in light of his working-class background. His re-jection of heterosexual sexual engagement as a test of his manhood runs fundamentally counter to one of the core behaviors associated with hege-monic masculinity (P. Collins 2004).

Respondents were also concerned that hegemonic and normative defi-nitions of manhood reinforced the negative aspects of masculinity. They were especially concerned about the negative behavioral characteristics of manhood that entailed harshness toward and domination of others. Among the dispositional characteristics enumerated were such behaviors as being rude or aggressive, insulting others' beliefs, and not listening when others spoke. Respondents also explicitly cited rejecting specific di-mensions of machismo, such as abuse of women by male family members. Instead of including negative characteristics as part of their definitions of manhood, they enumerated the desirable traits that men should ascribe to, for example, being supportive, being less selfish, and expressing emotions.

The last theme mentioned by respondents was the rejection of man-hood because it is a social construction that has no value—a construc-tion that respondents were openly rebelling against by questioning its meaning. As Jonathan Rosa, a twenty-three-year-old doctoral student in anthropology at the University of Chicago, stated, "[Manhood] means a constructed image of masculinity . . . it means an idea that I am trying to fight against; something that I am trying to unsettle personally, and in the world individually, and among the social networks where I occupy different positions . . . manhood is bullshit, basically."

Jonathan, as well as other respondents, equated manhood with patriarchy and undeserved male privilege. Patriarchy hurts everyone, and therefore manhood is a flawed ideology that should be deconstructed and eventually obliterated and replaced with more equitable arrangements between people. Jonathan's and other respondents' views toward manhood endorse this theme and echo the words of other feminist men (Vicario 2003; White 2008) who advocate for a fundamental restructuring and transformation of social relationships and an outright rejection of masculinities as a social construction.

Most Admired Men

We turn now to whether these 36 respondents were consistent in identifying the characteristics of manhood of the men they admired most. One question that might arise is whether the respondents rejected machismo for themselves but in fact admired its characteristics in other men, especially those they held as worthy of emulation. In other words, at times, it may be difficult for young men to not align themselves with other men, even when those men may not be viewed as admirable in terms of their gender attitudes toward women. Can male solidarity be broken when the costs for young Latinos may be very high?

Respondents' responses to the questions, "Who do you admire as a man?" and "Why?" were coded for the first person mentioned, followed by the reasons given for admiring him. For the second question, we used the same coding scheme as that applied to the definition of manhood. Consistent with their definitions of manhood, respondents' descriptions of the men they admired omitted the characteristics essential to the definition of machismo. Respondents did not feel that manhood entailed the domination of women, the denial of emotion, or the denigration of intellectual activities, nor did they admire men who displayed these characteristics.

Admirable Men

When respondents were asked whom they admired as a "man," the majority of the 36 respondents (61 percent) named their fathers (see table 3.5). Given these results, it is not surprising to learn that a large number

Table 3.5. Respondents' identifications of individuals admired as men

Individual named	Percentage of respondents (N = 36)
Father	61.0
Grandfather	12.1
Uncle	6.1
Professor	3.0
Nelson Mandela/Gandhi (one-person entity)	3.0
Roberto Clemente/sports figure	3.0
Arturo Islas/Chicano novelist	3.0
Pastor	3.0
Jamie Foxx/comedian/actor	3.0
Don't know because never met a man he admired	3.0
Total	100.0

Note: Responses are the first mentioned in list of admired men.

(80 percent) of the respondents were raised in two-parent households. Other family members, such as grandfathers and uncles, were cited as second most admired. Men outside the family, such as coworkers or scholars, were mentioned least. All told, respondents cited a family member as the most admired in nearly 80 percent of cases.

Characteristics of Admirable Men

When we asked why respondents admired certain men, the characteristics they offered were very similar to those themes that emerged when they defined manhood and fit within the three dimensions of manhood that had been identified: relational engagements, positive ethical positionings, and rejection of hegemonic masculinity (see table 3.6).

Relational Engagements

Within the relational engagement category, respondents mentioned that the men they admired demonstrated commitment to their families by supporting and loving them and by working in jobs that were undesirable and low paying. Edgar González, a twenty-four-year-old who graduated from Princeton University with a bachelor's degree in politics and was employed by Wells Fargo as an investment analyst, responded as follows when asked whom he admired as a man:

> My father . . . he is a very good family man. He did what he had to do to provide for his family . . . he [worked the] graveyard shift for over fifteen years. He did [it] day in and day out and didn't complain . . . he did it for us and that to me is like what a man should do. . . . He's great to my mom, great to my brother, sister. We all get along great. . . . I respect him a lot. . . . Growing up you see a lot of males who are heads of households who don't treat their families with the same amount of respect as my dad did and he's been a wonderful person.

As part of the commitment to family, the respondents explicitly mentioned family members, primarily fathers, who immigrated to the United

Table 3.6. Noted themes in characteristics of admired men

I. Relational engagements

Commitment to the family by supporting them financially, morally, emotionally; selfless acts for the family's survival; ability to survive the immigration experience for the sake of the family; grit and determination in surviving the immigration process to provide a better life for children and family

Personality characteristics that are admirable (e.g., funny, energetic, charismatic, strong, perseverance, self-empowerment, lovable, jovial, a listener)

Political commitment to those less fortunate (e.g., "What I respect about my father is his connection to the common man")

II. Positive ethical positionings

Responsible human being; having a work ethic

Succeeded educationally or supports education (e.g., "he is a thinker," "I really admire someone who can teach me things")

Overcome personal obstacles and tragedies to become a better human being (e.g., having a brother murdered, experiences in Vietnam, alcoholism, family abuse, breaking the cycle of violence)

III. Rejection of hegemonic masculinity

Exhibits the opposite of dominating characteristics (e.g., confident but not arrogant, humble, gentle, service to others, selfless, not loud or forceful, treats his mother like queen, loves wife, treats people with dignity, respect, and caring)

Never saw a man the respondent admired

States from their native countries to seek a better future for their families. As noted in the earlier discussion, 83 percent of the respondents were born in the United States (the remainder came to this country before the age of eleven); however, 80 percent of the respondents came from families in which at least one parent had immigrated to the United States.

Immigration experiences were often traumatic and fraught with difficulties. Family members explained that they endured these problems to provide a better future for families left behind in their native countries, as well as for future families they might establish in the United States. Israel García, a nineteen-year-old sophomore at the University of Colorado, Boulder, discussed extensively his father's travails in coming to the United States from Mexico:

> My father's story, my father is my hero. And there's no other way to go around it but saying it. He was the second oldest of eleven children. And his father was killed when he was twelve, murdered. . . . He dropped out of school in sixth grade and began to work so he could help his mother support the family. And when he was sixteen, he left the household because he felt himself more as a burden and that he could help her more by immigrating to the United States and getting a job here. So that's what he did. . . . He was alone here in the states . . . when he was only sixteen.

Israel's father went through a difficult time growing up with no family in this country. Eventually, he learned English and found refuge in a church where he ultimately became a pastor. He also became a "court interpreter, so he works in court alongside judges and lawyers. From a poor boy in Mexico to come to America and be able to accomplish that much, it's hard to say anything but that he's a strong man and that he persevered." Israel took inspiration from his father's struggles and found his dedication to his family admirable and worth emulating. His father's Intersectional Identities as manifested in his gender, ethnicity, race, and class status, coupled with these immigration experiences, formed the core of Israel's views on manhood.

Ethical Positionings

Respondents also expressed admiration for individuals who "did the right thing," even when they were not obligated to do so. James Aranda,

a twenty-seven-year-old master's degree student in community and regional planning at the University of New Mexico, was born when his
mother was sixteen. His father left soon thereafter. His maternal grandfather, whom he considers his father, raised him. James's grandfather was
committed to doing the right thing; he did the same for James's cousins
and other family members. James grew up regarding his cousins, uncles,
and aunts as siblings because they had been raised together as a family.
James responded in the following way when asked whom he admired as
a man:

> Definitely my pops; he's taken . . . me and my brother [James's uncle]
> and he didn't have to . . . he's done it with cousins who were in trouble
> and in and out of the criminal justice system, going to jail. He took them
> into his home just because—that's his responsibility to his family. That's
> what comes first—his family, his sisters, his brothers, his cousins, he
> takes care of business . . . he'll drop everything right there for his family.
> I definitely say I admire him more than any other man.

The ethical commitment James's grandfather felt toward his family
was a source of guidance for James. James knew how selfless his (grand)
father had to be in order to "do the right thing." James also understood
how unusual it was for individuals to exhibit such a high level of sacrifice.
His grandfather's ethical positionings were implicitly central to James's
definition of manhood.

Respondents also admired men who showed conviction and personal
strength in overcoming seemingly impossible obstacles and personal
tragedies. They mentioned such impediments as alcoholism, childhood
abuse, and Vietnam. Joseph García, a thirty-three-year-old master's degree student of Latin American studies at the University of New Mexico,
stated that "someone he admired as a man" was his father, who, "having
limited education, growing up in an abusive household, being forced to
go to Vietnam—he could have come out a lot worse." Instead, he felt his
father had made a contribution to democracy by serving in Vietnam. According to Joseph,

> There's all this patriotic discussion about democracy but in the history
> of this country it's the people at the local level, at the very community
> level, that have done something to create positive change in actually
> doing something about what makes this country a true democracy; they
> are the heroes of this country. Those that have gone and fought wars that

were initiated by white supremacists . . . utilizing people of Color to fight these wars as well as working class, poor people. As we see overwhelmingly, many of the frontline soldiers are people of Color and to come back recognizing the ideal . . . of what this country is about; and being able to make positive change and understanding one's faults but understanding also that one is a human being. The ability to enjoy life . . . no matter the pain, or the oppression they are under.

The commitment to country exhibited by Joseph's father moved him to reflect on the nature of war and its inherent injustice in deploying the poor and people of Color to fight for rights that everyone enjoyed and only a small number paid to have those rights. He was moved by his father's commitment and renewed his admiration for his father's courage and patriotism.

Rejection of Hegemonic Masculinity

The direct contradiction of the definitions of machismo was another prominent theme in the list of admired characteristics enumerated by respondents. For example, Xavier Márquez, a twenty-five-year-old who had received his master's degree in physical therapy at the University of New Mexico, explicitly stated that his father, the man he most admired, had always "given us everything we've needed" and "was always there, he never abandoned us." But most important, his father was "good to my mom; he treats her like a queen, like whatever she wants or needs he's going to give it to her before he gets something for himself. He knows how valuable my mom is; I think that's definitely another mark of a man."

Xavier's father not only treated his wife with the utmost respect, he also bestowed similar esteem and love on other women in his family. According to Xavier, his father had always wanted to go to college. However, his sister (Xavier's aunt) also wished to go to college, so Xavier's father resolved this conflict by sacrificing his own education and paying for his sister's degree. As told by Xavier, "He always wanted to go to college, and his older sister wanted to go to college, too, so instead of him going, he worked so he could pay her tuition. She ended up becoming a teacher . . . that's crazy for him to do that in the late sixties, early seventies."

Respondents also looked to the men they admired for shaping a "new masculinity," one that did not include harshness and domination. Respondents were still unsure what this new masculinity would look like, so they picked men whom they thought embodied a different brand of manhood. For example, the elementary school teacher Issaac, introduced earlier, stated that he was trying "to think politically" in selecting the man he admired most, but "it's slim pickings lately, politically." After some consideration, he picked "the coach of the Indianapolis Colts, Tony Dungy" because of "his presence, like he's not a very loud forceful presence on the field." Instead of forcefulness, the coach exhibited "a certain dignity about the way he interacts with his players and the media . . . his presence is strong and his character is strong even though it's not necessarily through his voice." The coach's quiet strength appealed to Issaac: "I've been thinking about my own teaching and working with young children. It's like I struggle as a young teacher . . . learning how to work and collaborate and manage and facilitate with children." For Issaac, teaching was the "biggest struggle because it's like I have all these great ideas but we can't do anything if we can't create a safe space for children to think and to learn." Issaac was having difficulty embodying the middle ground where he could be authoritative but at the same time gentle so that his elementary school students could feel supported. For Issaac, "it's hard as a male teacher, especially with young children, because you don't have too many role models." According to Issaac, of the thirty-six teachers he worked with,

> there's three [male teachers]; one of them is in his first year of teaching and there's another one who I don't perceive as a good model. So I look elsewhere—I look in sports or in reading Paulo Freire [a Brazilian scholar] that embodies some kind of critical liberation. . . . Where we build community and move people, not only ourselves but each other in a quiet way with strength. I think those are the kind of men that I admire or look toward [as examples].

Finally, one respondent claimed he had never met a man he admired because the concept of manhood was so reactionary that men should not be admired on that basis.

Changing Definitions, Changing Norms

As early as 1982, the Chicana sociologist Maxine Baca Zinn was calling for the study of Latino manhood to go beyond gender: "We must understand that while maleness is highly valued in our society, it interacts with other categorical distinctions in both manifestation and meaning" (1982,

38). Furthermore, "it could be argued that energy expanded in refuting machismo may devote too much attention to the concept, and overlook whole areas of inquiry" (34). We have heeded Baca Zinn's call to go beyond gender by examining definitions of manhood using Intersectionality that considers Social Identities in addition to gender. The results indicate that Intersectionality is a fruitful approach because the respondents did indeed look beyond machismo and provide expanded definitions of manhood for themselves and for the men they admired. The results are also consistent with Social Identity Theory and Intersectionality as the respondents are feminist-identified men and therefore question hegemonic definitions of manhood.

Privilege and Oppression in Respondents' Social Identities

Tajfel's (1981) theory of Social Identity predicts that when individuals become aware of the illegitimacy that privileged Social Identities afford them, they are more likely to modify the content of their Social Identities or even reject them. Indeed, the respondents in this study discarded the dimensions of manhood associated with machismo, such as the domination of women, suppression of emotion, and rejection of intellectual endeavors. Instead, they revised the definition of manhood to include such positive, nonsexist characteristics as collaboration, honesty, and gender equity. Their questioning of manhood went as far as to suggest the elimination of the concept altogether, focusing instead on positive values and behaviors, such as providing financial and emotional family support. By highlighting the behavioral aspects of manhood, they show that individuals who are not biologically men, such as women, or who are perceived as "failed" men, such as gay men, may still fulfill the requisites of manhood.

Furthermore, respondents also responded according to an Intersectional analysis: they acknowledged the disadvantages they and the admired men in their lives suffered because of their class background, race, and ethnicity but simultaneously questioned their privileges as men. Respondents also acknowledged the advantages of being heterosexual. Heterosexually identified respondents explicitly stated that the concept of manhood had to be modified because of its oppressiveness toward and exclusion of gay sexualities. Respondents who identified as gay also acknowledged their additional disadvantage because of their sexuality, race, ethnicity, and class background while simultaneously recognizing their privileges because of their gender.

In summary, the historical emphasis on the concept of machismo for studying Latino men's gender identification has limited the inclusion of significant Social Identities that at times turn into Intersectional Identities that could facilitate a broader range of knowledge production. None of our 36 respondents identified the three dimensions of machismo as essential to the definition of manhood. In identifying the men they admired in their lives, they focused primarily on their fathers and other family members. The reasons given for finding these men worthy of admiration were because they also did not conform to the three dimensions of the core attributes of machismo. Quite the opposite, respondents admired the men they mentioned because of their work ethic and commitment to sacrifice in the service of others, especially their children, so they could succeed in life.

The young Latinos who have come to identify as feminists may be outlining new conceptions of manhood that go beyond machismo and that are aligned with other oppressed groups. They see themselves in alliance with women, the poor, gays, and other disadvantaged groups. Furthermore, they view being a man as something to question and redefine, leading to a possible new model for more equitable social arrangements.

CHAPTER 4

The Latino/a Gendered Educational Pipeline: Vulnerabilities and Assets in Pathways to Achievement

Drugs, prison, discrimination, poverty, immigration raids, racism, and limited educational opportunities continue to threaten children of Color at an alarming rate in the United States. The loss of or harm to children is a major reason for the anger felt by many Latina/o parents and other parents of Color. There is a contemporary ring to Sojourner Truth's words of over 100 years ago: "I have borne thirteen children and seen them most all sold off to slavery" (Stanton, Anthony, and Gage 1889, 117). Given the Trayvon Martin case, the loss of boy children has become urgently worrisome.[1] For parents of Color, class privilege does not trump the exposure to risk suffered by many young Latinos and other young men of Color. In fact, when George Zimmerman was acquitted of Trayvon Martin's murder, President Obama stated,

> You know, when Trayvon Martin was first shot I said that this could have been my son. Another way of saying that is Trayvon Martin could have been me 35 years ago. . . . I think it's important to recognize that the African American community is looking at this issue through a set of experiences and a history that doesn't go away. . . . The African American community is also knowledgeable that there is a history of racial disparities in the application of our criminal laws—everything from the death penalty to enforcement of our drug laws. And that ends up having an impact in terms of how people interpret the case.[2]

President Obama continued by delineating the experiences of public surveillance he has endured as an African American man, regardless of his accomplishments:

There are very few African American men in this country who haven't had the experience of being followed when they were shopping in a department store. That includes me. There are very few African American men who haven't had the experience of walking across the street and hearing the locks click on the doors of cars. That happens to me — at least before I was a senator. There are very few African Americans who haven't had the experience of getting on an elevator and a woman clutching her purse nervously and holding her breath until she had a chance to get off. That happens often. . . . And I don't want to exaggerate this, but those sets of experiences inform how the African American community interprets what happened one night in Florida. And it's inescapable for people to bring those experiences to bear.

To demonstrate the commonality of Trayvon Martin's experience of stereotyping with that of other men of Color, athlete LeBron James and his Miami Heat teammates and actor Jamie Foxx were photographed wearing hooded sweatshirts like the one Martin wore the night he died.[3]

Parents of Color have engaged in the public discussion surrounding Martin's shooting and the subsequent verdict, expressing the terror they feel about their sons' vulnerabilities: the way they dress, how they walk, and, ultimately, the color of their skin make them victims of violence in ways that are gender-specific to boys and young men. Parents have expressed their despair over the futility of inculcating a set of guidelines to protect their boys when, in fact, it appears nothing can be done to avoid the possibility of harassment or even death. Scholars have noted that Martin's fate "spans the historical arc from Emmett Till's murder in 1955" (B. Alexander 2013) to the murders of other young men of Color, such as Amadou Diallo and Michael Brown.

Latino parents live with a dilemma: many believe that their sons, in order to be "men," should not be restricted in the same way their daughters are (Hurtado 2003b). At the same time, they are deeply aware that the freedom they allow their sons may make them vulnerable to surveillance by agents of the state. They may also be subject to stereotyping as the "dangerous, dark [men] of color" who engender such fear that "women clutch their purses" when they see them coming. They are routinely "stopped and frisked" (Hurtado, Haney, and Hurtado 2012), and may even be shot to death, as were Isaac Torres and Daniel Márquez, two of the three young Latinos to whom we dedicate this book. It is within the perils of growing up in this society as a male of Color that the respondents in this book have attempted to navigate the gendered educational pipeline.

The Contradictions of Masculinities

The contradictions in masculine vulnerabilities and privileges, as described above, deeply affect the educational achievement and opportunities of Latino men. Educators and researchers have argued that the disparity in educational achievement between Latinas and Latinos is due to differences in gender socialization; that is, young women are highly restricted, both socially and sexually, whereas young boys are allowed considerable freedom and male privilege. This divergence leads to different expectations: Latinas are often socialized to marry, have children, and care for a family as the primary basis for a successful life; in contrast, Latinos are commonly socialized to enjoy freedom and male privilege, are not expected to perform household chores, and are expected to succeed outside the home.

In this chapter we address the contradictory gender socialization of the Latino respondents in the Latino Masculinities Study (LMS) and compare this to the socialization process of the Mexican-descent Latinas in the Chicana Feminisms Study (CFS). From the larger samples in both studies we selected interviews of the highest-achieving Latinos and Latinas—those in doctoral programs—and examined the gender socialization in their families and communities. We were interested in exploring the gender Intersectional Identities of Latino and Latina respondents. By holding constant two social identities—ethnicity (all respondents were Latino/a) and race (all respondents were racially mestizos)—we focused on the Intersectional node of gender (young men versus young women) and on the differences in the students' gender socialization at home and how this affected their educational pathways.[4]

We begin by presenting the results of our interviews examining differences in gender socialization, specifically, the differences around sexual and social restriction and household responsibilities. We then examine whether potential differences in socialization led to different parental educational expectations for Latinas and Latinos or whether, despite differences in gender socialization, respondents received similar parental messages about the importance of educational success.

Gender Socialization and Educational Achievement: Where the Girls Are

In 2001 the American Association of University Women (AAUW) Educational Foundation released the highly regarded study "¡Sí Se Puede! Yes, We Can—Latinas in School" (Ginorio and Huston 2001). This study documents that in the years under study Hispanic women and men had the highest dropout rate from high school (30.0 percent), in comparison to Black (11.1 percent males; 12.9 percent females) and white respondents (9.0 percent males; 8.2 percent females).[5] These findings captured the media's attention as the results of this study appeared in newspapers around the United States, including the *Monitor* (McAllen, Texas), *USA Today*, the *Houston Chronicle*, *Santa Cruz Sentinel*, *Los Angeles Times*, and the *New York Times*. The newspapers attributed the high dropout rates of Latinas (*not* Latinos) to "cultural values": "Schools must do more to recognize cultural values that saddle Hispanic girls with family responsibilities, such as caring for younger siblings after school, that take away from educational endeavors. . . . 'Many Latinas face pressure about going to college from boyfriends and fiancés who expect their girlfriends or future wives not to be "too educated" and from peers who accuse them of "acting white" when they attempt to become better educated or spend time on academics,' the study said" (Gamboa 2001, 1A).

The reports of this study failed to mention or recognize in their analysis of Latinas' "school failure" the conditions of poverty many families lived under, the inferior school facilities, the overcrowded classrooms, the substandard teaching in many minority schools, and the constant threat of violence many poor students had to negotiate daily. By relying on a cultural explanation for the educational failure of Latinas, newspapers fell prey to what anthropologist Virginia Domínguez (1992) calls "culturalism," that is, the overreliance on "cultural" factors in attributing causation and the ignoring of powerful structural influences like poverty on Latinas' behavior. Furthermore, because the media's narratives used a gendered cultural explanation to frame the study's results, those results could not be applied to Latino men. Therefore, newspaper reports simply ignored the fact that Latinos were also not graduating from high school and that those reasons deserved analysis too. In addition, early marriage of young women can be detrimental to educational achievement, but this is also true for young men.

Gender Socialization and Educational Achievement:
Where the Girls Still Are and the Boys Have Fallen Further Behind

Nearly a decade later, in 2008, the AAUW published a long-awaited report, *Where the Girls Are: The Facts about Gender Equity in Education* (Corbett, Hill, and St. Rose 2008). The report addresses studies done in conjunction with a research agenda established in the organization's 1992 landmark study, "The AAUW Report: How Schools Shortchange Girls." That report sparked a national debate on gender equity in education; the 2008 publication presents updated empirical analyses on a range of inter-related topics, including "school climate and sexual harassment, girls in science and technology, race and gender on campus" (xi). Although the 2008 report identifies a number of obstacles that girls still face in the educational system, it also documents the ways that many of the research-based policy recommendations were implemented over the years and the education achievement of girls and women facilitated as a result.

In the same report, however, a new and important educational "crisis" is identified. The report notes that the successful implementation of many of the policy recommendations that the AAUW had helped generate over the past decade and a half had led to an unexpected turn of events, one in which certain populations of boys—not girls—could be "cast as the disadvantaged gender" (Corbett, Hill, and St. Rose 2008, xi). Although it was clear that the overall educational achievement of girls *and* boys had improved dramatically compared to that of nearly a generation earlier, these overall improvements masked large disparities based on "race/ethnicity and family income level" (4), particularly among African American and Hispanic children.

The first AAUW report, released in 2001, directly cites Latino culture as the source of Latina girls' lack of educational success (Ginorio and Huston 2001). By extension, the report also blames Latino parents as transmitters of these cultural values and norms. However, the 2001 report fails to distinguish between different parenting styles within poor Latino communities. In rushing to judge and condemn Latino culture and, indirectly, Latino parents, the report does not allow for the examination of educational success, including that found within the poorest Latino communities in this country. In short, this study failed to acknowledge similarities and differences related to gender, diversity in performing Latino culture, and structural factors such as poverty that may have influenced the educational outcome of poor Latino/a students. This failure thus makes the only viable solution for students' educational success to be assimilation into mainstream white culture; otherwise, they risk school failure, condemning them to a lifetime of underachievement.

The second AAUW report does not fully acknowledge that while white girls (and white women) may indeed have begun to succeed in education, they, in fact, have reached parity with white boys (and white men) and, in some instances, have started to exceed white boys' (and white men's) educational and professional achievements. The report blames boys' lagging behind girls in some venues, regardless of ethnicity and race, on the successes of the women's movement and on feminism in general. Further, the report does not fully integrate into its analysis the role of structural disparities by race and ethnicity in explaining the differences in educational achievement. Thus, according to the report, the crisis at the time was "not specific to boys; rather, it is a crisis for African American, Hispanic and low-income children" (Corbett, Hill, and St. Rose 2008, 4). The authors conclude that the inequalities that were identified by race and ethnicity are both pressing and "longstanding." However, the report fails to fully address the gender differences in educational attainment between Latino boys and Latina girls.

Both of these studies focus on educational underperformance; consequently, we learn very little about the Latino students of both genders who experience educational success. By not taking an Intersectional approach in the study of educational attainment (or the lack thereof), neither report fully analyzes the fact that educational attainment is a gendered pathway that is also affected by ethnicity, race, class, and sexuality.

With the AAUW analyses as a backdrop, we examine some dimensions of the educational inequality crisis using Intersectionality.

Deciphering the Gender Knot: Studying Latino/a School Success

The plight of young Latino men in the educational system has been examined by others (e.g., Figueroa and Garcia 2006; Sáenz and Ponjuan 2009). Despite the clear value of these previous discussions, our focus is on some of the issues that remain largely unanalyzed, including why, despite the important commonalities between young Latino men and women (or boys and girls), their schooling experiences are so very different. For example, we note that both the boys and the girls are likely to attend poorly funded schools, to represent the first generation in the family to enter higher education, to be raised in poverty, to share immigrant status, and so on. These common structural positions would seem to trump the effects of gender differences, but they do not. As we suggest here, each group experiences and manifests the effects of these structural disadvantages in different ways, which helps explain their different educational achievements. We argue that important differences in their life experiences and socialization histories account for their varying levels of educational achievement.

Core societal institutions use Intersectional Identities to allocate power and privilege, which has enormous consequences for the members of the groups to which they are applied. Therefore, Intersectional Identities are critically important to interpreting research results where within-group differences might otherwise be masked or ignored. In this chapter we use these intersectional axes of difference to focus on the ways life experiences of young Latino men differ from those of young Latinas, which helps explain their disparate educational outcomes. We suggest that the level of Latinos' educational performance can be understood only as a function of the multiplicity of powerful macro and micro forces over the course of their lives.

In addition, when only educational underperformance is examined, as in the AAUW studies, it is second nature to assume that Latina/o cultural values are responsible. An alternative lens focuses on the schooling process of the most educationally successful students in this group, that is, those who have reached the highest levels of educational achievement. If these students are given the same cultural messages as those who underperform, then what explains their educational success? As predicted in both AAUW reports, we assume that there are gender-related similarities as well as differences in Latinos'/as' socialization. We also assume that Latino families enforce, question, and modify cultural values, as all ethnic groups do, when they encounter new environments and when they develop as parents and human beings. Therefore, Latino culture is not static and immune to influence and change. Indeed, when Latino culture does change, the change is not necessarily in linear ways to emulate "white culture," but in intricate, complicated ways to accommodate parents' history, language, social class, and social environment. As such, we expect messages about education and Latino/a culture to reflect Latino parents' complex social contexts rather than to follow a for-or-against educational achievement binary or to inculcate or deny Latina/o cultural norms.

Respondents in Doctoral Programs

In this chapter we focus on the seventeen Chicana respondents in the CFS and the eleven Latinos in the LMS who were enrolled in doctoral programs at the time of the interviews. The remaining respondents (84 young women and 94 young men) were not doctoral students. None of the respondents in either study at the time of the interviews had yet earned his or her doctorate. We use the data from the two sets of interviews both to examine differences and similarities between these young Latinas'/os' educational trajectories as these young women and men navigated their doctoral programs and to study how their gender socialization diverged and converged, hampering and facilitating their educational achievement.

Table 4.1 lists the doctoral programs and institutions the respondents were attending at the time of the interviews. Eight of the women were enrolled in programs in sociology, and most of the men were enrolled in doctoral programs in sociology and literature (3 in each field). Of the 17 women doctoral students, 12 were first generation in college, and 5 had at least one parent who had graduated from college (although in two instances the parents were divorced and the respondents lived with their mothers, who did not have a college education). The 5 women respondents with college-educated parents were of mixed Mexican and white heritage. Of the 12 women respondents who were first generation in college, both parents were of Mexican origin. Of the 11 men in doctoral programs, 9 were first generation in college, and 2 had parents who had attended college. In these two instances, both parents had some college. One father, who was Puerto Rican, had attended college but had not earned a degree. His wife, who was also Puerto Rican, had a master's degree. In the second instance, the mother, who was white, had an associate's degree, and the father, who was Mexican, had a bachelor's degree.

Table 4.2 summarizes the backgrounds of the respondents. Most respondents grew up in two-parent households (11 Latinas and 8 Latinos) and most came from families where both parents were of Latino ancestry (12 Latinas and 9 Latinos). Most respondents identified their social class while they were growing up as either poor or working class (14 Latinas and 9 Latinos). Only a few respondents considered their class background to be middle class (3 Latinas and 2 Latinos), and none of the respondents considered themselves upper middle class or wealthy. Nine Latinos and 14 Latinas were not married (although one Latina had a child) and most did not have children (15 Latinas and 11 Latinos). Most were born in

Table 4.1. Doctoral programs of respondents

Doctoral program	Latina respondents (N = 17)	Latino respondents (N = 11)
American culture		
University of Michigan	1	
Anthropology		
New York University, University of Chicago	1	1
Chemistry		
UC Berkeley		1
Education		
UC Berkeley, UC Los Angeles, University of Michigan	4	
Engineering		
UC Santa Cruz		1
Literature		
Stanford University, UC Berkeley		3
Political Science		
University of New Mexico	1	
Psychology		
CUNY, UC Santa Cruz	1	1
Sociology		
Columbia University, Harvard University, UC Berkeley, UC Santa Cruz, University of Michigan	8	3
Urban planning		
UC Berkeley	1	
Zoology		
UC Berkeley		1

the United States (16 Latinas and 9 Latinos); if born outside the United States, they had been raised in largely Latino communities.

The Restrictions of Femininity, the Freedom of Masculinity

The Girls' Point of View

Latina respondents uniformly reported that they were heavily supervised by their parents, primarily by their mothers. This was the case regardless of sociodemographic distinctions such as whether they lived in two-parent or single-parent households. There were well-specified curfews and explicit consequences if rules were violated. Furthermore, parents, primarily mothers, monitored the Latinas' friendships and peer networks to safeguard them from inappropriate people. While they were growing up, most Latinas were not allowed to "date" in the traditional sense, that is, being picked up at the house by a boy and leaving with him. Even when they went away to college (and, in some instances, graduate school), upon returning home they were expected to abide by a curfew or at least check in if they were going to be out beyond a certain time.

Familial proscriptions regarding dating served in many instances to ensure that respondents' sexuality developed within a culturally sanctioned framework. Many of the respondents described themselves as "late bloomers" who were not particularly popular in high school. It was un-

Table 4.2. Respondents' backgrounds

Background	Latina respondents (N = 17)	Latino respondents (N = 11)
Grew up in single-parent household	5	3
First generation in college[a]	12	9
Mixed heritage		
White and Latino	5	1
Salvadorian and Panamanian		1
Puerto Rican and Canadian		1
Social class identification while growing up		
Poor	6	4
Working class	8	5
Middle class	3	2
Upper middle class	0	0
Wealthy	0	0
Marital status		
Married (no children)	2	2
Married (with children)	1	0
Single (no children)	13	9
Single (with children)	1	0

[a]Neither parent attended college.

clear whether respondents' lack of one-on-one dating was because of their parents' unusually strict rules or because of their academic inclinations and comparative lack of interest in boys. Their social life took the form of having strong friendship networks and going out with groups of friends.

Most Latinas raised with these social restrictions did not perceive them as particularly punitive, as most of their female friends had similar rules. A few also saw their parents' socialization practices as a reflection of cultural differences between their families and those of white students in their high schools. Most did not admire white students' freedom to come and go as they pleased and preferred their parents' concern about their whereabouts.

As a component of dating restrictions, the majority of Latinas stated that their parents valued virginity until marriage. Sometimes there was an explicit discussion of these values, but most simply "knew" their parents' preference without an outright conversation on the topic. Virginity was to be preserved both to increase the probability of securing a husband and a happy future and, just as important, to avoid pregnancy outside of marriage at all costs. Several mothers had gotten pregnant before marriage and felt that their lives had "ended" once they were required to get married. Monitoring their daughters to avoid pregnancy was also seen as essential for their daughters' educational achievement. Once a girl got pregnant, according to most of the mothers of our respondents, all plans had to be refocused on raising the child.

Premarital cohabitation was likewise taboo, even among Latinas who were engaged to be married. The only exception, for the most part, was found in mixed-heritage families. For example, Sonya Smith, a twenty-four-year-old doctoral student in the American Culture Program (Chicano studies/Asian American history) at the University of Michigan, whose father was white and mother was of Mexican descent, received a bouquet of yellow roses from her mother when she found out by "finding condoms in the garbage" that Sonya had "lost her virginity":

> I was in high school, and I was petrified because I thought what is she [my mother] going to think of me? I'm not a virgin. I was very nervous about it but then it turns out everything I feared that she would do, it was completely the opposite. She was like, "I just want to make sure you are safe. I'm glad you are using condoms. Let's get you on the pill." The next day I woke up in the morning and I had a dozen yellow roses from her. I was just like, "Oh, okay. Why didn't I tell her earlier?" But in terms of telling my dad, he has never been told, but I think by now he knows.

Although her father was white and had a master's degree in business administration from the University of California, Berkeley (which might imply that he would be more open-minded about sexual issues), Sonya was very reluctant to speak to him about her sexual behavior.

Latinas in our study did not necessarily follow their mothers' admonishments, reporting that they did engage in premarital sex. However, they had to maneuver secretively so that their families would not find out. Most Latinas eventually told their mothers, but not their fathers, about their sexual activity. Although most mothers did not approve, they did not threaten to disown their daughters. The mothers, however, did express sadness and loss when their daughters did not conduct themselves sexually the way they considered proper.

Most Latina respondents reported being given specific household chores that started with age-appropriate tasks when they were relatively young. As they grew older, their responsibilities increased. Several Latinas stated that every Saturday was "cleaning day." They, their sisters, and their mother cleaned the entire house. Soledad, who was twenty-seven years old and a graduate student in the doctoral program in education at the University of Michigan at the time of our interviews, stated, "We'd wake up very early on Saturdays. We thought we were the only family in America that woke up at 6:30 to clean house."

A few of the Latina respondents did not have chores or had parents who were lax about enforcing compliance. Several of these mothers wanted their daughters to focus on their schoolwork, and others felt that their daughters were going to be saddled with housework when they married so they wanted to spare them the burden of "women's work" while they were young. Sara, who was twenty-nine years old and a doctoral student in sociology at the University of Michigan, stated that her mother "cleaned and cleaned. She made my bed, she washed dishes. I didn't wash dishes." Her mother's rationale was, "Your day will come, when you are going to have to do this for the rest of your life. So as long as I'm alive and I can do this, I will." Sara was well aware that her mother was providing a "privilege" that would be short-lived, although Sara's mother was only partially correct because in Sara's case, her "husband does all the housework."

In the majority of the respondents' families, however, the only viable excuse for avoiding housework was to claim homework commitments. Most mothers deferred or suspended household chores for the sake of their daughters' schoolwork. Thus, Soledad could escape the Saturday morning cleaning rituals if she said she had "lots of homework; that was the tactic I came up with."

Most Latina respondents who had brothers reported that the brothers were exempt from household chores and from curfews. In the most extreme cases, economic resources were unfairly distributed according to the children's gender. Soledad's brother Ben is a drastic example, albeit not the only one, of the privileged position Latino sons occupy. Ben was allowed to leave the house as he pleased and was not required to perform household chores or to have a job during the school year. During Saturday morning cleanings, Soledad's mother told her daughters, "Hush, [because] your brother is asleep," and do not "run the vacuum yet." After Ben woke up and left his bedroom to watch television in the living room, his sisters would clean his room. Soledad recognized that "the freedom that my brother has, even as a twenty-year-old, is incredible to me." Throughout high school Ben simply announced, "Mom, I'm doing this" instead of asking, "Mom, may I do this?" Everybody in the family indulged him, "the baby," including Soledad's father, who routinely handed him spending money because he empathized with a young man "wanting to do things and not having money." When Soledad jokingly challenged her father— "What about me and Julie [her sister]? When we ask for money you didn't say 'Here's fifty bucks.' You said, 'Go get a job!'" He replied, "Well, you're going to end up taking care of Ben anyway, so I need to groom you to be independent, 'cause someone's going to have to take care of him."

The privileged position of the Latina respondents' brothers also existed in ethnically mixed families. Mariposa was thirty years old and a doctoral candidate in sociology at the University of Michigan. Her father was of Mexican descent and her mother was white. Her parents were divorced, and Mariposa was raised by her mother in San Francisco. She recalled that her brother had all the "privileges that my father would have had if he lived in our house. My mom surrendered everything to my brother." Mariposa was well aware that "it definitely had to do with the fact that he was a boy and I was a girl." Similar to the situation with Ben, Mariposa's brother's privileges extended to not "having a curfew that stuck. He pretty much had freedom." Mariposa picked up the slack by doing chores usually assigned to boys; she "mowed the lawn out of embarrassment. He had his own room—the works."

Most Latina respondents recognized that their brothers had both privileges and vulnerabilities. They tried to be patient with their shortcomings and worried about them, but they also were perfectly capable of getting "pissed off" at them when they acted irresponsibly. Several respondents worried about their brothers' educational prospects. For example, Valerie, a twenty-nine-year-old doctoral student in education at the University of California, Los Angeles, stated that her mother worked several jobs so that Valerie could attend Catholic school. Valerie's mother reasoned that a Catholic education would maximize Valerie's educational achievement. When Valerie's much younger brother graduated eighth grade, her mother wanted him to attend Catholic high school, but Valerie's father disagreed because he wanted his son to attend public school to learn to be "streetwise." Valerie wanted her brother to obtain the same educational benefits she had received. She also recognized her brother's vulnerability as a man when he later had to serve in the armed forces in Operation Desert Storm and participated in combat.

Latina respondents offered several justifications for gender differences in privileges: their brothers were the youngest, or the oldest, in the family or they were the only boys, or they (the respondents) were the only girl in the family. Whatever the justification, many times, male privilege remained unchallenged. Some respondents, however, did not accept gender differences within their families. In these cases, many of them succeeded, after years of struggle, in changing the family dynamics, making their brothers accountable to more equitable standards.

Several Latinas reported much more egalitarian treatment in their families. For example, Ruth N. López Turley was twenty-four and a doctoral student in sociology at Harvard University. Her parents were of Mexican descent, and her mother raised her in Laredo, Texas. Ruth was allowed to date boys, although her mother questioned her extensively after she went out, asking, "¿Y qué hicieron? ¿Y adónde fueron?" [And what did you do? And where did you go?], which resulted in Ruth's "rarely coming home past eleven." However, unlike in other Latina families, her brothers were treated the same way in terms of curfews and household chores. According to Ruth, "The expectations were pretty much the same for all of us as far as the household work. My mother had this cause that she was going to fight against machismo. She was very into not going along with the typical Mexican practice of expecting the women to do the housework from a very young age. My mother kept insisting that her boys were not going to grow up like that."

It was a similar situation for Valerie, whose mother "was the oldest and . . . she didn't have a childhood because she was too busy raising her brothers and sisters and changing the diapers and stuff. So she wanted me and my brother to have [a childhood]." Valerie felt that both she and her brother "were given a lot of freedom" and that "things were pretty equal between [us]."

The egalitarian families were not necessarily the ones with the most education. Ruth's mother, for example, was an orphan who had lived on the streets of Mexico until she was nine. At that age she walked across the bridge connecting Mexico and the United States and ended up in an orphanage in Laredo, Texas, where she remained until she married at the age of fifteen. Both of Valerie's parents were born in El Paso, Texas; her mother was raised in Compton, California, her father in Florence, which are predominantly working-class areas in Los Angeles. Valerie's father had a sixth grade education and worked as a cabinetmaker, and her mother graduated from high school and was a homemaker most of her life, eventually working as a secretary to help pay for Valerie's tuition to Catholic school.

The Boys' Point of View

The socialization patterns described for Latinas were reversed in the Latino respondents. All of the Latino respondents reported being allowed to date and having very little supervision and few curfews as they entered their teenage years. Of the 11 Latinos, 8 had sisters and 7 reported that their sisters had different rules from the boys in the family (one Latino respondent did not live with his sister). Jorge Morales, a twenty-seven-year-old doctoral student in comparative literature at the University of California, Berkeley, stated that while he was growing up his parents never told him when he could start dating. "I was never given an age, where I was allowed . . . I never really asked for permission . . . I never felt like there was a prohibition on dating." In comparison to him and his brother, his sisters "weren't allowed to date by my father throughout high school." Jorge's response was very similar to those of the rest of the Latino respondents.

While Latinas reported that their parents (with the exception of two mixed-heritage parents) emphasized virginity until marriage, the boys received a similar message, but there was an unspoken understanding that they would more than likely violate this restriction. Nava, a thirty-year-old doctoral student in sociology at the University of California, Santa Cruz, stated that although his parents preferred that he abstain from sex until marriage, he was "from an early age . . . given a lot of freedom . . . in the ninth or tenth grade when my parents let me stay out—until two or three in the morning . . . I had a lot of freedom to move around." When Nava went out on dates, his father would simply say, "Wear a raincoat" to avoid pregnancy.

Even though most parents did not speak about sex directly to their daughters or their sons, they did communicate the importance of virginity until marriage, especially for women. As Jorge Morales stated:

> It was implied, you know, that you don't have sex until you get married because it's supposed to be like the traditional Mexican family. But, I mean, there was certainly a more implied stigma towards women, you know, having sex before marriage than for men. I think for men, for us, for the males in the family, the big fear was "what if you get your girl-friend pregnant" then you're going to have a lot of responsibilities and troubles and you may not end up going to college for those reasons. The emphasis was more on how that would possibly hinder your future. Although, sex doesn't imply having a child, but that was sort of like the fear that my parents had.

Parents would point to the occurrence of pregnancy in the family or community to emphasize the importance of avoiding the problem in order to secure an educational future. Jorge noted, "They would just express a lot of disapproval when someone, a friend, a family's son, got his girl-friend pregnant and they would point out and emphasize that that was really bad and how we should be careful about that. Also, I guess, at least in the Mexican American community, abortion wasn't really an option. It was not something that people even really thought about. You got preg-nant, you had the kid. That's just the way it was."

The Culture of Silence about All Things Sexual

As striking as the differences are between the young women and men in both studies, one of the most important similarities was the almost com-plete silence in their families around the subject of sexuality. In describ-ing the discussions she had with her mother, Soledad stated, "I mean we just don't really talk about those things. We talk about like emotions and feelings towards someone, but when you start getting into the realm of the actual sexuality thing, she just does not . . . it's just not something I think she's comfortable talking about. So . . . we don't really go there." There was no discussion with her parents about the mechanics of sexual intercourse, menstruation, sexual development, pregnancy prevention, or sexually transmitted diseases. Even in the age of AIDS and with families either openly promoting young men's sexual activity or ignoring it, there was no open discussion of condom use.

The young Latino men had a different relational style to both parents than the young women had. Whereas most respondents in the CFS spoke daily to their mothers, many referring to their mothers as their "best friend," when it came to sexual matters, there was almost no discussion of sexuality. Young men in the LMS did not speak to either parent as frequently as the young women did, and when they did, conversations were not as intimate, but they too experienced almost complete silence around sexual matters.

Many of the young women felt that the lack of sexual discussion about sex led to confusion and, in several instances, to unplanned pregnancies. In a few instances, it led to abortions, which the young women felt had changed them for life. Among the young men, lack of meaningful conversation about sex led to fathers at times encouraging their young sons' sexual activity before they were emotionally ready. Joel Gills, a thirty-year-old doctoral student in psychology at the University of California, Santa Cruz, stated,

> I'll tell you this one experience that I had. . . . My parents were having marital problems. He [my father] was having an affair and they had basically separated . . . so he was hardly ever home. . . . And then one day he was taking me somewhere, and we're in the car, and he was asking me about my girlfriend that I had at the time, like "How's that going?" and everything like that. And I go, "It's going fine." And he asked me, "Have you all had sex yet?" And I said, "No," because we hadn't. And he's like, "Have you ever had sex?" And I said, "No, I haven't." So he's like, "Well, maybe I should do something about that. Maybe I should hook you up." Not in those words, but he's like, "Maybe I should help you out or something." I felt really awkward and was like, "No, no." Kind of like "That's okay, thanks, though." Because I really didn't know what he meant by that. I was fifteen, and I knew he was having an affair, but I didn't really know anything about that. . . . And so I didn't know what the hell he meant, if he was going to try and hook me up with a prostitute or something, and I was like, "That's nasty."

In this instance Joel obviously was not at the stage in his development where he could clearly express to his father his preference for engaging or not engaging in sexual intercourse. However, his father assumed that of course Joel was ready, and he was willing to facilitate the action. Because Joel was male, his father thought of him as a "little man" rather than as a young adolescent in the midst of his social, psychological, physical, and sexual development. Although we did not ask Joel whether his father would have made the same offer to his sister, none of the Latina respondents mentioned either of their parents offering to facilitate their first sexual encounter.

Chicana feminist writers have urged researchers to move away from dichotomies of victim/victimizer, oppressed/oppressor, powerful/powerless and to take seriously the simultaneity of Intersectionality according to ethnicity, race, class, gender, sexuality, and physical ableness. Therefore, it is important to examine more closely the construction of sexuality among young women as well as that among young men of Color (Roa 2003; Sinha 2003). If young women, as Chicana feminist writers posit, are not solely victims, then neither are all young men victimizers. They too experience vulnerabilities as they attempt to enact a hegemonic masculinity that is psychically brutalizing to all who try to fulfill it.

Chicana lesbian writers have been at the forefront of bringing sexuality to the center of Chicana feminist debates (Anzaldúa 1987; Moraga 2011; Trujillo 1991; Zavella 2003). These scholars' incisive intervention is echoed in the study of Latinos and Latinas. Their findings indicate that most respondents negotiate their sexuality within various significant relationships in their lives—from that with their parents to that with their partners, to that with their communities, to that with institutions like the church and universities. Chicana feminist writers have also proposed dropping the usual assumptions about young people's sexuality and going beyond the popular rhetoric to not being beholden to fads when determining what to analyze. Placing the respondents' voices at the forefront, listening carefully to the nuances of their lives, and avoiding objectifying them will, according to these scholars, avert colluding in their oppression as they are socialized to become "women" and "men."

In examining the Latino/a responses in our studies, it is important to observe that expressed cultural values were not necessarily followed and that not all restrictions entailed compliance, especially around sexual matters. As Zavella's (2003) work on Chicana and Mexiana sexuality indicates, her respondents dealt with both restriction and desire, often weaving in and out of controlling their passions or indulging them. Zavella's work underscores that in addition to restriction, the young women she interviewed also sought pleasure albeit a las escondidas (under the radar); nonetheless, there was not absolute submission.

Our analysis indicates that although young Latino boys are allowed considerable liberty, this degree of freedom may not always be desirable; that is, sometimes freedom, including sexual freedom, can be confusing and painful. Because of the emphasis on machismo in most research on Latino boys, there is an absence of analysis of the fact that Latino boys are sometimes pushed into the public realm or the sexual realm when the desire is either absent or not fully developed. Although Latino boys and men are supposed to be hypermasculine and seek independence, some, or perhaps many, may not be prepared to embrace such "privileges." Studies on machismo have assumed that Latino boys and men desire freedom without restraint; within this paradigm it has been difficult to anticipate the finding that they might be fearful and exposed to dangers they are ill prepared to handle.

On the other hand, Latina girls and young women may be stronger, more resilient, and more independent than the expressed cultural values attributed to them. Culturalism leads to a myopia that does not allow for the full complexity of these young people's humanity to be appreciated and analyzed. Such lack of insight and investigation may in part explain why research has not focused or explained the emergence of gifted Latino students from the poorest, most vulnerable communities to become first-generation college students with few economic resources but who succeed in the most competitive educational environments in the world. The over-emphasis on machismo leaves these successes unexplained.

The assumption in most of the literature has been that the differences in gender socialization will lead to Latinas' educational failure and to a privileging of Latinos' educational achievement. Obviously, the Latinas in our study who were enrolled in doctoral programs had already excelled educationally. The question was, in order to succeed educationally, did they have to overcome their gender socialization, or were there other messages and resources their parents were providing besides the values described above? Furthermore, how did these messages compare to those that parents were providing to equally successful Latinos?

Parents' Point of View

Several researchers (Apple 1978; Oakes 1985; Rendón 1992; Skemp 1978) have emphasized the importance of *instrumental knowledge* (the factual and procedural information necessary for entering college and succeeding in higher education) to a student's educational success. Achieving instrumental knowledge, or "know-how," is crucial, especially in higher education, where a large part of student accomplishment is negotiating the bureaucratic structures necessary to design courses of study, approach professors, and gain access to resources such as libraries, computer labs, and financial aid. Scholarly work has emphasized the role of parents in providing instrumental knowledge to their children. Therefore, it is not surprising that most successful students in higher education come from households in which both parents (or at least one parent) attended college. Implied is that the instrumental knowledge provided by educated parents leads to other resources, such as social support, as well as financial help. In other words, parents' educational attainment has been examined as a whole, and the research generally is in agreement that educated parents are best equipped to instruct, support, and otherwise encourage their offspring to succeed in higher education.

The effect educated parents have on their offspring's educational success is so overwhelmingly powerful that there is a mostly undocumented assumption that less educated parents are not very helpful to successful students, and, in fact, may be a hindrance to their children's educational achievement. This assumption is even stronger for students of Color, in particular, for Latinos. Latino parents with low educational levels not only lack instrumental knowledge but also have rigid views of gender that favor sons in every way, including encouraging them to succeed educationally. In contrast, they tend to encourage their daughters to stay at home and marry early, and they view raising a family as more important than gaining an education.

According to the respondents in our studies, most Latino parents want the best for their children, including education. However, given that most of the respondents' parents had not attended college and, in many cases, had not attended high school, parents could not provide instrumental knowledge. Indeed, most respondents were first-generation college students (12 of 17 Latinas; 9 of 11 Latinos), and therefore parents could not provide the know-how to navigate higher education. For example, Nava stated,

> I think my parents, even though they didn't understand the whole college thing in the beginning, they were always supportive and wanting us to do well in school. It's just that they didn't necessarily have the skills to help us. Like my dad couldn't really help me with my writing, he couldn't even write himself. So yeah, there are certain things that we had to do

for ourselves, but the fact that our parents put value on education was important—they valued education, they just didn't understand what it's all about.

Nava reported differences in gender socialization between him and his younger sister concerning curfews and virginity; nonetheless, his parents wanted an education for both of them.

We asked doctoral students about their parents' views on their educational success. We found that parents without a college education provided other types of knowledge or support, such as encouragement, financial contributions (no matter how limited), and an explicit emphasis on education. Parents who had attended college provided these assets in addition to instrumental knowledge. However, the amount of guidance for their children varied. Some college-educated parents discussed the respondents' career choices and requirements extensively, and others provided only minimal guidance. Gabriella González, who was twenty-six years old and in the doctoral program in sociology at Harvard University, was one of the few respondents with college-educated parents. Her father was a biophysicist and read her papers in graduate school. He talked to her about her research interests extensively. Her family provided wide-ranging guidance for her professional aspirations.

Although Soledad's family privileged her brother, Ben, in many ways (as mentioned above), Soledad was encouraged by both her mother and her father to value educational achievement. During her childhood, her family had limited resources. When she turned fifteen, her father gave her the choice of celebrating with a traditional quinceañera or "we can take the money and do something else."[6] Soledad said her parents were very "focused on us going to college. They had sent me to a very expensive private school." Instead of a quinceañera, Soledad's parents suggested that she apply the money "toward a Stanley Kaplan SAT prep course." Soledad's extended family, including "my aunts, my uncles, and my grandma said, 'She's got to have a quinceañera; everyone's got to have one.'" Her father did not bow to family pressure and replied, "That's not the way she's going to enter society. I want her to enter society with a degree. That's more important." In fact, Soledad's parents were so invested in their children's education that they worked extra jobs to send the three of them to private school from kindergarten through twelfth grade and contributed to Soledad's and her sister's education at private colleges:

> My parents really scraped and saved and did everything they could to make sure that we went to a private Catholic grammar school. We all went to private high schools. . . . [My brother] Ben goes to a public college, but Julie and I went to private colleges. . . . Sometimes my dad had three jobs. Most times he had two. He was always doing something. We'd call them his "side jobs." And mom has always worked—she's been working since she was seventeen. Her mom died when she was very young. She was the oldest in her family and had to take care of them. She's a secretary for an insurance company in Chicago. My dad is a sergeant in the Chicago Police Department.

Although Soledad's parents were unable to provide instrumental knowledge about the workings of higher education, they worked hard to earn the extra income needed to give their children, including their daughters, the edge to succeed educationally.

The area where most parents, especially mothers, provided the greatest support was in the form of what various respondents called "moral support" or "affirmation" of their life choices. There was no gender difference between Latinas and Latinos in the closeness they felt toward their mothers, the main providers of this type of support. There was far greater variation in respondents' reported closeness to their fathers, and again, in this, there was no gender difference between Latinas and Latinos. The type of support mothers provided for respondents also did not vary. As Soledad stated, even though her mother was in Chicago and she was attending the University of Michigan in Ann Arbor,

> I speak to my mom almost every day and we're very close. It's the kind of intimacy where, she'll know the minute I'm on the phone what kind of day I'm having. Do you know what I mean? There's nobody in the world that knows me like she does. I can go weeks without talking to my father you know? But his thing is always like, "Have you talked to Soledad; have you talked to Julie?" And she says, "Yes," so she's kind of like our filter.

The communication pattern in most of the respondents' families consisted of mothers speaking directly to children, especially daughters, then reporting back to fathers. Fathers rarely spoke directly to children about sensitive topics, especially sex or menstruation, or about the day-to-day details of their children's lives. Fathers also provided moral support, but it was not as intimate as that provided by mothers. For example, Marie, who was a twenty-eight-year-old doctoral student in sociology at the University of Michigan, described the kind of relationship she had with her father in comparison to that with her mother:

> I mean there's certain topics you cannot talk to dad about. But I think he's a very loving and tender and caring man. So there are things you can do with dad that are actually fun, like you can go and have ice cream. . . . I think that makes it kind of close or we can take walks together. But you know you can't talk to him about sex or anything like that. I mean, it's just different; it's a different kind of closeness.

Jaime Humberto Cruz, who was a thirty-year-old doctoral student in comparative literature at the University of California, Berkeley, felt his family's support, mainly initiated by his mother, because

> they showed up! When I was in high school my mom would drag my father to all the award ceremonies, all the open houses, and I thought that was cool. I don't know why most students were like, "Oh my God, my parents are here." I was a good student, I wanted them to come. I knew the teachers were not going to say bad things so I liked it. They showed an interest and they were concerned, they always looked at my grades, they always asked how school was [going]. . . . I think that the idea they always had was that we can't give you anything else but the opportunity to get an education, and they followed that through to this day.

Jaime Humberto's experience of complete family affirmation of his school activities was not uncommon. The support many parents expressed was unconditional, even when they did not fully understand their children's career choices. For example, Jorge Morales reported that his father was extremely supportive of his career choice to become a literature professor even if that was not the best-paying job. His father, who had not finished high school and worked as a laborer in a seed company, did not fully understand what being a professor entailed:

> I admire my father for many things, for pushing college, you know, being supportive of me going to college when a lot of members of my family didn't really see the value of education; they did see it but it was the kind of thing where you go to college and you get a good job and you make good money. My father has been very supportive of me pursuing an academic career and going to college for the sake of learning, for the sake of getting an education itself. That's something that a lot of members of my

family, they're somewhat supportive, but somehow they're also puzzled by it. Like they're always asking me, "Why so many years of college? Isn't it bad for you to study so much? Why don't you stop school now and just get a job and make money?" As you know, academia is not the place to make money. My father is certainly someone I really admire for really being supportive.

Only one Latina, Sandra Sáenz, reported that her father, when they lived in Mexico, did not support her educational aspirations. However, her mother challenged him about his close-mindedness and won. At the time of the interview Sandra was thirty years old and writing her doctoral dissertation in higher education at the University of California, Los Angeles.

Our interviews revealed some important clues suggesting what attributes and conditions contribute to the educational achievement of Latina and Latino doctoral students. Some of the traditional gender socialization documented for Latinos and Latinas was indeed practiced by our respondents' families, especially around the gender division of household labor and women's restrictions on sexuality. In addition, however, both Latinos and Latinas were told that education was important not only for gaining better employment but also for living a fulfilling life. The emphasis on getting married and having children held for Latinas and Latinos. In fact, all of the respondents had internalized these values as their own; they expressed a desire to be married, if they were not married already, and, with one exception (a Latina), all wanted to have children. However, these personal goals did not detract from their commitment to finish their doctoral programs and to have a career.

Another important conclusion derived from our studies refutes the assertion that "cultural values" alone are responsible for Latinas' educational failure. While the description of home and community life at the beginning of this chapter, as reported in numerous newspapers across the country, was similar to what Latinas in the CFS reported, our respondents were not high school dropouts. In fact, they were among the most educationally successful Latinas in this country, attending top doctoral programs in the most prestigious universities in the world. How to explain the discrepancy?

The cultural values outlined at the beginning of this chapter were not the only values their parents were imparting; such values were embedded within other messages concerning academic achievement and discipline. The discipline lesson many Latinas learned by doing chores and caring for siblings was later applied to the structuring of academic courses of study.

Many of the Latinas in the CFS reported that their brothers were less academically successful than they were, despite male privileges in the family. Lack of structure and discipline did not help these young men succeed. Of course, the 101 respondents in the CFS had many successful brothers, because family socialization emphasizing achievement is not the only determinant of success.

Both studies also indicate that although the majority of Latino parents were unable to provide instrumental knowledge, they provided support in the form of money (usually small amounts), affirmation whenever their children succeeded educationally, babysitting (when respondents had children), moral support (especially from mothers), and sometimes private school educations (which entailed working additional jobs).

Contrary to the master narrative (Stewart and Romero 1999), Latinas have developed strengths and skills that are a direct outcome of what appears to be detrimental gender socialization. While growing up, girls are taught skills that they as young adults can refurbish into assets when entering educational settings. Latinos' unexamined vulnerabilities are an outcome of boys' and young men's gender privileges and ordinarily are thought of as their initiation into machismo. They have therefore not been examined as drawbacks that may make educational achievement a tough road for even the most accomplished Latinos.

The Hidden Injuries of Manhood

We turn now to the social and psychological macro and micro processes that affect boys of Color disproportionately. These processes were not reported by the Latina doctoral students. The increasing incarceration of men of Color, especially of young men between the ages of eighteen and thirty, has been thoroughly documented. Haney (2008) has argued that the massive increases in the "prison-industrial complex" and the corresponding growth of correctional influence in social and political arenas have insinuated a criminal justice mindset—a kind of *carceral consciousness*—into the way many young men of Color think about themselves and others. The carceral consciousness has drawn increasing numbers of people into vicarious and direct participation in the crime and punishment process such that punitive, prisonlike norms, practices, and points of view have become increasingly merged with the everyday life of the larger society. From Haney's perspective, in the United States, the industrialized country that incarcerates the greatest number of its citizens, individuals are turning either into law enforcement agents or potential criminals.

There is no doubt that the carceral consciousness is extremely gendered and racialized. The state has decided that women are not as dangerous as men: they earn less; they are victimized more; and they do most of the emotional and social-reproductive labor necessary for society to survive (women head most single-parent households).[7] Yet Latina women absorb many of the consequences of the increased incarceration and state surveillance of Latino men. Latino men returning to their communities after stints in juvenile detention halls, jails, and prisons rarely receive social or other government services designed to undo or ameliorate the effects of institutionalization. Instead, their families—primarily the women in their families—are called upon to fill this void. As a consequence, communities of Color have a disproportionate number of formerly incarcerated individuals returning to their communities with the experience of prison in their background, bringing back into the community the norms and brutality of prison.

Many of the respondents in both the CFS and the LMS reported having someone in their immediate or extended family who had experienced prison. Hurtado, Haney, and Hurtado (2012) propose that the cycling between prison and Latino communities results in many of the norms learned in prison spilling into the everyday life of young Latinos as they get exposed to the repressive norms learned in total institutions. Haney (2003) has termed *prisonization* the process undergone by individuals as they adjust to prison's punitive norms. Because of the brutality of prison life, many inmates learn coping skills that allow them to survive inside prison that are difficult to abandon once they are no longer institutionalized. Furthermore, young Latinos, regardless of their educational achievement, repeat these norms.

Among the characteristics of prisonization are the dependence on outside sources to structure one's daily life, hypervigilance and distrust of others, psychological distancing from others, social isolation and reluctance to ask for help, incorporation of exploitive norms of prison culture (an eye for an eye), and a diminished sense of personal value. As we document in chapter 5, Latino respondents were more likely than white respondents to have had a relative in prison, someone in their family be a gang member, or gang members in their neighborhoods while they were growing up.

The effects of prisonization can be manifested in young Latino men even when they have not been in prison and even when they have been educationally successful. As Angela Valenzuela's (1999) important work indicates, young Chicanas in high school were more likely to deal with teachers and the principal so as to advocate on behalf of their "guys." They had sufficient self-efficacy to do not only their own schoolwork but their boyfriends' as well. In addition, they would "supervise" the comings and goings of their guys and negotiate their status with school authorities when their guys skipped school or did not turn in assignments. In contrast, young Chicano men were erratic in school attendance and could not focus enough to accomplish the minimum requirements to survive in high school. Instead, many hid behind a posture of detachment, silence, and withdrawal that might be functional behavior in prison but that obviated any real engagement or investment in schoolwork. The women in their lives negotiated their survival while they remained more or less aloof. The adaptation of these young Chicanos was predicted by the exposure to the prisonization of those around them, who, in turn, might have learned these survival tactics while in prison.

The respondents in the LMS withstood exposure to the adaptations to prisonization by entering institutions of higher education. However, their educational success did not mean that they were free from the continuing reinforcement of these tactics. They were retraumatized through their exposure to microaggressions, which are defined as "subtle, innocuous, preconscious, or unconscious degradations, and putdowns, often kinetic but capable of being verbal and/or kinetic. In and of itself a microaggression may seem harmless, but the cumulative burden of a lifetime of microaggressions can theoretically contribute to diminished mortality, augmented morbidity, and flattened confidence"; they are "probably the most grievous of offensive mechanism spewed at victims of racism and sexism" (Chester Pierce, quoted in Yosso et al. 2009, 660).

The Latino doctoral students in our study were no strangers to harassment by police, security guards, and other representatives of the state. Congruent with previous research on "stop and frisk" policies (Ogletree 2012), Latinos were stopped by police when driving because of their appearance. Nava, a doctoral student in sociology at the University of California, Santa Cruz, related an incident when he and a friend were pulled over by the police for no apparent reason other than his friend "looked ethnic and I looked ethnic": "I was pulled over once with a friend of mine . . . he was half white and half Mexican American and he had long hair and we were driving from a bible study . . . it was in high school and the cop pulled us over and said [that] we looked like shady characters and then we pulled out our Bibles and he was like, 'Oh, okay, go ahead, go study the Bible.'"

For Nava, this incident combined with other experiences, as predicted by the theory of cumulative microaggressions, resulted in a hypervigilance characteristic of prisonization. As Nava described it,

> I've always felt every time I go to a store, even now, I still have that internal nervousness about whether people think I'm stealing because that's just kind of the way I grew up, [that] is people always looking at me that way, [looking at] me and my friends that way. So even as an adult, you know it's funny because like I'm completely in a different world now and I still feel that way; I still feel like people are watching me and thinking that I'm stealing; it's just kind of something that you grow up with and it's hard to shake that feeling that you're different even if you don't look different on the outside to some people, you always feel that way.

Nava's words find resonance in President Obama's observation that "there are very few African Americans who haven't had the experience of getting on an elevator and a woman clutching her purse nervously and holding her breath until she had a chance to get off. That happens often." The hypervigilance that results from the ever-present suspicion of others is a burden that even the most educationally successful men of Color have to cope with as they try to stay focused on their studies.

The burden for Latinos and other men of Color is even heavier now because, as Trayvon Martin's mother indicated about the not-guilty verdict handed down by the Zimmerman jury, "the case is sending a terrible message to other little black and brown boys—that you can't walk fast, you can't walk slow. So what do they do?" These were exactly the sentiments expressed by Anselmo Ontiveros, a twenty-four-year-old doctoral student in engineering at the University of California, Santa Cruz, who related the incident of being stopped for driving "too slow" by an off-duty policeman who was out of his jurisdiction:

> I was going to work. . . . And I was in the fast lane going 65 miles an hour and the cop was on a motorcycle behind me, he was tailgating me, but I was at 65 . . . I was like, "I'm not going to go over 65 he's going to pull me over." And we go up a little hill and my car slows down a little bit, you know 5 miles an hour . . . I speed up back to 65 and he puts the lights on, he pulls me over . . . he says, "Do you know why I pulled you over?" and I was like, "No, . . . I know I didn't go past 65." And he says, "I pulled you

over because you were going too slow." I was dumbfounded . . . he wrote me up, he gave me a ticket for going slow, and he goes, "The speed limit is 65, you were blocking traffic." I didn't want to argue.

The harassment did not stop with the policeman writing a ticket:

Then he steps back and I wasn't being rude. I was like, "Okay, fine," and he takes out the vehicle code out of his back pocket, and I was like, [thinking] "Oh crap!" Then he started going around my car, and he started giving me "fix-it" tickets, he gave me one for my windshield being cracked, he gave me a "fix-it" ticket for having too much grease and dirt around my tire, he gave me a "fix-it" ticket for having a cracked bumper. He said it was unsafe that it can fly off and the bumper was just cracked . . . walking around my car looking for stuff and giving me all these "fix-it" tickets, and the worst part of that was he wasn't even a highway patrol, he was an off-duty Watsonville [town twenty miles south of Santa Cruz] police officer. I don't know why he was going to Scott's Valley [a nearby town] and he stopped me right here on [Highway] 17, and he also put that on the ticket that I disobeyed a sign that said slower traffic keep right . . . and there's not a sign there, the sign is about three miles down the road . . . and he seemed upset but he wasn't like rude to me, he didn't pull me out of the car or nothing like that, he was just writing me up for stuff . . . I was even late to work.

When Anselmo "called the courthouse, the first thing the people at the courthouse asked was 'What does the ticket say?' I said 'Watsonville Police Department.'" As it turns out, not only did the policeman harass Anselmo, but he did not have the jurisdiction to give Anselmo a ticket "because he was off duty and he pulled me over for a technicality, he said I was going too slow . . . and he didn't have a radar gun." Anselmo challenged the tickets in court and won on all of the offenses except for the cracked windshield, which he had to pay "300 dollars" to fix.

Anselmo related this incident with a sense of sardonic humor and, as predicted by the process of prisonization, emotional detachment that denied the burden of a student's having an unexpected expense for fixing a cracked windshield, having to spend a full day going to court, and being late for work. All of these microaggressions, which "may seem harmless," can lead to "flattened confidence" (Chester Pierce as cited in Yosso et al. 2009). Anselmo concluded ironically that in the past he had "gotten a speeding ticket for going too fast on 17," and then he corrected his behavior, and "I got a ticket for going slow so I don't know what speed to drive now [laugh]. I'm going to fly over there now."

For young men of Color nothing seems to work to keep police harassment at bay. Anselmo overcomplied by going the speed limit and acquiesced to the policeman's charges by not arguing or challenging his overextension of authority at the time. His compliance did not appease the officer, though. For students who come from strained resources (Anselmo was raised by a single mother), $300 was a financial drain and could have had a deleterious effect on his continuing with his studies. Furthermore, students who are used to excelling in school find it difficult to be accused of wrongdoing because their entire lives are based on following rules meticulously in order to succeed educationally.

In 2010 the overall high school graduation rate for Latinos was 58 percent in comparison to 54 percent for African American males and 78 percent for white, non-Latino males (Schott Foundation 2012). Given these graduation rates, it is not surprising to find that the number of Latinos in the field of engineering is abysmally low; thus Anselmo's accomplishments were beyond even those of outstanding students. The harassment by the police and the continued pressing by adding more tickets probably affected Anselmo more than he was able to admit even to himself—distancing and emotional numbing were the only outs available to him as alternatives to harassment for his driving, other than "flying" to work.

An option many young men of Color take when encountering public harassment by police officers is to assume that there is a simple misunderstanding that can be clarified with objective evidence, for example, running car plates to confirm that the car is not stolen or presenting identification to confirm that the driver is indeed a university student. That is exactly the tactic taken by nineteen-year-old Trayon Christian in an incident at the luxury store Barney's of New York in 2013. Christian, a New York City College of Technology freshman from Queens, was arrested at Barney's after buying a $350 Salvatore Ferragamo belt. Following the purchase, he was stopped by undercover officers who were allegedly called to the scene by a Barney's sales clerk who believed the transaction was fraudulent. The officers asked Christian how he could afford to purchase such an expensive belt. He was then handcuffed and taken to a local precinct despite showing the officers the receipt for the belt, his student identification card, and the debit card he used. According to his lawyer, "Christian was told that his identification was false and that he could not afford to make such an expensive purchase" (Wilson 2013). Christian had saved the money for the purchase from his part-time college job.

Applying the same tactic of documentation taken by Trayon Christian, David García, a twenty-three-year-old doctoral student in chemistry at the University of California, Berkeley, related an incident that took place after he and a group of friends of various ethnicities had a late-night dinner at Denny's restaurant after a long outing at the Magic Mountain amusement park. The friends were leaving the restaurant to drive the two miles back to their dorms. They were piling into the truck when there was a sudden flash of lights directed at their vehicle. An officer with a loudspeaker ordered them not to move as a siren sounded. The group was startled because they did not know what was going on. David and his friends waited five to ten minutes before the officer approached their vehicle. He asked them what they were doing and they answered. According to David,

> Apparently there had been some people who had been throwing rocks at pedestrians and I guess they had been driving a Ford Ranger and [my friend] Matt drove a Ford Ranger as well. So he really thought it was us. All of us were like, "No, we just got back from Magic Mountain, we'd been in Denny's for the last hour or so. We can go back inside and ask the waitress if you don't believe us. Here are our receipts." We each had a receipt because we bought our meals separately.

David concluded that the officer's doubt stemmed from the fact that "Matt looks pretty Asian, I guess I look Latino enough, and Wendy was Black and Christy was white. So we were a very mixed group. And Wendy is also part Jamaican and she has a thick Jamaican accent." David felt that the officer

> just wouldn't let it go. And I felt like, you know, if we had been a group of white people, this would not have happened. And, he even called for backup. We ended up sitting in the parking lot for like about twenty, twenty-five minutes while a bunch of other cops showed up. And then, [the police officers] took one look at us and were like, "No, those aren't the people and then drove off." And then he [the policeman] made us sit there for like, another five or ten minutes after all of the other cops had driven off. He was just like, "OK, well you guys stay here." And then he went back to his car and held us there for like another five to ten minutes before he finally came back and told us we were free to go.

Even though David was not naïve about the officer's bias, he still kept asking the question, "Why didn't the cops let us go?" when the other officers told him, "That's not the Ford Ranger, those aren't the people. I mean, there really was no reason to hold us there any longer." David's attempts to document the legitimacy of his and his friends' claims by showing the restaurant receipts and producing the server as an eyewitness, as well as the other officers' visual confirmation that they had done nothing wrong, did not convince the original officer. Furthermore, there was no apology from the officer. Instead, they were treated as potential criminals. Given this officer's behavior, young men of Color could conclude that they should be placed under constant surveillance because eventually they will transgress.

The harassment that young men of Color are subjected to is not confined to that received from police officials. According to our respondents, any public space is a potentially threatening situation. The unexpectedness of harassment and its unpredictability make it especially stressful. Even when respondents thought they were following the rules and conducting themselves as "upstanding citizens, to conduct themselves [well] in public" (as Trayvon Martin's father had taught his sons), there was still the possibility of harassment. This was the case for Raúl Coronado, a thirty-two-year-old doctoral student in comparative literature at Stanford University who was visiting a gay and lesbian center in San Francisco. Raúl stated, "I walked up to their balcony, and I had been there that morning, I was told I could go up there and I wanted to read, and the security guard followed me up there . . . [he] said 'Excuse me sir, this place is open to the public but we don't want any gang activity so if you could please leave.'" Although the security officer never stated explicitly why he thought Raúl fit the profile of a gang member, Raúl concluded that it was "because I was Latino, and I wasn't sort of the stereotypical kind of gay-looking man, like, the crew cut or things like." The respondents' visual Intersectional Identities were fertile ground for multiple sources of misunderstanding and potential allocation of stigma. Had Raúl visually conformed to the "stereotypical" look of a "gay-looking man," there was a greater probability that his presence in the gay and lesbian center located in San Francisco, one of the most gay-friendly cities in the world, would have remained unchallenged. Instead, his Intersectional visual representation triggered a fear of "gang activity" in the security officer, outing Raúl from one of the few public safe spaces available to gay and lesbian people.

Reflections on the Educational Success of Girls and Boys

Our purpose with the Chicana Feminisms Study and the Latino Masculinities Study was not to explore the determinants of educational success. Rather, both studies were conducted to examine educationally successful Latinas' and Latinos' views on feminism. As a component of this exploration, we asked respondents about their childhood and family life and about their gender socialization. As education was such a central part of their lives, the interviews inevitably led to discussions about their educational success as well as their parents' views on education. Below are a few of the attributes respondents mentioned as relevant to their educational achievement.

Almost all respondents in both studies explicitly mentioned the positive role that institutional programs played in their educational accomplishments. Most respondents, including those with college-educated parents, admitted having benefitted greatly from recruitment programs, special summer programs, and affirmative action policies directed at students of Color. In spite of their families' commitment to and support of academic achievement, the respondents felt it unlikely that they would have succeeded to the degree that they did without structural interventions. Ruth N. López Turley, the Harvard doctoral student, had one of the most egalitarian mothers in the study. She took it upon herself to directly contradict cultural messages of machismo. However, Ruth attributed her educational success to a combination of factors, which included her mother's encouragement and sacrifice, as well as the educational programs designed for students of Color (such as the summer high school program Ruth attended at Harvard University), guidance from teachers and peers who knew more about college, and, most important, financial assistance directed at students of Color and low-income students. In other words, academic success was dependent on a variety of factors, including parents, but not solely parents. In fact, several of the respondents commented that if their parents had been born later and had had the educational benefits they experienced, they considered their parents capable and disciplined enough to have succeeded as much if not more than they.

Intersectionality requires the examination of gender within the context of Intersectional Identities. The research on Latinos and education many times has overemphasized gender socialization as conceptualized through a cultural lens to the exclusion of other important Social Identities and structural factors. Respondents did not isolate their ethnicity or culture, offering both as explanatory factors for their academic failures or success.

They did not objectify themselves as being solely "Mexican" or "Latino/a" and then make attributions about their educational experiences based only on their ethnicity. From a social-psychological perspective, this makes perfect sense. People think of themselves as integrated human beings and take into consideration all circumstances when providing an account of their lives. Respondents mentioned poor schools, underprepared teachers, and subpar curriculum as school characteristics associated with being poor and Latino/a. None of the respondents made statements about having difficulty in school because of their Latino "culture" or because of "culture conflict." Also, none of the respondents mentioned distancing themselves from their families as a result of their experiences in higher education. In fact, many reported including their families in school activities once they arrived at the university, bringing home books and other resources to educate their families as well as relatives, and many times inspiring their parents to pursue degrees. The educational experiences of many of the respondents spilled over into their families and communities.

Understanding Latino and Latina academic achievement requires an analysis that takes into account culture, language, structural opportunities, and family socialization to provide a more complete picture of what makes Latino and Latina students succeed even when all odds are against them. The respondents' stories show that poverty is not destiny — "Querer es poder" (Where there is a will, there is a way). Such values have to be undergirded by special programs and by proactive institutions of higher education to help them overcome structural barriers such as poverty and geographic isolation.

This chapter underscores that the gender socialization these Latino and Latina doctoral students received earlier in life was not determinative of their educational achievement. In the next chapter we also discuss evidence that Latinos' views on women's equality and feminism are not determined solely by the gender socialization they receive at home. Instead, their exposure to education, travel, and mentors influences their views on gender and allows them to reflect on and reenvision the norms and practices they have been exposed to.

Postscript: After the Trayvon Martin Verdict

Trayvon Martin's parents publically grieved after their son's death. Both parents felt their son was a "perfect boy" with enormous potential. They thought he was safe walking at dusk on a rainy night inside a gated community with security. Trayvon had grown up in a diverse community, and his father, Tracy Martin, had never felt the need to talk to his sons about how to deal with race. Instead, he talked to his children about "how we prepare them to become teenagers, to become upstanding citizens, to conduct themselves in public" (www.cnn.com/2013/07/18/justice/trayvon-martin-parents/).

Although Trayvon's parents attended every day of Zimmerman's trial, they chose not to attend the day the verdict was announced. They were afraid of losing their composure when the outcome was revealed. When they finally heard about the not-guilty verdict, Trayvon's dad stated, "My heart is broken, my faith is not" (www.cnn.com/2013/07/18/justice/trayvon-martin-parents/). Sybrina Fulton, Trayvon's mother, stated, "When I heard the verdict, I kind of understand the disconnect. . . . Maybe they [jurors] didn't see Trayvon as their son. They didn't see Trayvon as a teenager. They didn't see Trayvon as just a human being that was minding his own business" (www.cnn.com/2013/07/18/justice/trayvon-martin-parents/). The sense of futility was made apparent when Fulton stated, "The case is sending a terrible message to other little black and brown boys— that you can't walk fast, you can't walk slow. So what do they do? I mean, how do you get home without people knowing or either assuming that you're doing something wrong? Trayvon wasn't doing anything wrong" (www.cnn.com/2013/07/18/justice/trayvon-martin-parents/).

The last time a family member saw Trayvon Martin alive he was stepping out of his home to play a pickup game of basketball and buy a snack afterward. The next time they saw him was when a body bag was unzipped at the morgue. The experience of Trayvon Martin's family is not uncommon, as more and more young men of Color are the objects of senseless violence. However, instead of being filled with feelings of bitterness and revenge, Trayvon's parents committed themselves to preventing future tragedies like the one they suffered:

> The Trayvon Martin Foundation was established by Sybrina Fulton and Tracy Martin in March 2012 as a not-for-profit organization under the auspices of the Miami Foundation. The Foundation's purpose is to create awareness of how violent crime impacts the families of the victims and to provide support and advocacy for those families in response to the murder of Trayvon Martin. The scope of the Foundation's mission is to advocate that crime victims and their families are not ignored in the discussions about violent crime[,] to increase public awareness of all forms of racial ethnic and gender profiling[, to] educate youth on con-

flict resolution techniques and to reduce the incidences where confrontations between strangers turn deadly (http://trayvonmartinfoundation.org/about-us/).

Trayvon's mother said that she hoped that a foundation started in her son's name would allow for something good to come out of his death: "The change that we hope to [effect] is with the law," Fulton said. "We want to make sure any teenager who is walking down the street won't be killed, that they will make it home safe" (www.cnn.com/2013/07/18/justice/trayvon-martin-parents/). When asked if the justice system worked, Trayvon's father stated, "It didn't work for us," but "we remain prayerful that through this injustice, we can close that gap and hopefully the system can start working for everyone equally."

May the prayers of Trayvon's parents be answered and more young men of Color end up in higher education instead of facing the same fate as Martin and Fulton's beloved son met.

CHAPTER 5

Relating to Feminisms: Intersectionality in Latino and White Men's Views on Gender Equality

In *The Color of Privilege: Three Blasphemies on Race and Feminism*, Hurtado (1996) proposes that different feminisms have developed based on the differential racial positioning women have to white patriarchy. The feminisms of white women has evolved largely from their position vis-à-vis white, privileged men while the feminisms of women of Color are defined by their relation to men of Color, whose status, in turn, is determined by their position relative to white patriarchy. Thus the economic positioning within this racial order further defines the feminisms of all women:

> White middle-class women are groomed from birth to be the lovers, mothers, and partners (however unequal) of white men because of the economic and social benefits attached to these roles (de Beauvoir 1952, xxiv; Lorde 1984, 118–19). Upper- and middle-class white women are supposed to be the biological bearers of those members of the next generation who will inherit positions of power in society. Women of Color, in contrast, are groomed from birth to be primarily the lovers, mothers, and partners (however unequal) of men of Color, who are also oppressed by white men. The avenues of advancement through marriage that are open to white women who conform . . . are not even a theoretical possibility for most women of Color (Ostrander 1984). Ramón Gutiérrez (1991, xviii) rightly indicates that marriage provides a "window into the social, political, and economic arrangements of a society," and that it is through marriage that people "create social alliances, establish a new social unit, change residence, exchange property, and gain rights to sexual service." It is the most intimate linkage, besides biological ties, that two individuals may engage in—therefore, it is not surprising that

like tends to marry like because it is through the ritual of marriage that
we define the contours of class and status. (Hurtado 1996, 10–11)

Because white women could "relate to privilege" through their familial
relationships to white patriarchy, their feminisms by definition had to be
different from those created by women of Color, who could not cross the
biological divide to produce "pure" white offspring for the reproduction
of white, patriarchal race privilege.

In this chapter we propose that the same is true for different groups
of men and their relationship to patriarchy. If men are to be considered
allies of women in their struggle for equality, *their relationship to feminisms*
will also be affected by their relationship to white patriarchy, creating a
difference in their manifested views on gender. Thus we examine the attitudes and views of both Latino and White men here. We use the Brown
and White Masculinities Study (BWMS) as the source of data to examine
the different views on feminisms of these two groups of men and, given
all men's access to patriarchal privilege, the similarities.[1] All women suffer the consequences of male privilege but not all are similarly situated
with regard to white men, who have the most access to its benefits. Thus
we delineate in this chapter the dimensions Brown men have in common
with white men and highlight how Brown men's experience of a "lesser"
masculinity (Connell 1995) affects their views on gender inequality.

Machismo and Masculinities

The historical antecedents for the popularization of the use of the concept
of machismo, particularly in the academic realm, begin in 1961 with the
publication of Oscar Lewis's *The Children of Sanchez*.[2] Renowned anthropologist Lewis writes that the book "is about a poor family in Mexico
City, Jesús Sánchez, the father . . . and his four children. . . . My purpose
is to give the reader an inside view of family life and of what it means to
grow up in a one-room home in a slum tenement in the heart of a great
Latin American city which is undergoing a process of rapid social and
economic change" (xi). Those who grow up in this environment inhabit
a "world of violence and death, of suffering and deprivation, of infidelity
and broken homes, of delinquency, corruption, and police brutality, and
of the cruelty of the poor to the poor" (xi).

The dysfunctional Sánchez family became the prototype for the concept known as the "culture of poverty," [3] which crossed Mexico's national borders into the United States and made its way into the Moynihan Report. [4] Both Lewis and Moynihan attribute poverty to the highly gendered and dysfunctional nature of poor families and their failure to fully embrace the assumed egalitarian gender roles of the white, middle-class, nuclear family unit as the pathway to the American dream—that is, a successful occupation, a nuclear marriage, and well-adjusted, successful offspring.

Lewis's classic study captured the US imaginary and still holds currency (Small, Harding, and Lamont 2010). His description of the dynamics of a poor Mexican family with an abusive father and four dysfunctional children became iconic of all Latino families, whether residing in the United States or in Latin America. Cultural specificity, historical moment, or social context was irrelevant in the obfuscating presence and predominance of machismo. As stated by Lewis, "It seems to me that the culture of poverty has some universal characteristics which transcend regional, rural-urban, and even national differences" (1961, xxv).

A few years later and approximately 600 miles north of Mexico City, a second and, arguably, more influential study of Latino masculinity was conducted by another US-trained anthropologist, William Madsen (1964). After conducting his fieldwork in South Texas, Madsen reinscribed the predominance of machismo in all Latino familial relationships:

> The ideal male role is primarily defined by the concept of *machismo* or manliness. Every Mexican-American male tries to make his life a living validation of the assumption that the man is stronger, more reliable, and more intelligent than the female. He strives to achieve the respect of his society by acting like a "real man" in every situation. Perhaps the most common anxiety found in male Latin society is the fear of failure in the role of manly behavior. . . . As one Latin male explained, "To us a man is a man because he acts like a man. And he is respected for this. It does not matter if he is short or tall, ugly or handsome, rich or poor. These things are unimportant. When he stands on his own feet as he should, then he is looked up to." (18)

In particular, Madsen documents in great detail the patriarchal privileges Mexican Americans enjoy: "The wife is expected to give comfort and pleasure to her husband. She must acknowledge his authority and superiority and think of his needs before her own. She is supposed to accept abuse without complaint and avoid resentment of his pastimes and extra-marital affairs. Her in-laws may criticize her and her husband may beat her for demanding that he spend too much time at home" (48).

According to Madsen, for a man to be a "macho," the wife must be submissive: "She sets the tone of the home atmosphere, ideally by radiating love and understanding. In her role as wife and mother, she is frequently compared with the Virgin of Guadalupe. This holy model for female behavior possesses all the most prized values of womanhood: purity, sanctity, tolerance, love, and sympathy. By extension but rarely by direct comparison, the husband and father is seen as a human image of God. He is aloof, absolute, and forceful in administering justice" (48).

Following the publication of these two seminal studies, much of the academic work by Chicana/o scholars in the 1970s and 1980s was aimed at debunking the dysfunctionality of Chicano families caused by machismo (Baca Zinn 1975; Paredes 1977). In an effort to counteract the negative portrayal of the male dominance of families, Chicana/o scholars focused on the economic and social oppression that many Chicano families suffered in the United States (Baca Zinn 1994).

The year before the publication of Madsen's *Mexican-Americans of South Texas* and two years after the publication of Lewis's *The Children of Sánchez*, Betty Friedan published her groundbreaking book *The Feminine Mystique* (1963), which is credited with sparking the second wave of the feminist movement. Friedan most notably articulated "the problem that had no name":

The problem lay buried, unspoken, for many years in the minds of American women. It was a strange stirring, a sense of dissatisfaction, a yearning that women suffered in the middle of the twentieth century in the United States. Each suburban wife struggled with it alone. As she made the beds, shopped for groceries, matched slipcover material, ate peanut butter sandwiches with her children, chauffeured Cub Scouts and Brownies, lay beside her husband at night—she was afraid to ask even of herself the silent question—"Is this all?" (15)

The "problem" delineated by Friedan was based on the unquestioned, and therefore normal, white patriarchal privilege. According to Friedan, the system of white male privilege required an emotionally stunted wife who was not capable of taking care of herself and her children if she worked outside the home; the education of bright, middle-class, white women was only the means to the end of obtaining the title of Mrs. A woman's main role was to support her husband as he built a career because his success translated into the economic and social achievements of the nuclear family. In other words, the dominant role of white men within the white, middle-class family described in the *Feminine Mystique* had very similar dimensions to those attributed to the concept of machismo. However, in this instance, there was no structural oppression to explain the behaviors—no poverty, no blocked opportunities, no racism, no segregation, and no culture of poverty. Instead, sexist, macho dominance was the "normal culture" instilled in white nuclear families, where white men were viewed as "naturally" superior. Because white patriarchy was considered normal and natural, there were no words to problematize the problem; hence it had "no name." Most important, unlike machismo in Latino families and men's putative familial neglect in African American families, white patriarchal privileges had the full support of the state through an elaborate web of laws that were accepted as normal and natural until the white feminist movement shone a light on them and forced them to be dismantled: "In 1963, most women weren't able to get credit without a male co-signer. In some states they couldn't sit on juries; in others, their husbands had control not only of their property but also of their earnings. . . . newspapers were allowed to divide their help-wanted ads into categories for men and women, or . . . it was perfectly legal for an employer to announce that certain jobs were for men only. Even the federal government did it" (G. Collins 2013, MM42).

In commemorating the fiftieth anniversary of the publication of *The Feminine Mystique*, *New York Times* columnist Gail Collins wrote that the book contained "a very specific cry of rage about the way intelligent, well-educated women were kept out of the mainstream of American professional life and regarded as little more than a set of reproductive organs in heels." Of course, Collins should have said "white women," given the biological requisites of whiteness as manifested in the "one-drop" rule, under which, until recently, any individual with "one drop" of "Black" blood was assigned the racial category of Black. However, economically privileged white men were never accused of machismo.

Because the analysis of white and Brown patriarchies has been segregated, there is no formal acknowledgment in the literature of the overlapping nature of the construction of masculinities in relation to the sexist construction of femininities—those constructions that happen in the intimacy of family life and therefore affect men's and women's *personal* identities regardless of race, ethnicity, and class. The variations in masculinities and access to patriarchal structural privileges are dependent on men's *Social* Identities of race, class, ethnicity, and sexuality. Therefore, we can predict that the white and Latino men in the study presented here may display overlapping views on gender, particularly regarding attitudes about behaviors within the intimacy of personal relationships (e.g., who should be responsible for housework, who should be dominant in the home) and divergent views on structural gender disadvantages (e.g., women's employment outside the home).

The Study

Comparing Brown and White Masculinities

In this chapter we examine the intersections of race, class, ethnicity, and gender with quantitative questionnaire data from the BWMS. We compare the commonalities and differences in young Latino and white men's gender attitudes and views toward feminisms. We employ three statistical techniques to explore the data: independent sample t-tests, chi-square tests, and principal components factor analysis. We then address three interrelated research questions: (1) What are the factors underlying Latino men's and white men's attitudes toward gender and feminism? (2) How do the structure and content of these factors differ across race and class lines? (3) How does Intersectionality help us explain the potential commonalities and differences in factor content and structure?

About the Respondents

In the BWMS there were 301 young men who had some college experience. Approximately half of the sample identified as Latino (150 respondents) and the other half as white (151 respondents).[5] Ages of the Latinos ranged from 18 to 37, with an average age of 27. Seventy percent of Latino respondents (105) were undergraduates and 15 percent (23) were graduate students. Eight percent (12 respondents) had completed their bachelor's degree, and 4 percent (6 respondents) had completed a graduate degree (PhD, MA, or MD). Approximately 3 percent (4 respondents) had some college experience (e.g., community college) but were not enrolled at the time the questionnaire was administered. Most of the Latino respondents were recruited from Northern California (61 percent) and were attending four-year institutions (92 respondents). The remaining respondents were recruited from colleges in the Southwest and Midwest and on the East Coast. In describing their economic background, 70 percent (105 respondents) of Latino respondents identified as being poor to lower middle

Table 5.1. Social-class identification of Brown and White Masculinities Study respondents

Social-class identification	Number of Latinos (% of total) N = 150	Number of whites (% of total) N = 151
a. Poor	30 (20)	2 (1)
b. Working class	51 (34)	7 (5)
c. Lower middle class	24 (16)	16 (11)
d. Middle class	33 (22)	58 (38)
e. Upper middle class	12 (8)	62 (41)
f. Rich	0	4 (3)
No information provided	0	2 (1)

Note: Respondents were asked, "How would you describe the economic background of your family when you were growing up?"

class, and 30 percent (45 respondents) identified as middle class or upper middle class. None of the respondents identified as rich (table 5.1).

Ages of white respondents ranged from 18 to 36, with an average age of 24. Almost all of the white respondents were undergraduate students (95 percent, 144 respondents) with only one attending graduate school. Approximately 3 percent (4 respondents) had completed a bachelor's degree, and 2 respondents had attended some college (e.g., community college) but were not enrolled at the time they completed the questionnaire. All white respondents were recruited from Northern California. In describing their economic background, 79 percent (120 respondents) reported that they considered themselves middle to upper middle class while growing up, 17 percent (25 respondents) identified as lower income to lower middle class, and approximately 3 percent (4 respondents) identified as rich (2 respondents did not provide this information) (see table 5.1).

About the Questionnaire

Respondents were asked to complete a twenty-eight-page self-administered questionnaire addressing a wide range of topics; in this chapter we examine the sections on gender and legal issues. Gender issues included fifty attitudinal statements on gender roles, women's rights, and feminism, which respondents were asked to address using a four-point scale (1, strongly disagree; 2, disagree; 3, agree; 4, strongly agree). The attitudinal statements were derived from three previously published scales that had been empirically validated and shown to be reliable indicators of gender-based attitudes.[6] The remaining items were based on prior qualitative research conducted with Chicanas and Latinos on the topic of feminisms (Hurtado 2003b; Hurtado and Sinha 2005).

We also analyzed responses to six closed-ended questions presented in the legal issues portion of the questionnaire. These items asked respondents to address experiences with police harassment, incarceration of family members, gangs in their neighborhoods and within families, and the ethnic composition of their neighborhoods and high schools.[7] We also compare the respondents' parental income and education. Taken together, the analyses of these questions illustrate the different structural positions held by these two groups of men.

Locating Men's Standpoints within Different Masculinities

The Intersectional positions occupied by Latino men, as well as those occupied by other men of Color, make them vulnerable to the criminal justice system (Ríos 2011), which in turn provides them with experience, knowledge, and insights into the country's apparatus of social control. Economically privileged white men are often protected from such experiences. As of 2009, men accounted for 93 percent of all prisoners in the United States. Even direr than this statistic, of those men incarcerated in state or federal prisons, almost 39 percent were African American and 21 percent, Latino (West, Sabol, and Greenman 2010). These incarceration rates are of special concern when one takes into account that African Americans compose only 14 percent (Rastogi et al. 2011) and Latinos only 16 percent of the total US population (Ennis, Ríos-Vargas, and Albert 2011). In 2009 African American men were incarcerated at a rate six times higher than that of white men and almost three times higher than that of Latinos (West, Sabol, and Greenman 2010). If these trends continue, one in three African American men, one in six Latino men, and one in seventeen white men can expect to be in prison at some point (Haney 2006; Mauer 2011). When we consider the death penalty, the harshest and most irrevocable punishment meted out by the criminal justice system, African American men receive this sentence in disproportionate numbers (Haney 2005).

The racial disparities in incarceration rates have been attributed to gender-, race-, and class-specific mechanisms of social control (Alexander 2010; P. Collins 2004; Haney 2006). They are considered a result of the accumulation of racially biased practices at various points in the justice system, ranging from law enforcement practices to sentencing (Alexander 2010; Haney 2006; Mauer 2011). Ríos's (2011) research with young African American and Latino men in Oakland, California, paints a vivid picture of respondents' experiences with the criminal justice system. His book focuses on the common policing practices of judges, probation officers, and school personnel in many working-class communities of Color. His analysis highlights the impact of surveillance on young Latinos' and African Americans' perceptions of their life chances. In some cases, these perceptions result in practices of resistance that are informed by the development of a consciousness politicized around social relations; other times, the young men succumb to the deleterious effects of oppression and enter the cycle of defiance, apprehension by police, imprisonment, and release, and then the cycle begins again. In general, white men, especially if they are economically privileged, do not experience the criminal justice system as directly and harshly as Latinos and African Americans; this experience influences their perceptions of social justice in general. Because Latinos and African Americans may see inequality in the justice system as a result of the intersection of race and class, there is an increased probability that they are also aware of the advantages of social movements, including feminism.

In an effort to demonstrate empirically the differences in structural position between Latino and white respondents, we conducted a series of t-tests and chi-square analyses on the questionnaire data, focusing on the respondents' experiences with the criminal justice system, exposure to gangs, racial composition of neighborhoods and high schools, and parental measures of achievement in terms of education and income. Before presenting the results of these analyses, we provide a review of t-test measurement.

The measures called t-tests belong to a class of statistical analyses called parametric inferential statistics. A t-test indicates whether there are reliable differences in mean (average) scores across two groups of respondents;[8] it is one of the most commonly used statistical analyses to examine group differences (Kranzler 2007).[9] In reporting results from t-tests, significant differences are assessed using a p value.[10] The accepted p value in the social sciences is less than .05, which indicates that there is a 5 percent or less chance that the difference found between the two groups is purely random.

Social Class Measured by Parental Income and Education

We conducted t-tests to determine whether there were reliable differences between the Latino and white respondents in terms of parental income and education, which are established indicators of socioeconomic class. The results indicate that the mean parental annual income for Latinos (approximately \$30,000–\$39,999) was significantly lower ($t[279] = -7.929, p < .001$) than the mean parental income reported by whites (approximately \$60,000–\$74,999) (see table 5.2). The same was true for parents' education, with t-test analyses confirming a reliable difference in average parental education across the two groups (for mothers, $t[297] = -8.483, p < .001$; for fathers, $t[296] = -10.457, p < .001$). The average parental education level reported by Latinos ("some college, no degree") was significantly lower than that reported by whites ("bachelor's degree")

Table 5.2. Parents' income, Brown and White Masculinities Study respondents

Annual income	Number of Latinos (% of total) N = 150	Number of whites (% of total) N = 151
Less than \$6,000	4 (2.7)	2 (1.3)
\$6,000–9,999	4 (2.7)	2 (1.3)
\$10,000–14,999	7 (4.7)	4 (2.6)
\$15,000–19,999	6 (4.0)	2 (1.3)
\$20,000–24,999	17 (11.3)	2 (1.3)
\$25,000–29,999	9 (6.0)	4 (2.6)
\$30,000–39,999	18 (12.0)	5 (3.3)
\$40,000–49,999	19 (12.7)	9 (6.0)
\$50,000–59,999	11 (7.3)	4 (2.6)
\$60,000–74,999	21 (14.0)	6 (4.0)
\$75,000–99,999	15 (10.0)	26 (17.2)
\$100,000–149,999	8 (5.3)	36 (23.8)
\$150,000–199,999	2 (1.3)	19 (12.6)
\$200,000 or more	3 (2.0)	17 (11.3)
No information provided	6 (4.0)	13 (8.6)

Note: Respondents were asked, "What is your parent's/parents' yearly income? If your parents are divorced, check the income of the parent who raised you."

(see tables 5.3 and 5.4). On average, the respondents in each group occupied different structural positions as indicated by parents' income and education.

The next question was whether these structural differences led to differences in the context in which respondents grew up, which, in turn, may have led to a different relationship with the state apparatus of social control and with residential and school segregation. To this end, we conducted chi-square analyses on six items in the section on legal issues in the questionnaire. Before presenting the results of the analyses, we provide a brief review of what a chi-square indicates when examining quantitative data.

While t-tests are parametric measures, chi-square tests (χ^2) belong to a class of statistical techniques called nonparametric inferential statistics. The key distinction between a parametric and a nonparametric test is the type of data analyzed. In the case of parametric tests (e.g., the t-tests), data must be continuous and measured on a scale (e.g., for the t-tests in the previous section, the data for parental education were measured on scales ranging from "less than high school" to "graduate degree"). In the case of nonparametric tests, data are measured categorically (e.g., a yes/no answer to a question about police harassment) and analyzed in terms

Table 5.3. Mothers' education levels, Brown and White Masculinities Study respondents

Education level	Number of Latinos (% of total) N = 150	Number of whites (% of total) N = 151
Less than high school	50 (33.3)	1 (0.7)
Graduated from high school	29 (19.3)	18 (11.9)
Some college, no degree	17 (11.3)	22 (14.6)
Associates degree	6 (4.0)	7 (4.6)
Vocational certificate	5 (3.3)	5 (3.3)
Bachelor's degree	21 (14.0)	42 (27.8)
Some graduate school	3 (2.0)	9 (6.0)
Graduate degree (MA, PhD, JD)	17 (11.3)	47 (31.1)
No information provided	2 (1.3)	0 (0.0)

Note: Respondents were asked, "How many years of education does your mother have?"

Table 5.4. Fathers' education levels, Brown and White
Masculinities Study respondents

Education level	Number of Latinos (% of total) N = 150	Number of whites (% of total) N = 151
Less than high school	61 (40.7)	1 (0.7)
Graduated from high school	17 (11.3)	8 (5.3)
Some college, no degree	19 (12.7)	21 (13.9)
Associate's degree	3 (2.0)	5 (3.3)
Vocational certificate	4 (2.7)	0 (0.0)
Bachelor's degree	19 (12.7)	42 (27.8)
Some graduate school	2 (1.3)	13 (8.6)
Graduate degree (MA, PhD, JD)	22 (14.7)	61 (40.4)
Missing	3 (2.0)	0 (0.0)

Note: Respondents were asked, "How many years of education does
your father have?"

of frequency counts (Kranzler 2007).[11] Below we present the results of the
analyses using chi-square.

Residential and School Segregation, Gangs, and Incarceration

Communities of Color are closely monitored by police, and it is not uncommon for schools in these communities to report high rates of student
expulsion, punitive monitoring of students (e.g., metal detectors at school
entrances), and an overall high police presence on the premises (Hurtado,
Haney, and Hurtado 2012; Ríos 2011). We asked respondents about the
level of racial segregation in their neighborhoods and schools while they
were growing up to provide context for their answers on the criminal justice system. Latino respondents were more likely to have lived in neighborhoods where the ethnic composition was "mostly people of Color" (47
percent, 70 respondents) than whites were (6 percent, 9 respondents), and
white respondents were more likely to have lived in neighborhoods that
were either "mostly Anglo/white" or "almost all Anglo/white" (70 percent, 106 respondents) than Latinos were (28 percent, 42 respondents;
see table 5.5).

Table 5.5. Racial/ethnic composition of respondents' neighborhoods, Brown and White Masculinities Study

Racial/ethnic composition	Number of Latinos (% of total) N = 150	Number of whites (% of total) N = 151
Mostly people of Color	70 (47.0)	9 (6.0)
Approximately even number of people of Color and Anglos/whites	35 (23.0)	33 (22.0)
Mostly Anglo/white	26 (17.0)	59 (39.0)
Almost all Anglo/white	16 (11.0)	47 (31.0)
Other	2 (1.0)	3 (2.0)
No information provided	1 (0.7)	0 (0.0)

Note: Respondents answered the following open statement: "The approximate racial/ethnic composition of your neighborhood was _____."

A chi-square test indicated that there was a significant interaction between race and ethnic composition of respondents' neighborhoods ($\chi^2[4, N = 300] = 75.42, p < .001$). Consequently, Latinos were more likely to have attended high schools where the majority of students were people of Color than white respondents were (10 percent, 15 respondents), and white respondents were more likely to have attended high schools where the student body was mostly white or almost all white (62 percent, 94 respondents) than Latinos were (28 percent, 41 respondents; see table 5.6). Chi-square analysis of the ethnic composition of respondents' high schools indicates that these patterns were significant ($\chi^2[4, N = 298] = 58.86, p < .001$).

The structural segregation and lower socioeconomic origins of Latino respondents result in a wider range of experiences with gangs than reported by white respondents. Two-thirds of Latinos (66 percent, 99 respondents) grew up with gangs in their neighborhood in comparison to about one-fifth of whites (21 percent, 32 respondents; $\chi^2[1, N = 300] = 62.43, p < .001$), and nearly half of Latinos (45 percent, 67 respondents) had a family member who had belonged to a gang at some time in comparison to 8 percent (12 respondents) of the white sample ($\chi^2[1, N = 299] = 53.56, p < .001$). Racial segregation resulted in other consequences. Over half of Latinos reported being harassed by the police (54 percent, 81 respondents) in comparison to about one-third of white respondents

Table 5.6. Racial/ethnic composition of respondents' high schools, Brown and White Masculinities Study

Racial/ethnic composition	Number of Latinos (% of total) N = 150	Number of whites (% of total) N = 151
Mostly people of Color	68 (45.3)	15 (10.0)
Approximately even number of people of Color and Anglos/whites	37 (24.7)	39 (25.8)
Mostly Anglo/white	34 (22.7)	60 (39.7)
Almost all Anglo/white	7 (4.7)	34 (22.5)
Other	2 (1.3)	2 (1.3)
No information provided	2 (1.3)	1 (0.7)

Note: Respondents replied to the following open statement: "The approximate racial/ethnic composition of your high school was _____."

(35 percent, 53 respondents; $\chi^2[1, N = 300] = 11.26, p = .001$). Finally, almost three-quarters of the Latinos (73 percent, 110 respondents) indicated that they had a family member who had been incarcerated or in jail at some point in comparison to less than half of whites (41 percent, 62 respondents; $\chi^2[1, N = 299] = 32.23, p < .001$).

In sum, the majority of Latino respondents grew up in low-income neighborhoods populated predominantly by people of Color and where gang activity, police harassment, and familial incarceration were not unusual. White respondents came from much more economically privileged backgrounds (or standpoints) and did not experience the familial and environmental vulnerabilities Latino respondents were exposed to while growing up.

Intersectional Standpoints and Exposure to the Criminal Justice System

From a feminist theoretical perspective, differences in structural privilege can result in differences in standpoints, or backgrounds. Standpoint Theory is an approach concerned with the acquisition, construction, and interpretation of knowledge (Tanesini 1999). The theoretical origins of the concept of standpoints is rooted in Marxist thought regarding the "standpoint of the proletariat," which asserts that members of the working class have access to knowledge less readily available to members of the ruling class. The "subjugated knowledges" of the oppressed (Sandoval 1991) provide the subordinated with insights into the multilayered nature of social relationships and practices that constitute capitalist social structures. The material experience of oppression shapes an individual's standpoint in a given social structure and provides access to particular types of knowledge. Chicana feminist writers and other feminists of Color have expanded Standpoint Theory to include the intersections of ethnicity, class, sexuality, and gender (P. Collins 2000; Crenshaw 1989; Hurtado 2010; Pérez 1999; Saldívar-Hull 2000). The emphasis is on the importance of understanding the exercise of power between groups as a historically and culturally specific process, one that is embedded in social relationships (Hurtado 1996; Sandoval 1991).

The differences in social location result in Latinos having a different standpoint than whites, and these differences have the potential to influence respondents' attitudes and beliefs about gender and feminism. To explore this proposition, we conducted separate analyses for Latino and white respondents on the fifty attitudinal statements presented in the questionnaire's section on gender issues by using exploratory factor analysis (EFA). Before presenting the results of these analyses, we provide a brief explanation of the factor analysis statistical technique.

What Is Factor Analysis?

EFA is a statistical technique used to understand complex data by identifying correlational patterns in respondents' answers to a set of questions that have the same response categories. The purpose of an EFA is to identify the latent structure (called a factor) underlying a set of interrelated variables (usually derived from a set of questions or attitudinal statements) (Child 2006; Kline 1994; Tabachnik and Fidell 1996). The EFA technique is used most commonly in the social sciences and is based primarily on correlations, which are mathematical calculations indicating a relationship (positive, negative, or no relationship at all) between two or more variables (or questions/attitudinal statements).[12] When a set of variables systematically correlates, or "hangs together" (i.e., responses to a set of questions covary with each other), the variables are understood to be indicative of a factor. A factor can be defined as a conceptual "construct that is operationally defined by its factor loadings" (Kline 1994, 5). Factor loadings are the correlations (indicated with a number between −1 and +1) of a variable (or question) with a factor (Kline 1994, 5). Hence, a factor is the underlying construct that drives people's responses to a given set of variables (or questions); factor loadings are numerical values expressing the degree to which a variable (a response to a question) correlates with similar questions and, taken together, indicate an underlying construct. The construct is thus defined by the respondents' answers to a particular set of questions (variables); how strongly the answers correlate with each other becomes the factor loadings (indicated by numbers between +1 and −1). EFA is primarily concerned with the identification and naming of factors by examining the patterns of correlations between a set of variables (responses to a set of questions) and the underlying construct(s).

Factor analysis in the social sciences is usually used in the development and evaluation of scales (Kline 1994; Tabachnik and Fidell 1996).[13] A scale is a set of questions that together are a good (robust) measurement of a concept.[14] Factor analysis is a technique used to ensure that the scales do in fact measure what they purport to measure (construct validity) and are replicable across different samples of respondents (reliability). The scales used in the BWMS have already been established in the literature as being reliable and valid (Morgan 1996; Parry 1983; Renzetti 1987; Twenge 1997). Therefore, our purpose here was not to validate the scales (usually done by using a confirmatory factor analysis),[15] but, as its name implies, we used EFA to explore the differences in the attitudinal structure of these two groups of men's views on gender and feminisms. EFA permitted us to interpret the way the attitudinal statements on gender and feminism hung together to identify differences and similarities in the underlying structure of Latino and white men's attitudes at the intersections of race, ethnicity, and class.

Our decision about which factors to keep was related to the conventional criteria used in determining "significant" factor loadings.[16] We opted to interpret factor loadings (or correlations) of .4 or greater, as these coincided with the standards described by Tabachnik and Fidell (1996) and were more conservative than those described by Kline (1994).[17] We combined multiple criteria in deciding the number of factors to extract.[18] We used Kaiser's eigenvalue criterion, the scree plot,[19] and the total amount of variance explained by a factor simultaneously in making this decision. We extracted factors after consulting the scree plot that had eigenvalues greater than 2 and that explained 40 percent of the overall variance.[20]

Exploratory Factor Analysis

Latino Respondents

When examining the factor structure for the fifty attitudinal statements made by the Latino respondents, five principal factors emerged.[21] These five factors account for approximately 40 percent of total variance.[22]

The first factor that emerged for Latinos was traditional gender roles, with factor loading patterns that are supported in the literature (Hurtado 2005). These patterns consisted of nine attitudinal questions with loadings of .46 or greater on this factor, and the coefficient alpha was .657 (see table 5.7 for factors and individual item loadings).[23] The attitudinal statements loading on factor one addressed gendered behaviors in the context of a traditional heterosexual marriage. The three highest loading items (a–c) included agreement that the wife take her husband's last name (factor loading .734), fathers have ultimate authority over children (factor loading .7), and the rejection of normative marriage traditions like the wife not taking the husband's last name (factor loading .67). Some of the other items loading on this factor addressed the public display of femininity, such as women not appearing drunk in public (item e, loading .584) and women taking care of their physical appearance (item g, loading .477). The endorsement of gendered, hegemonic norms within heterosexual marriage was coupled with the rejection of equal opportunities for women (item h, loading −.475) and nonnormative, gendered behaviors, like husbands stepping in to take over household duties when wives were employed (item i, loading −.467).

The second factor was labeled feminist consciousness, which included ten items on the respondents' relationship to feminism and the feminist movement (the items had factor loadings of .42 or greater, and the coefficient alpha was .259).[24] The factor structure captures many of the cornerstones of all feminist movements: the claim that employment and gender equality do not detract from motherhood (items c and h, loadings .554 and −.488, respectively) and a rejection of statements that demean women's participation in the workforce (items d and g, loadings −.550 and −.524, respectively). The remaining attitudinal statements in this factor are a strong endorsement of feminism in general (items a, b, and e, loadings .613, .566, and .526, respectively) and the acknowledgment of the existence of family members who identify as feminists or believe in the goals of feminisms (items i and j, loadings .445 and .429, respectively).

Factor three for Latino respondents was labeled marriage and household division of labor and consisted of six attitudinal statements with fac-

Table 5.7. Latinos' factors and item loadings on gender and feminisms attitudes, Brown and White Masculinities Study

Factor	Item loading
Factor 1: Traditional gender roles (alpha = .657; 9 items)	
(a) A wife should willingly take her husband's name at marriage.	.734
(b) As head of the household, the father should have final authority over his children.	.7
(c) It is insulting to the husband when his wife does not take his last name.	.67
(d) If a husband and wife each have an equally good career opportunity, but in different cities, the husband should take the job and the wife should follow.	.594
(e) It is worse to see a drunken woman than a drunken man.	.584
(f) The first duty of a woman with young children is to home and family.	.49
(g) Women should be more concerned with clothing and appearance than men.	.477
(h) Women should have completely equal opportunities in getting jobs and promotions as men.	−.475
(i) If a woman goes out to work, her husband should share the housework, such as washing dishes, cleaning, and cooking.	−.467
Factor 2: Feminist consciousness (alpha = .259; 10 items)	
(a) I believe in the goals of feminism.	.613
(b) In general I am sympathetic with the efforts of women's liberation groups.	.566
(c) An employed woman can establish as warm and secure a relationship with children as a mother who is not employed.	.554
(d) Women have less to offer than men in the world of business and industry.	−.550
(e) I consider myself to be a feminist.	.526
(f) A woman can live a full and happy life without marrying.	.524

Table 5.7. *Continued*

Factor	Item loading
Factor 2: Feminist consciousness (alpha = .259; 10 items) (continued)	
(g) Career women tend to be masculine and domineering.	−.524
(h) Women should worry less about being equal with men and more about becoming good wives and mothers.	−.488
(i) There are females in my family that are feminists.	.445
(j) There are males in my family who believe in the goals of feminism.	.429
Factor 3: Marriage and household division of labor (alpha = .77; 6 items)	
(a) When I am married, I would be willing to take the responsibility of doing the laundry.	.729
(b) When I am married, I would be willing to take the responsibility of cooking meals for the family.	.686
(c) When I am married, I would be willing to take the responsibility of cleaning the bathroom.	.676
(d) When I am married, I would be willing to be responsible for mowing the lawn.	.647
(e) When I am married, I would be willing to take the responsibility of cleaning the kitchen.	.629
(f) When I am married, I would be willing to be responsible for maintaining the family car.	.444
Factor 4: Gender-based discrimination (alpha = .722; 6 items)	
(a) When you get right down to it, women are an oppressed group and men are the oppressors.	.664
(b) Women in the United States are treated as second-class citizens.	.632
(c) Men still don't take women's ideas seriously.	.583
(d) Men tend to discriminate against women in hiring, firing, and promotion.	.562

Table 5.7. Continued

Factor	Item loading
Factor 4: Gender-based discrimination (alpha = .722; 6 items) (continued)	
(e) Women have been treated unfairly on the basis of their gender throughout most of human history.	.471
(f) All men receive economic, sexual, and psychological benefits from male domination.	.467
Factor 5: Relational gendered privilege and subordination (alpha = .679; 4 items)	
(a) In obtaining government positions of leadership, men are taken more seriously than women only because they are men.	.667
(b) As a group, men have more power in society than women.	.627
(c) Daughters in a family should be encouraged to stay on at school and go to college as much as the sons in a family.	.597
(d) All other things being equal, men have advantages over women in gaining employment because they are men.	.442

Note: Responses were elicited to the following instruction: "Please indicate how strongly you agree or disagree with the following statements." Response scale: 1 = strongly disagree; 2 = disagree; 3 = agree; 4 = strongly agree.

tor loadings of .44 or greater and the coefficient alpha of .77. An important feminist goal at the start of the movement was to blur the division between work outside the home and household chores, the latter being traditionally within the purview of women's gendered activities. The second-wave feminist movement was dedicated to promoting the sharing of household duties with men, not only for ideological reasons but also because these chores were seen as the "second shift" (Hochschild 1989), which could stall women's achievement outside the home. The unpaid labor performed by women in all cultures and societies has led to men's unfettered success in the public realm. The attitudinal statements in factor three gauge Latino respondents' willingness to perform household tasks after marriage. The respondents endorsed taking responsibility for both "female" household chores such as doing the laundry (item a, loading

.729), cooking (item b, loading .686), and cleaning the bathroom (item c, loading .676) and kitchen (item e, loading .629). Respondents were also willing to take responsibility for male-oriented tasks such as mowing the lawn (item d, loading .647) and maintaining the family car (item f, loading .444).

Factor four was labeled gender-based discrimination, which describes the disadvantaged position of women as a result of their gender. The six items had factor loadings of .46 or greater, and the coefficient alpha was .722. Gender-based discrimination addresses women's mistreatment in two areas: discrimination in general, and discrimination associated with the workplace. The general gender-based discrimination items acknowledge that women are oppressed as a group and that this unfair treatment has been consistent throughout history (items a, loading .664; e, loading .471). Another set of items point to women's disadvantages in public and workplace situations (items d, loading .562; b, loading .632). Because of discrimination, women do not enjoy the full benefits of citizenship, and the lack of full public participation may lead to their ideas not being taken seriously (item c, loading .583). Similarly, because women are not perceived as equal to men, employment discrimination is more common among women, including unequal access to promotions. Therefore, men as a group benefit from women's disadvantages at multiple levels: economic, sexual, and psychological (item f, loading .467).

The fifth factor for Latinos was labeled relational gendered privilege and subordination. Unlike the gender-based discrimination factor, the attitudinal statements in this factor address gender subordination and privileges in *relational* terms. The four items in this factor had loadings of .44 or greater, and the coefficient alpha was .679. The attitudinal statements highlight men's unearned advantages at the expense of women's subordination. In contrast, gender-based discrimination focuses on the disadvantages suffered by women in absolute terms; that is, individuals can endorse the notion that women suffer gender discrimination, but they can simultaneously believe that it has very little to nothing to do with men's behaviors and gender privileges. From this perspective, an individual can attribute discrimination against women to structures that were set up in the past that persist even when men have changed and are not directly responsible for sexist outcomes. In contrast, the items in factor five make it clear that men benefit directly because of the relational differences in power based on gender where men are the beneficiaries of women's oppression. Three of the four attitudinal statements in this factor state directly that men generally have more power than women (item b, loading .627) and that men's leadership is more valued than women's (item a, loading .667), which also affects women's employment opportunities in comparison to those of men (item d, loading .442).

White Respondents

When examining factor structure for the original fifty attitudinal statements with the white respondents, three factors emerged.[25] These factors explain approximately 40 percent of total variance.[26] The attitudinal structure of white respondents is less differentiated than that of the Latino respondents as manifested in fewer factors — three for white respondents and five for Latinos. Although white respondents had fewer factors, the number of items in several factors is almost double (seventeen items in factor one, fourteen in factor two) that for Latino respondents (nine items in factor one, ten in factor two). Factor three, labeled marriage and household labor, had the same six items load together for the white and Latino respondents, although not in the same order of importance (see tables 5.7 and 5.8). Latinos had two additional factors — gender-based discrimination and relational gendered privilege and subordination.

White respondents' factor one, traditional gender roles, had seventeen items with factor loadings of .4 or greater, and the coefficient alpha was .775 (see table 5.8 for factors and individual item loadings). Of the seventeen items, seven (b, c, e, g, j, k, and q) also loaded on Latinos' traditional gender roles factor (items a, b, c, f, g, d, and e for the Latino respondents in table 5.7), which had a total of ten items.[27] Five of these items (d, h, i, m, and p) loaded on the Latinos' feminist consciousness factor, and five items (a, f, l, n, and o) did not load on any of the Latino factors. Overall, the white respondents' traditional gender roles factor combined attitudes delineated by the norms of heterosexual marriage and white respondents' views on women's participation in employment outside the home, a dimension that for Latinos was separated from marital obligations and instead belonged in the realm of feminisms (feminist consciousness). Nonetheless, both white and Latino respondents agreed on a majority of the items included in the traditional gender roles factor (41 percent of the white respondents' items were in agreement with Latinos'; 77 percent of the Latino respondents' items were in agreement with those of white respondents).

Similar to the Latino respondents' results, factor two for white respondents was also labeled feminist consciousness. Fourteen items had factor loadings of .41 or greater, and the coefficient alpha was .812. Of

Table 5.8. Whites' factors and item loadings on gender and feminisms attitudes, Brown and White Masculinities Study

Factor	Item loading
Factor 1: Traditional gender roles (alpha = .775; 17 items)	
(a) For a woman to be truly happy, she needs to have a man in her life.	.66
(b) A wife should willingly take her husband's name at marriage.	.652
(c) As head of the household, the father should have final authority over his children.	.626
(d) Women should worry less about being equal with men and more about becoming good wives and mothers.	.617
(e) It is insulting to the husband when his wife does not take his last name.	.587
(f) Many women in the workforce are taking jobs away from men who need the jobs more.	.554
(g) The first duty of a woman with young children is to home and family.	.542
(h) Career women tend to be masculine and domineering.	.541
(i) A woman can live a full and happy life without marrying.	−.54
(j) Women should be more concerned with clothing and appearance than men.	.539
(k) If a husband and wife each have an equally good career opportunity, but in different cities, the husband should take the job and the wife should follow.	.538
(l) In general, the father should have more authority than the mother in bringing up children.	.536
(m) Women have less to offer than men in the world of business and industry.	.512
(n) For a woman in college, popularity is more important than grade point average.	.498
(o) If the husband is the sole wage earner in the family, the financial decisions should be his.	.462

Table 5.8. *Continued*

Factor	Item loading
Factor 1: Traditional gender roles (alpha = .775; 17 items) (continued)	
(p) An employed woman can establish as warm and secure a relationship with her children as a woman who is not employed.	−.411
(q) It is worse to see a drunken woman than a drunken man.	.401
Factor 2: Feminist consciousness (alpha = .812; 14 items)	
(a) Women in the United States are treated as second-class citizens.	.759
(b) Even though some things have changed, women are still treated unfairly in today's society.	.738
(c) When you get right down to it, women are an oppressed group and men are the oppressors.	.697
(d) I consider myself to be a feminist.	.657
(e) I believe in the goals of feminism.	.598
(f) All other things being equal, men have advantages over women in gaining employment because they are men.	.573
(g) In general, I am sympathetic with the efforts of women's liberation groups.	.554
(h) Men tend to discriminate against women in hiring, firing, and promotion.	.552
(i) As a group, men have more power in society than women.	.548
(j) If women want to get ahead, there is little to stop them.	−.544
(k) Men still don't take women's ideas seriously.	.525
(l) All men receive economic, sexual, and psychological benefits from male domination.	.496
(m) There are males in my family who believe in the goals of feminism.	.469
(n) There are females in my family that are feminists.	.41

Table 5.8. *Continued*

Factor	Item loading
Factor 3: Marriage and household division of labor (alpha = .833; 6 items)	
(a) When I am married, I would be willing to be responsible for mowing the lawn.	.716
(b) When I am married, I would be willing to take the responsibility of doing the laundry.	.66
(c) When I am married, I would be willing to be responsible for maintaining the family car.	.65
(d) When I am married, I would be willing to take the responsibility of cleaning the bathroom.	.61
(e) When I am married, I would be willing to take the responsibility of cleaning the kitchen.	.583
(f) When I am married, I would be willing to take the responsibility of cooking meals for the family.	.58

Note: Response scale: 1 = strongly disagree; 2 = disagree; 3 = agree; 4 = strongly agree.

the fourteen items, five (d, e, g, m, and n) also loaded on the Latinos' feminist consciousness factor, which had a total of ten items. Five items (a, c, h, k, and l) loaded on Latinos' gender-based discrimination factor, and two items (f and i) loaded on Latinos' relational gendered privilege and subordination factor. Two items (b and j) did not load on any Latino respondents' factor.[28] Attitudinal statements loading on this factor addressed identification with feminism and an awareness that women were treated unfairly in various spheres of society. A key difference between the two groups was that there were fewer statements loading on this factor for Latinos in comparison to whites. Many of the statements loading on this factor for whites were distributed across the Latinos' gender-based discrimination factor and relational gendered privilege and subordination factor.

Factor three for the white respondents, marriage and household division of labor, was identical to factor three for Latinos (see tables 5.7 and 5.8), including the following six items (a, b, c, d, e, and f) with factor loadings of .58 or greater and with coefficient alpha .833.

We eliminated a fourth factor for white respondents because of lack of interpretability. The coefficient alpha was .555, and there were fewer than four items with factor loadings greater than .6 (Stevens 2002). This factor is therefore not included in the discussion of the results.

In comparing the attitudinal structure of white and Latino respondents, three general patterns emerged. First, Latinos had more nuanced attitudes about gender and feminisms, as indicated by the number of factors in comparison to those of white respondents (five factors for Latinos, three for white respondents).

Second, in comparison to Latinos, white respondents' attitudes were more homogeneous, tending to cluster a large number of items into one factor or construct. For example, when expressing their views on acceptable gendered behaviors within a heterosexual marriage, white respondents also included norms about women's employment outside the home. For Latinos, women's employment outside the home was consistently clustered with issues of having a feminist consciousness rather than with intimate behaviors within a heterosexual marriage. Similarly, white respondents' attitudes about feminist consciousness also had more items than were selected by Latinos (ten items for Latinos versus fourteen for whites). White respondents' feminist consciousness made fewer distinctions between different types of sexist or oppressive behaviors, whereas Latinos had three factors to cover their views on gender as a mechanism of control (feminist consciousness, gender-based discrimination, and relational gendered privilege and subordination). White respondents clustered all the discriminatory items into the construct of feminist consciousness.

Third, the marriage and household division of labor factor was exactly the same for both Latino and white respondents, indicating a solid node of connection on one dimension, the gendered division of chores within the home. Below we elaborate on these patterns.

Intersectional Understandings

To understand all dimensions of the results, it is important to also consider and evaluate the impact of the individuals' Social Identities and their intersections. Intersectionality Theory as proposed in this book begins with the radical notion that all racial, gender, ethnic, and class formations in society have a core of human similarity that resides in their personal identities. Regardless of the Intersectional Identities of individuals, all human beings have personal identities that overlap considerably with regard to what they desire as human beings (Hurtado 1997). Also, personal identity is socialized within the family unit (however it is defined). Most family units are motivated by similar values and desires, although these may be manifested in different ways. For example, all cultures value children and desire what is best for them. How this appreciation of children is manifested varies from culture to culture, and the degree to which the desire is realized is very much constricted by the context in which raising children takes place.

We argue that variations in normative and attitudinal outcomes are a result of the power, economic, and social dynamics that are regulated through Social Identities and their intersections. We begin by reviewing the results of the factor analysis to explore similarities between the Latino and white respondents regardless of the differences in the structure (as manifested in the number of factors for each group) of their attitudes. We then turn to differences as predicted by their Intersectional Identities to explore further the nuances of the respondents' understandings of gender and women's liberation.

Similarities

In spite of the differences in the attitudinal structures between these two groups of respondents, there was considerable overlap in the items within the resulting factors. Factor three, marriage and household division of labor, had the greatest amount of overlap (all six items loaded for Latinos and whites); factor one, traditional gender roles, had the second-highest degree of overlap (seven out of nine items chosen by Latinos were also chosen by whites); and factor two, feminist consciousness, had the least amount of overlap (five of the ten items chosen by Latinos were also chosen by whites). Latino respondents had two more factors than the white respondents had (factor four, gender-based discrimination, and factor five, relational gendered privilege and subordination).

As mentioned above, of the five factors that emerged for Latino respondents, marriage and household division of labor had complete overlap of items with the white respondents. Although the items had different loadings for each group (see tables 5.7 and 5.8), the level of agreement cannot be underestimated in its significance:

- When I am married, I would be willing to take the responsibility of doing the laundry.

- When I am married, I would be willing to take the responsibility of cooking meals for the family.
- When I am married, I would be willing to take the responsibility of cleaning the bathroom.
- When I am married, I would be willing to be responsible for mowing the lawn.
- When I am married, I would be willing to take the responsibility of cleaning the kitchen.
- When I am married, I would be willing to be responsible for maintaining the family car.

If the literature on machismo that has been reported over the years is an accurate depiction of Latino men, then very few of the Latino respondents would have uniformly answered the items on the gendered division of household labor in the same way as the purportedly more liberal, less sexist, and less macho white respondents. It is worth mentioning that we did not conduct the analysis separately for feminist-identified Latino or white respondents. These results indicate that the respondents in our analysis, regardless of their feminist or nonfeminist identification, did not differ in their commitment to an egalitarian sharing of household chores once they were married. In fact, this factor accounted for the same amount of variance for both Latinos and whites (5 percent).

The traditional gender roles factor had the second-highest level of agreement between Latino and white respondents, with seven out of nine Latino items in agreement with white respondents and with white respondents having seven out of seventeen items in agreement with Latino respondents. The items that both whites and Latinos had in common, though not in the same order of importance as part of their traditional gender roles factor, are as follows:

- A wife should willingly take her husband's name at marriage.
- As head of the household, the father should have final authority over his children.
- It is insulting to the husband when his wife does not take his last name.
- If a husband and wife each have an equally good career opportunity, but in different cities, the husband should take the job and the wife should follow.
- It is worse to see a drunken woman than a drunken man.

- The first duty of a woman with young children is to home and family.
- Women should be more concerned with clothing and appearance than men.

The core items that all respondents agreed with adhere to a rather traditional view of how women should conduct themselves in a heterosexual marriage and how they should conform to public and conservative standards of decorum. The level of agreement between Latinos and whites here is remarkable: white respondents were surprisingly conservative in views that measure what is thought of as machismo, such as wives accepting the husband's name, fathers' authority over children, and women deferring their professional success to their husbands'.

The feminist consciousness factor had the third-highest level of agreement between Latino and white respondents; Latinos had five out of ten items in agreement with the white respondents, and the white respondents had five out of fourteen items in agreement with the Latino respondents. The items that both whites and Latinos had in common (though not in the same order of importance) as part of their feminist consciousness are as follows:

- I consider myself to be a feminist.
- I believe in the goals of feminism.
- In general, I am sympathetic with the efforts of women's liberation groups.
- There are males in my family who believe in the goals of feminism.
- There are females in my family that are feminists.

This factor in several ways appears to illustrate both Latino and white respondents' *personal* commitment to feminisms and its goals. It also documents that others in the respondents' families share their personal commitment to feminisms.

We turn now to the differences and explore their possible origins. Whereas the similarities in the two groups' factors may stem from the overlap in respondents' personal identities, the divergences may stem from the differences in the respondents' Intersectional Identities.

Differences

The differences in lived experience between the two groups of men as organized by racial and class intersections can provide an explanation for the divergences in attitudinal structure and content found in the feminist consciousness, gender-based discrimination, and relational gendered privilege and subordination factors. Latinos' experiences at the intersections of race, ethnicity, and class were shaped by mechanisms of subordination and by firsthand experience with the human consequences of these mechanisms. Latino respondents experienced their male privilege in significantly different social contexts than did white respondents. The higher rates of police harassment for Latinos exposed them to vulnerabilities as they moved, unencumbered by family curfews and restriction, through public spaces. At the same time, freedom from strict family rules and monitoring was one of many manifestations of male privilege in the context of their nuclear and extended families. Latinos' male privilege therefore intersected with oppression based on race, ethnicity, and class oppression, creating particular experiential junctures.

In contrast, most white respondents' male privilege intersected with advantages based on race and class while they still enjoyed family-granted male privileges similar to those experienced by Latinos. Most of the white respondents grew up in more affluent neighborhoods, experienced less police harassment, and were less likely to have a family member incarcerated, which is suggestive of a different relationship with the social structures producing inequality—the same social structures that undergirded their race, class, and gender privilege. The larger number of Latino factors may be a reflection of Latinos' experiences with state control and subordination facilitating a more nuanced vision of the nature of gender oppression in comparison to the more general view held by white respondents (as reflected by a lower number of factors).

The differences in lived experience may also explain the divergence in the traditional gender roles factor, in which Latino respondents *disagree* with the conservative gender views expressed in this factor even while they *agree* with the two items that address women's employment: "Women should have completely equal opportunities in getting jobs and promotions as men" (for Latinos, loading −.475); and, "If a woman goes out to work, her husband should share the housework, such as washing dishes, cleaning, and cooking" (for Latinos, loading −.467). Both of these items did not load on any of the white respondents' factors. This added nuance to the Latinos' traditional gender roles factor may in fact make white respondents appear to harbor more traditional gender views than Latinos.

Latinos' economic vulnerability while growing up may have influenced their views in such a way that those who supported women's employment opportunities did not endorse traditional roles in the domestic sphere.

This finding is consistent with that of Mason and Lu (1988), who found that African American men were less likely to view women's employment outside the home as detrimental to their children's upbringing. African Americans and Latinos growing up in economically stressed environments and in families that struggled to make ends meet might have had shared experiences that shaped their views on women's roles inside and outside the home.

Lived experience, however, may not fully explain the differences in attitudinal structure and content among the respondents. All of the respondents were or had been university students exposed to a critical mass of scholarship on feminisms and the questioning of gender, race, class, sexuality, and ethnic privileges. Exposure to higher education interacted with lived experience and added significantly to the analysis. Firsthand experiential knowledge of race- and class-based discrimination at the institutional level lends understanding to other aspects of US society and culture that are also structured in discriminatory and interconnected ways (White 2008). Exposure to higher education provides the opportunity for Latinos to relate to feminist literature and ideas differently from white respondents with very little or no experiential knowledge of systematic exclusion and subordination.

Another potential source of variation in respondents' exposure to higher education is the number of courses they took in feminist and ethnic studies and their knowledge of various feminist authors. Table 5.9 summarizes several indicators of the respondents' exposure to formal undergraduate and graduate courses in women's studies and Chicano/a studies, and their knowledge of three major Chicana feminist writers (Gloria Anzaldúa, Sandra Cisneros, and Cherríe Moraga), three major African American feminist writers (Audre Lorde, Barbara Christian, and bell hooks), one major white feminist writer and activist (Gloria Steinem), and three major Chicana feminist texts. Uniformly, Latinos claimed more exposure to Chicana feminisms, African American feminisms, and even white feminisms.[29] As expected, given their university education, white respondents were also exposed to different academic feminisms, though not nearly as many as reported by Latino respondents. Whereas none of the Latino respondents lacked exposure to any of the items that asked about academic feminisms, white respondents had never been exposed to the African American feminist writer Barbara Christian, and they had not read *This Bridge Called My Back* (although five white respondents had heard of the book). *The House on Mango Street*, by feminist Chicana writer

Table 5.9. Exposure to academic feminisms, Brown and White
Masculinities Study respondents

Course	Number of Latinos (% of total) N = 150	Number of whites (% of total) N = 151
Women's studies Undergrad/grad	28 (18.7)	11 (7.3)
Chicano studies Undergrad/grad	67 (44.7)	18 (11.9)
Gloria Anzaldúa	42 (28.0)	10 (6.6)
Sandra Cisneros	75 (50)	22 (14.7)
Cherríe Moraga	23 (15.3)	5 (3.3)
Audre Lorde	16 (10.7)	5 (3.3)
Barbara Christian	5 (3.3)	0 (0.0)
bell hooks	41 (27.3)	28 (18.7)
Gloria Steinem	22 (14.7)	11 (7.3)
This Bridge Called My Back		
Read	11 (7.3)	0 (0.0)
Heard of it	32 (21.3)	5 (3.3)
Borderlands/La Frontera		
Read	39 (26.0)	10 (6.6)
Heard of it	43 (28.7)	40 (26.5)
The House on Mango Street		
Read	71 (47.3)	47 (30.9)
Heard of it	47 (31.3)	28 (18.5)

Note: Respondents were asked, "Did you take any women's studies/Chicano
studies courses in undergraduate/graduate college?"; "Have you read or
heard her [the author] speak?"

Sandra Cisneros, was the book most read by both Latino (47 percent) and
white (31 percent) respondents.[30]

The different experiences and knowledge Latinos and whites brought
to their understanding of social inequality may have created a different
relationship with the feminist materials encountered in their university
education. For white respondents, their lived experience at the intersections of gender, race, and class was characterized by convergent forms of
privilege (and not subordination); it is possible that their understanding
of social inequality occurred mostly at the intellectual level. This could

have shaped the more linear and unidimensional structure of their attitudes toward gender and feminism.

Latinos' Stand-Alone Feminisms

In the exploratory factor analysis, Latino respondents had two more factors than did white respondents: gender-based discrimination (factor four) and relational gendered privilege and subordination (factor five) (see table 5.7). Although both groups of men held relatively traditional attitudes toward gender roles, they were simultaneously aware that women were disadvantaged in various arenas of US society. The multilayered attitudinal structure of the Latino respondents was indicated in the factors' coefficient alphas across groups (see table 5.10). Higher alphas indicate that the items clustered together to a higher degree and suggest more homogeneity in responses loading on a particular factor. Overall factors that emerged for white respondents had higher coefficient alphas than all of the factors that emerged for Latinos (see table 5.10).

Latinos' combination of education and life experience lowered the probability of internalizing narratives that hindered the perception of the devastating consequences of disparate treatment. Their two additional factors indicate that they did not believe the United States was an unfettered meritocracy (Apfelbaum 1979; Haney and Hurtado 1994), or that color blindness existed (Haney-López 2003) and psychological individualism (Haney 1982) was a feasible strategy for women to use to avoid discrimination. In other words, they avoided the pitfalls of "blaming the victim" or excusing the fruits of patriarchy—all characteristics of the social landscape surrounding discussions of structured inequality in contemporary US society. Therefore, it was not completely unexpected that strong statements characterized the content of Latinos' two additional factors: that women's gender has historically been the basis for differential treatment in employment opportunities and leadership positions, and that women's achievements and contributions are discounted. Furthermore, the items in factor five also clearly stated that men, as a group, had benefitted from women's disadvantages not only economically but also sexually and psychologically.

Agreement with items in both factors four and five outlines the major tenets of Chicana feminisms, which, of course, overlap with feminist claims in general. All 150 Latino respondents had some academic exposure to many aspects of feminisms in their education, which, coupled with

Table 5.10. Exploratory factor analysis comparison alpha coefficients, Brown and White Masculinities Study

Latinos		Whites	
Factor	Alpha	Factor	Alpha
Traditional gender roles	.657	Traditional gender roles	.775
Feminist consciousness	.259	Feminist consciousness	.812
Marriage and household division of labor	.77	Marriage and household division of labor	.833
Gender-based subordination	.722		
Relational gender privilege and subordination	.679		

their lived experience, provided a powerful platform from which to question their male privilege and begin the arduous process of understanding women's subordination. The Latino respondents asserted a much more forceful feminist stance than the white respondents.

Relating to Feminisms: Intersectionality and Men's Relationship to Feminism

In 1970 the first women's studies program was established at San Diego State College (now San Diego State University). The second was created at Cornell University the same year. Since then, feminisms has undergone many transformations, from the early stages, when men in general were perceived as the source of patriarchal oppression of liberal feminism (Jaggar 1983) and where the goal was to have equal rights, to more recent times, in which one of the goals is to construct inclusive paradigms for potential collaborations with feminist men (Anzaldúa 1987; Castillo 1994; Hurtado 2010). Patriarchy is now conceptualized as a system of privilege that is not independent of other systems of privilege such as race, class, ethnicity, physical ableness, and sexuality (Hurtado 2011). The rise of Intersectionality embodied in significant axes of power has provided a lens through which contemporary masculinities can be examined.

Understanding the experiential variation that exists within the category of "man" can facilitate a more nuanced analysis of privilege and sub-ordination. Intersectionality is an effective theoretical tool that can be used to understand within- and across-group variation in experience. An intersectional lens allows us to "see," in Anzaldúan terms (1987, 78–79), how contradictory experiences of privilege and subordination have the potential to subvert power emanating from interlocking systems of domi-nation. Both groups of men in the study exhibited commonalities in their views of traditional gender roles. The commonalities stemmed from their gender socialization, which can easily make heterosexual arrangements appear "natural." Most individuals grow up in families from which they receive their primary socialization with varying degrees of "traditional-ism." The socialization occurring in family contexts takes gender-specific forms, which include commonalities in the ways boys are socialized and differences organized by race, sexuality, ethnicity, and class.

Using Intersectionality to analyze the BWMS permitted our examina-tion of both the differences between and the similarities of these men's views on gender and feminism. Had we examined only how these two groups of men were different and neglected the intersections they had in common, for example, male privilege, our conclusions would have been misinformed and would have placed one group of men as implicitly su-perior to the other. Instead of deducing that one group was more (or less) macho than the other, we found that both the Latino and the white re-spondents had some traditional views on gender but, *at the same time*, they had some progressive views in common, such as the division of household labor after marriage.

We also arrived at an understanding that Intersectional Identities are an outcome of differences in social structure, which may lead to differ-ent perceptions about the nature of oppression and gender subordina-tion. The potential for future collaborations with men lies in increasing our Intersectional understandings, which may lead to social and political mobilization to address gender disparities and to sharpen men's insights about their own privilege and contributions to women's oppression.

CHAPTER 6

Relating to Oppression: Intersectionality in Defining Latino Men's Views on Chicana Feminisms

In her canonical feminist text *Borderlands/La Frontera: The New Mestiza*, Gloria Anzaldúa reminds us, "Que no se nos olviden los hombres [Let us not forget the men]" (1987, 83). Her construction for a new world order is devoid of hatred, patriarchy, and discrimination, all of which are supplanted by harmony, inclusiveness, and social justice. Within this context, she advocates for compassion and accountability for men. Anzaldúa was not alone in including men from Chicana/Latino communities in her vision for a feminist utopia. Chicana feminist writers have historically recognized that a true feminist movement must include men, especially men in their communities, for social justice to prevail. The question left unaddressed, however, is how this inclusion should take place. What are Latino men's roles in seeking inclusion in feminisms? How will Latino men define feminisms for themselves? What experiences might prompt them to undergo a transformation of consciousness that would compel them to traverse the gender divide and join a feminist standpoint? Equally important, would feminist Latino men stand in solidarity with feminists of all inclinations to fight against sexism and other forms of oppression?

These questions have not been answered in the Latino or feminist literature thus far. Latino men's views on feminism and their role in fighting gender inequality have not been examined. By adhering relentlessly to the concept of machismo, this scholarly inquiry has rendered the possibility of a feminist Latino man inconceivable. But we knew better, or at least we thought that the state of Latinos' gender consciousness might be better than that depicted in the research. Thus, in designing our study, we heard the call from Anzaldúa and other Chicana feminist writers to not forget the men. We asked Latino men whether they considered themselves feminist, and we explored what their feminisms would look like if they did indeed exist.

In this chapter we examine, through Intersectionality, questions posed to the respondents in the Latino Masculinities Study (LMS): "Do you consider yourself a feminist?" and if so, "Why?" In answering these two deceptively simple questions, respondents revealed the complexities of a life of intersectional existence. They fully acknowledged their precarious understandings of "what it feels like for a girl [woman]," to quote Madonna's popular song. The respondents admitted they could only "imagine" (to quote Adu-Poku [2001]) and "empathized" with women's trials and tribulations. Nonetheless, their "distance" and lack of direct experience of what women experienced did not prevent respondents from feeling "in the flesh" (Moraga and Anzaldúa 1981, xix, 211–212) the anger, sadness, frustration, rage, futility, and urge to do something about women's condition. They had seen close up and personal what the women in their lives went through—restriction, humiliation, discrimination, violence, rape, invisibility—and they were moved to identify with women's pain and struggles. Their identification with feminisms may have been initiated by exposure to books and intellectual analysis, but the passion they felt was fueled by the injustice of patriarchy and their potential role as co-conspirators in the pain experienced by the women around them.

This chapter begins with the respondents' definitions of feminisms followed by their reasons for considering themselves feminists. We conclude by reviewing the implications for Chicana feminist theory of Latinos' views on feminisms and the potential of forming political collaborations with women to work in behalf of Latino and women's issues in the future.

Latinos' Definitions of Feminisms

To begin, of the 105 respondents in the LMS, 63 identified as feminist with no reservations, 19 with some reservations,[1] and 23 did not identify as feminist. In this chapter we focus on the 82 respondents who proclaimed a feminist identification, with or without reservations. Similar to previous qualitative studies exploring feminist consciousness and masculinities in predominantly white samples (Christian 1994; Vicario 2003; White 2008), we are fundamentally concerned in this chapter with the social processes that Latino men undergo to facilitate a feminist identification and consciousness. The inclusion of respondents who identify as feminist allows for the exploration of experiences that shape the development of a feminist consciousness (Christian 1994) and does so in a systematic manner (White 2008). Because this project explores Intersectionality by examining the experiences of Latinos, we can more effectively identify factors that contribute to gender consciousness in the context of race, ethnicity, and, to a certain extent, sexuality and class.[2]

Overall, respondents provided a variety of responses in defining feminism and describing the various experiences that shaped their feminist identification and gender consciousness. Their definitions of feminism generally began with discussions about egalitarianism in their romantic heterosexual relationships and their ideal views of marriage. Respondents also moved beyond the intimacy of their personal relationships and discussed their beliefs in equality for women in a number of contexts, including equal rights in the workplace. Overall, respondents' definitions of feminisms were viewed through Intersectionality, taking into account race, sexuality, ethnicity, and class in analyzing women's struggles. Respondents provided definitions that emphasized inclusiveness rather than restriction, expanding both the definitions of womanhoods and manhoods. In general, these responses focused on the struggle for women's individual rights and questioning of the individual and structural privileges provided by patriarchy.

Feminisms That Are Personal

Respondents articulated their subjective understanding of feminisms while explaining at length their beliefs about gender equality in social and political contexts. Of particular concern was equality between heterosexual romantic partners in the context of a committed relationship, including marriage. Respondents' emphasis on equality in such relationships stemmed from a concern about women's individual rights. For instance, Andrés Elenes, a twenty-six-year-old Chicano majoring in managerial science at the Massachusetts Institute of Technology (MIT) discussed his views on how feminist relationships should function. He stressed the importance of "trust and honesty" between partners and the idea that "there's no role" that should be attached to a particular gender; rather, "you're just a partner . . . in a relationship everyone is equal, everyone has the same stake in the relationship." According to Andrés, equality was "almost business-like . . . you pull your weight, I pull my weight, kind of deal." Andrés's view of equality emphasizes the utilitarianism and functional aspects of feminisms. For Andrés, being feminist included equality in a relationship and roles that were defined not by a person's gender, but by the tasks that needed to be completed to maintain and further the relationship.

Matt Rojas, a twenty-five-year-old respondent of mixed ethnicity (Cuban father, white mother), was a first-year law student at the University of Michigan. He situated his definition of feminisms in the context of his heterosexual marriage:

> I've been married for three years, my wife is an artist, she has a BFA in painting. I think women should be able to choose the role they want to play . . . in life. . . . If they want to be lawyers, they can be lawyers, if they want to be moms, they can be moms, if they want to be pilots . . . they're just as capable as the majority of men, at pretty much anything. So I think that's someone who's feminist . . . who supports women and the things that they're trying to do in their life. So, I feel like when I support my wife and her painting, her art, and we also have a child and so, I feel like I'm a feminist because I support what my wife wants to do and I try and help her do those things.

For many respondents, feminisms were defined as a woman's right to choose in all contexts of human existence—personal relationships, professional work, and how to best live their lives.

Feminisms in the Workplace

One of the primary contexts mentioned in respondents' definitions of feminisms was the workplace because they saw it as a site of struggle for obtaining equal treatment. Douglas Arévalo, a thirty-one-year-old Colombian student at La Guardia Community College who was also working as a bicycle messenger in New York City, believed that women "should be paid the same amount of money that a man should be paid," and that "they shouldn't put up with sexual harassment at work." Douglas was aware that women were discriminated against in the workplace in terms of differential pay and sexual harassment and felt discrimination was unjust.

José "Nike" Martínez was a twenty-two-year-old of Mexican descent who had graduated with a bachelor's degree in computer science from California State University, Monterey Bay. His response also focused on equality in the workplace. However, in contrast to Douglas, he emphasized access to employment for women and people of Color. He defined feminisms in an expansive manner by saying that "equality [is] for everybody no matter who you are or where you come from." José then applied this idea to the issue of discrimination in the workplace: "If you have the qualifications for whatever you want to do, there is no reason they should degrade you because you're female or your race or anything like that." He explicitly couched his opposition to discriminatory employment practices in his belief in equality for everyone, including women.

Feminisms Inclusive of Race, Ethnicity, Class, Sexuality (and Men)

Respondents also viewed feminisms through an Intersectional lens that included women, men, race, class, ethnicity, and, at times, sexuality. Israel García, a nineteen-year-old Chicano with a double major in sociology and political science at the University of Colorado, Boulder, provided the following response in defining feminisms: "[Feminisms] strives to create equality on all levels, whether that'd be race, class, gender, any of those things. I think we need an equal playing field, and the way feminism is seen to me is that it's an equal opportunity for everyone. And if that's what it is, then I'm all for it, because I'm all for equality and I'm all for equal playing fields." Israel believed equality should cut across lines of gender, race, and class. He advocated for the creation of an "equal playing field" and saw feminism as a vehicle for accomplishing that goal, not only for women, but also for the poor and working class and for people of Color. He fundamentally defined feminism as an inclusive movement that could create equality for all disadvantaged people.

Congruent with Chicana feminist writings (Anzaldúa 1987; Baca Zinn 1982), Remberto Núñez defined feminism in a manner that was inclusive of women and men, as well as of race and class. He was twenty-one years old and from El Salvador, his family having immigrated to the United States when he was just a few months old. Remberto was an undergraduate majoring in social and behavioral sciences at California State University, Monterey Bay. In defining feminisms he said, "I think that it's a new consciousness arising in the minds of women and men who see the injustices that have been going on, the inequity between men and women . . . [it's] the mission to empower women somehow." Remberto discussed feminisms as a form of consciousness, as proposed by Gloria Anzaldúa (1987), which could emerge in individuals regardless of their gender. This consciousness appears to be predicated on the awareness that inequalities between women and men exist and that the situation needs to be remedied (Gurin, Miller, and Gurin 1980). Remberto's consciousness entailed concrete action to further "the mission to empower women." These actions included making visible the fact that the "inequalities that go on between women [and men] is just like the inequalities that go on between race[s], and between income."

Remberto's response aligns with the position taken by a number of feminists of Color (P. Collins 2000; Davis 1983; hooks 1984, 2000; Hurtado 1996). He viewed feminist identification as an achieved ideological position rather than one that was linked to a specific set of experiences and interpretations, thus removing what Ashe (2004) calls the "experiential bar" to men's participation in feminist movements. Some feminists have conceptualized men's lived experiences as obstacles to the development of feminist consciousness (Ashe 2004), assuming an essential component of masculine identity based on the notion that men's experiences are uniform and conform to a singular category. Remberto's delineation of feminism as a mode of consciousness and other respondents' description of material experiences contributing to their feminist consciousness contest such essentialized notions of feminist participation. Respondents' definitions demonstrate the diverse nature of masculine experiences and are indicative of men's complex relationship with feminist engagement.

Because respondents had Intersectional understandings of the nature of women's oppression they held a critical view of hegemonic white feminisms, which they viewed as giving gender primacy and not addressing issues of ethnicity, class, and race. Similar to those of the respondents in *Voicing Chicana Feminisms* (Hurtado 2003b), these responses were characterized by a critique of middle-class, white hegemonic feminisms as constructed in the United States. Joseph García, a thirty-three-year-old master's student in Latin American studies at the University of New Mexico, provided an example that illustrates respondents' complicated definitions of feminisms:

> [Feminism is] believing in a woman's rights, her basic rights, and that women can do anything that a man can do. . . . If it means that feminism is used to co-opt the rights of others, I'm not supportive of that. . . . I actually have strong views about feminism in the United States and how I think it's been [used]. . . . I think the civil rights movement was co-opted by the [white] feminist movement of the '70s, and the people who gained the greatest opportunities from feminism in this country [and] from civil rights [struggles] were white women, who are overwhelmingly well represented in academia and have created a situation that has limited the opportunities for people of Color.

Although Joseph recognized that *all* women had disadvantages because of their gender, he also acknowledged that it was not only gender that created disadvantages but race, too. Joseph's critique demonstrates the importance not only of flexible and inclusive definitions of feminism for building coalitions among different groups of women, but also of coalitions across intersectional lines of gender, race, class, sexuality, and ethnicity. His response also illustrates the importance of social location in the way that feminisms are defined because he felt his experiences of oppression at the intersections of race and class, like those of many of the respondents in *Voicing Chicana Feminisms*, were not addressed by hegemonic white feminisms nor were they relevant to the lives of working-class people of Color. Therefore, although white women experience disadvantages because of their gender (and sometimes class, sexuality, and physical ableness), they inherently benefit from race privilege, which may prevent them from constructing feminisms that consider the struggles of people of Color in general.

Why Feminist?

In their explanations of why they identified as feminists, respondents described different experiences they encountered in several areas of their lives. From their varied explanations, three themes emerged: (1) the importance of relationship experiences within and outside the family; (2) experiences of racial discrimination and exclusion; and (3) experiences in higher education. Regardless of the spheres in which the experiences took place, respondents' gender consciousness was influenced predominantly by the women in their lives (mothers, sisters, aunts, nieces, friends, romantic partners, and women coworkers, among others). While white women were relating to privilege through their relationships with white patriarchy (fathers, brothers, husbands, uncles),[3] the Latino respondents were relating to Latina women's oppression.

Some respondents recounted experiences with family members who acted in ways that contradicted societal expectations for their gender (e.g., mothers were active and strong, fathers valued equality in household obligations). Other respondents described the experience of female family members receiving differential treatment, such as sisters not receiving parental support for their endeavors. Experiences within the family included fathers who influenced respondents' commitment to feminist views through positive example, that is, not displaying oppressive behavior and not exhibiting sexist behavior toward the women in the family. Overall, respondents learned what actions to emulate and which to avoid by observing their fathers' behavior, and these experiences helped shape the respondents' self-reflexivity on their own actions.

Family Experiences Influencing Latinos' Feminisms

Hurtado's research with young Chicanas demonstrates what she calls the "centrality of women" in the respondents' definitions of feminisms (2003b, 211). In particular, she notes that respondents learned their feminisms by observing women's lives. In many cases, these women were family members, like mothers, aunts, and sisters. Respondents in Hurtado's study gleaned important lessons from their family members, in addition to receiving social and emotional support:

> My respondents inhabited a world filled with women — mothers, sisters, aunts, grandmothers, and women friends. Most of their primary relationships (aside from the lovers of the heterosexual women) were with women. . . . The people they talked to, they spent time with, and they depended on, and who returned much of what they gave, were women. It was from this female-dominated context that my respondents drew their map of feminisms "in the flesh." (Moraga and Anzaldúa 1981, xix, 211–212)

Similar to the respondents in *Voicing Chicana Feminisms*, the LMS respondents wove in and out of various experiences with women in their intimate family circle and described the influence these experiences had on shaping their gender consciousness and feminist identification. Some described the strength their mothers displayed in two-parent households, while others referred to the socialization they received from single mothers. Ronnie Rendón, a twenty-seven-year-old gay Chicano studying studio arts at the University of Texas, Austin, discussed his mother's strength when asked why he considered himself a feminist. He perceived her as contradicting the dominant societal discourse around notions of womanhood, which made the disjuncture between patriarchal ideology and lived experience visible to him. Ronnie's mother exposed him to the multilayered nature of social reality, particularly the way in which inequalities are sustained and perpetuated (Hartsock 1983). Ronnie made the connection between capitalist and patriarchal systems and their collusion in objectifying and oppressing women, including the fact that men are perceived to be worth more than women and that women's bodies are used to sell products to men.

Other respondents stated that their feminist identification was largely the result of being raised by a single mother, many times coupled with having families that were constituted primarily of women. Ryan Ramírez was a twenty-year-old undergraduate of mixed ethnicity (Mexican and white) majoring in philosophy at the University of Colorado, Boulder. A single mother who considered herself "a very big feminist" raised him. He "grew up in a family of women, my sisters and mom, and I definitely respect women." Ryan's awareness of gender inequalities extended to a critical view of violence against women. At the time of the interview, there was extensive media coverage of rape allegations levied against the football team at the university he was attending. Ryan stated, "I think it's good that it's getting national attention because I think it's ridiculous how many girls are date raped. . . . Rape [should be] totally intolerable . . . there is no reason you shouldn't respect women, in my opinion." The concern and respect Ryan displayed for women as a group highlights the love and compassion he felt for his sisters and mother—the women who were central to his family life and his feminist identification.

Respondents often mentioned becoming self-reflexive about sexism because they witnessed the differential treatment their sisters received in their families, ranging from not receiving positive support for their endeavors from parents to unequal application of family rules. Although responses varied on the specific experiences that were influential, concern for the well-being of their sisters was a core element permeating respondents' feminist views. Xavier Márquez, a twenty-five-year-old Chicano who received his master's in physical therapy at the University of New Mexico, illustrates respondents' concern for the welfare of sisters. In answering the question of whether he considered himself a feminist, Xavier said, "Yeah, definitely . . . especially with the experiences with my sister, like my parents not giving [her] support and stuff like that." In describing the impact his sister's experiences had on him, Xavier continued, "I try my hardest because it's probably ingrained, like I was probably raised not to be a feminist, so I try really hard to recognize any situations where I think I'd be in the wrong."

In addition to the influence their mothers and sisters had on their becoming feminists, at times, fathers' egalitarian behaviors and attitudes prompted respondents to commit to gender equality. Albert Domínguez III, a respondent of mixed ethnicity (Puerto Rican and Ecuadorian) who had earned a bachelor's degree from Syracuse University and was working as a student activities program coordinator at George Washington University, described the influence his father's behavior in the home had on his views toward feminism. According to Albert, "my father is not like that [macho], he's not like 'women are supposed to do that.'" Because Albert did not hear his father express restrictions based on gender, "there was no reason for me to ever believe [in those restrictions]." Although Albert's parents followed traditional gendered roles "they inherited from their parents," like his mother cooking "all the time," Albert perceived their adherence as not based on gender requirements but, rather, as the result of his mother's not working outside the home. Albert described his father's sensitivity and appreciation of his wife's housework and remembered that he never said things like "Where's my food" when he came home from work. Albert saw his father as valuing his mother's work as well as participating in some of the necessary activities to maintain the household: "My father came home and cleaned the house, and I think they had a good balance of what they needed to do to make the house run."

Observing the men in their families mistreating women also influenced respondents' gender consciousness. Chris Valásquez was twenty-three years old at the time of the interview and had completed his bachelor's degree in liberal studies from California State University, Monterey Bay. When asked why he considered himself feminist, he said, "When I was younger I had an uncle . . . I actually had to witness this, he's an alcoholic . . . and we got a call one time like at three, four in the morning. He was beating his wife, and I had to assist my dad in going to the house and pulling him off her and stuff. So that was a shocker, like, 'Wow, this goes on, it's not only on TV.'" Chris's identification as feminist was informed by witnessing domestic abuse in his family, making real the violence in women's lives.

Other respondents mentioned similar instances of men in their families mistreating women, which influenced their identification as feminist. Augie was twenty-four years old and was on leave from the master's program in ethnic studies at San Francisco State University. Elaborating on why he considered himself feminist, he said,

> I remember the last time I went to Mexico . . . my grandpa treated my grandma as a domestic slave, like "that's what you're for." It was weird the way the relationship worked, and when I got there I could see my grandma, her spirit was in a way killed. She almost felt, or at least I assumed that she felt, that there was really no purpose anymore to life,

right? All of her children are in the United States, most of them, she only
has one daughter over there [in Mexico].

Augie recognized that the emotional mistreatment his grandmother received at the hands of his grandfather was a function of specific gender roles, which in many ways normalized the sexist treatment. When
oppressive gender dynamics are part of everyday interaction, even odd
or oppressive practices become routine. As Augie observed, "They [his
grandparents] don't even sleep in the same room . . . it seemed like they
didn't even communicate. [Yet] you could tell that they loved each other
but it was just weird."

Augie continued with the story of his arrival at his grandparents' home
in Mexico:

> So I get there and right away we're having dinner or lunch and I could
> see that she was sad you know . . . and I was sitting there and one of my
> dad's brothers was there too, and we were all talking and I go, "Hey
> Grandma, Abuelita," you know we were talking in Spanish. "If I were to
> have seen you on the street, just randomly you know, I wouldn't have rec-
> ognized you and I probably would have tried to make you my girlfriend,"
> and she just got all red, just smiling and really happy because no one ever
> gave her attention and that's what she needed, at least at that moment.

Augie recognized that his grandmother did not receive the emotional support and recognition she needed from the men in her family, and he tried
to fill this gap during his visit. "I was just trying to make her happy, trying to make her laugh." The men in Augie's family did not appreciate his
efforts, "and my dad's brothers and my grandpa kind of tripped out on
me, because I said that." Augie continued to support his grandmother
"during the time that I was around" by taking "her out a lot, you know
what I mean, trying to talk to her." Augie recognized that he did "have
gender privilege," and he attempted to use that privilege to improve the
emotional well-being of his grandmother, at least for the duration of his
visit to Mexico.

Augie's feminisms clearly were influenced by his educational experiences and used for a critical examination of his family's everyday life, particularly the emotional mistreatment of women. He attributed his sensitivity to his grandmother's situation to the fact that, "as a student a lot of
the classes that I took within the Chicano studies emphasis were feminist
courses, just Latina life stories, you know, oral history courses, and when

I took those courses I learned a lot in terms of my family." The courses made Augie think "about some of the things that feminism stands for, realizing when I took these courses that I do have gender privilege and trying to take that into account in everyday life, in what you do."

Experiences Outside the Family Influencing Latinos' Feminisms

Respondents also emphasized the role of women outside the family in the development of their gender consciousness, most of whom they encountered through intimate relationships, through friendships, or in their jobs. In a few instances, respondents' gender consciousness was raised not by the presence of women but by their absence in particular settings, especially in the corporate workplace.

Respondents' interactions in intimate relationships with women created a space for dialogue that had ramifications for the way respondents viewed gender inequity. Edgar González, a twenty-four-year-old Chicano who graduated from Princeton University with a degree in political science, was working as an investment analyst for a bank. In responding to why he considered himself feminist, Edgar discussed the long-term relationship with his feminist female partner, who was in college at the time of the interview, as critical to his views on feminisms. They had been together for seven years and were considering marriage, although she was reluctant to have a traditional wedding, unlike Edgar, who wanted one to please his parents. Ultimately, Edgar convinced her to have a traditional Catholic Mexican wedding, although at her insistence, the ceremony was altered in significant ways. Edgar would wear white and be given away by his mother. In Edgar's words, she took "every tradition and turned it upside down." These changes made an impression on Edgar: "Some of those [discussions] stuck with me. We respect traditions because it's nice when you have a traditional ceremony, but certain things that I see, even if it is implied, that repress women's views or opportunities, I immediately get defensive and I don't like any of that." Even though Edgar felt that his partner's views on marriage were "radical," he was affected by the deconstruction of the gendered nature of the traditional Mexican wedding ceremony.

Edgar and his partner eventually married, and they did alter the wedding ceremony to reflect their feminist views, although the changes made to the ceremony were not as radical as initially proposed by Edgar's partner. The outcome was "a traditional wedding that was modified [only] in certain areas." Both Edgar and his partner were given away by their respective parents, as opposed to only the bride being given away by her father. They also altered some practices that were specific to Catholic Mexican weddings, such as the groom giving the bride gold coins as a symbol of his intention to provide for her financially. Edgar and his partner split the gold coins between them and placed them in each other's hands, symbolizing "that we would both contribute [equally] to the household, in terms of wealth or otherwise." Another culturally specific practice that was altered was the offering of a bouquet of roses to the Virgin of Guadalupe to request fertility. Instead they "asked for [the Virgin's] blessings and prayers, as she represented womanhood and motherhood to us, not just fertility per se." According to Edgar, his partner did not change her last name, nor did she wear a "princess dress," but, rather, a "simple elegant dress" to avoid being "the center of attention." She felt it was *their* wedding, "not just something for the bride." Sticking to tradition, Edgar wore the customary black tuxedo, not a white one as originally proposed by his partner. Finally, the couple honored their grandparents at the wedding because "it was our way of saying thank you to our families for all the support they gave to us while raising us. We thought of our wedding as a party to celebrate our love and also the joining of our families, not just as a 'giving away of the bride.'" Edgar and his partner's modifications to their wedding highlight the influence feminist practices have on intimate, heterosexual relationships.

Experiences outside of the family with women friends also influenced respondents' views on feminism. Russell Contreras, a twenty-nine-year-old editor working for the Associated Press in New York City, described the lessons he had learned from women friends while an undergraduate at the University of Houston: "They were always calling me out on things I said." He described how he would "get defensive" at first, but then, upon reflection, he realized that "I need[ed] to acknowledge some things that I do, or that men do" because "I reinforce that stuff" and it "will be something that I'm dealing with for the rest of my life." Russell also described how these conversations impacted his consciousness in professional endeavors as an editor:

If it's someone like Gloria Anzaldúa . . . if she came out with a new book like tomorrow or next week, I'd want to review it, but I'd also know that, wait a minute, I'm coming from a different position of privilege in reading this book and I would be very self-conscious about it throughout the review. I'd probably be paranoid, but it's not so much that I'm worried about what I'm going to say. It's just me knowing that I'm invading the space. And I think I feel the same way when a Latino comes out with a book, a piece of literature, and some white person is reviewing it, who may or may not understand the context of what this writer is talking about. And of course the review comes out, and they read it, and they exoticize the text and do all the things that I think are wrong, and I get mad . . . and I don't want to repeat that, especially with a feminist text.

The intimate and honest discussions Russell had with his women friends in college provided the details necessary to fill out the contours of his feminisms. These discussions taught him about the hardships women experience living in a patriarchal society, and he was extremely respectful in not invading their boundaries.

The relationships respondents had with women outside their families exposed them to the intricacies of patriarchal oppression. Without the intimate and often contentious discussions, Latinas' views on gender subordination would remain "underground feminisms" (Hurtado 2003c). It was touching to hear the respondents' narratives on the personal interactions that led to their deeper understanding of feminist issues and of themselves. It took courage on the part of all involved to break the silences that might lead to liberation.

Workplace Experiences Creating Latino Feminist Identification

Respondents also attributed their feminist identification to experiences in the workplace that affected them in several ways. First, the workplace provided them with an opportunity for consistent contact with women, and these interactions played an important role in shaping respondents' gender consciousness. Marcos Pérez was a twenty-six-year-old Chicano enrolled in the doctoral program in sociology at the University of California, Santa Cruz. He described some of his employment experiences after graduating from high school as important in developing a feminist outlook.

Marcos had always worked in fields where women predominated. After high school, he ran child care sites and summer day camps for the YMCA. He said, "Everyone I worked with were women," which led him to "realize how idiotic unequal gender practices really are." Marcos continued, "I do not believe that gendered relationships should be driven by power. Relationships should be driven by cooperation. In this process, men should reflect on their own power, even if it makes one feel uncomfortable." These views were further reinforced when Marcos entered higher education and majored in community studies, an academic discipline in which the majority of the professors were women.

There were also opportunities for consciousness building when respondents worked in the corporate world. Edgar González, the respondent whose nontraditional wedding was described earlier, discussed the sexism he witnessed while employed at a large corporation. He noticed the lack of representation of women at major company functions such as at a closing dinner that Edgar attended as a representative of his employer. He described the environment as a "clubby world"; "if you were a woman, you wouldn't feel comfortable there." Edgar was aware that women's absence resulted in an exclusionary space and that if "you just put a woman in that situation, it changes the whole dynamic." Edgar also felt uncomfortable in these spaces—being young and Latino, someone "whose last name is González." Edgar's exposure to sexism in the corporate world was one of the reasons he considered himself a feminist.

Discrimination Contributing to Latino Feminisms

Racial discrimination as well as other types of exclusionary acts influenced respondents' assessments about gender inequalities. They focused on the ways in which their feelings of marginalization informed their perceptions of women's oppression. Jonathon Rosa was twenty-three years old, of Puerto Rican and Canadian descent, and a doctoral student in anthropology at the University of Chicago. While growing up, Jonathon noticed "that girls were treated differently in different situations and in ways that I did not think were right or fair." He had had similar experiences in various social groups, which led to his feminist identification. He stated,

> I think being who I am and growing up where I grew up . . . feeling on the outside of masculinities and femininities and genders in general . . . feeling on the outside of groups for me personally. . . . The way that perception played out was that no one had to tell me that the girls were as smart as the boys or that the girls were as good as the boys or that the girls were as cool as the boys.

Jonathon grew up biracial in a predominantly white neighborhood in upstate New York. He described being excluded from different groups, particularly groups organized around gender, which was instrumental in leading him to believe that girls were as capable and competent as boys. His definition of feminisms was couched in his childhood experiences of exclusion, which was the springboard from which his gender consciousness emerged.

Experiences in Higher Education Contributing to Latino Feminisms

Respondents mentioned three experiences in higher education as the impetus for their feminist identification: (1) the exposure to feminist literature; (2) the opportunity for cross-sex friendships in university settings; and (3) related experiences provided through higher education. One of the most frequently mentioned aspects of university attendance was the exposure to a formal curriculum in feminist academic materials that included Chicana feminist writings.[4] Many times, respondents emphasized the importance of reading specific feminist authors, while others discussed the impact of reading feminist literature in general. Feminist readings left a deep impression on many of them, exposing respondents to radical ways of thinking about gender.

Some respondents talked explicitly about strands of social theory as instrumental in shaping their thoughts and influencing their intellectual work. Comments from Jorge Morales, a twenty-seven-year-old Chicano doctoral student in comparative literature at the University of California, Berkeley, illustrates this point:

> To make a long story short because I believe women's oppression is tied to other kinds of oppressions, racial, ethnic, sexual, I think all oppressions are tied to each other, and I think that Mexican women struggle simply because they are women. . . . I don't think they should have to suffer simply because of their gender and also I'm a graduate student in comparative literature. . . . My work has really been informed by feminist theories and a particular slant of poststructuralism, Marxism, and Chicana feminist thought so I think that must have been part of it.

Jorge felt that his exposure to academic writings on Intersectionality in the context of his graduate training influenced him on a personal level as well as on an intellectual level. His response demonstrates the influence Chicana feminist writings have on the acquisition of discourses for respondents to articulate gender consciousness.

Raúl Coronado, a thirty-two-year-old gay Chicano doctoral student at Stanford University, also demonstrated the importance of being exposed to feminist literature, specifically Chicana feminist authors. In responding to why he considered himself feminist, Raúl stated that "when I got into college and took my first feminist studies classes and read Gloria Anzaldúa, *The Borderlands*, Cherríe Moraga, *Loving in the War Years*, I just identified with that so much and I knew then that in order to be able to become more aware about power relations and aspects of queer Chicano sexuality, I had to . . . understand sexism in order to understand queer sexuality." Chicana feminist writings exposed the workings of patriarchal power in oppressing gay men as well as women.

University-sponsored activities outside the classroom also contributed to respondents' gender awareness. Marcos Pérez underwent a significant transformation while conducting fieldwork in Mexico as part of his undergraduate requirements for his major:

> I did community studies and it's a major that is predominantly attended by women. I had to do six months of fieldwork working with the labor union in Mexico, and I guess people consider union work kind of a masculine thing, but I went down there because I had heard of a transnational company that was basically exploiting women workers. . . . I worked at the labor union and I saw how a lot of the men from the labor union basically silenced and had the power control over women and also how the power control existed in the factory setting and also how it figured into home life and life within community. So it was like this cycle of power that women couldn't get out of.

Marcos observed the treatment women received at the hands of men within seemingly progressive organizations like labor unions. At times, men's authority over women extended to committing violence against them. As Marcos related, in one instance a woman's

> husband had migrated to the United States and came back and found out that his wife had been organizing but she was organizing with a man so he suspected that there was an affair and basically beat the shit out of her for a couple of days 'til she left him. Another woman, a lot of the women actually that I met had husbands who had either passed away or were severe alcoholics. . . . Because I got to meet a lot of these women I realized the shit that they have to go through, so it made me reflect on

> my own personal life outside of that community that I was working in. Where do my sisters stand, and where does my mom stand. . . . It made me reevaluate gender dynamics within my own life.

Seeing women under the direct control of men, some of those women being abused physically, affected Marcos's notions about gender and initiated a process of self-reflexivity about the gender dynamics around him, including in his family.

In sum, women inside and outside the family were important in awakening the respondents' feminisms. Women's presence (or the lack thereof) in employment contexts was as formative. In addition, respondents learned empathy for all women from the work of Chicana feminists. The respondents' narratives highlight the multiple paths traversed by Latino men to reach a feminist identification.

Theorizing Latinos' Gender Views

What do Chicana feminist writers hope to accomplish by including men in their feminist theorizing and activism? One obvious answer, as proposed by Intersectionality, is the recognition of multiple oppressions. Chicana feminist writers understand "in the flesh" (Moraga and Anzaldúa 1981, xix, 211–212) that liberation for their communities cannot be based solely on gender, because most of the writers come from working-class, racialized Latino communities with a history of colonization in what was once their homeland (Anzaldúa 1987; Castillo 1994; Saldívar-Hull 2000). The inclusion of men in these writers' communities is based on the understanding that liberation requires the inclusion of everyone, not only women. By including men, Chicana feminist theorizing expands into providing a comprehensive social justice agenda.

We turn to integrating Latinos' views on gender as expressed by respondents in the LMS to examine two propositions: the expansion of a Chicana feminist liberation theory, and the utility of Chicana feminist constructs.

Core Concepts in Chicana Feminisms

One of the greatest victories of all feminisms is the decoupling of gender from biological sex, that is, the recognition that the outward, sometimes called "performative," aspects of maleness and femaleness are independent of biological embodiment. The expression of gender as independent of a person's biological sex has liberated individuals from Freud's dictum, "biology is destiny." Individuals, regardless of biological makeup, can be male, female, transgendered, or not gendered at all. Furthermore, the performativity of gender is socially constructed and should not determine a priori individuals' abilities or roles in life. Conceptualizing of sexuality independent of gender and sex—that is, whom individuals are sexually attracted to is not predetermined by gender or sex—is another expression of decoupling. Every combination of sex, gender, and sexuality is possible, and no one should be judged because of their preferences or, some would argue, their desires. All feminisms have this core value in common. Chicana feminists have been at the forefront of fighting against the social restrictions imposed by the trinity of gender, sex, and sexuality (Anzaldúa 1987; Castillo 1994; Pérez 1999; Trujillo 1991).

The respondents in the LMS implicitly agreed with this conceptualization of the feminist struggle. At a minimum, they explicitly decoupled sex and gender in defining their feminisms. Of paramount importance was their sophisticated understandings of gender. None of them expressed a biological basis for gender assignment, for men or women, thus moving beyond a physical essentialism that would limit participation in a feminist movement. Instead, respondents assumed that both men and women (and anyone in between who does not fully identify as male or female) could benefit from feminisms. Their quarrel was not with whether they could be feminists or not; their concern was more with whether their male privilege would result in an unconscious domination of feminist issues—a very self-reflexive position central to Chicana feminisms (Hurtado 1996; Hurtado and Cervantez 2009).

Within Chicana feminisms, self-reflexivity acknowledges individuals' Intersectional Identities and potential commitment to multiple subjectivities. Inherent in this standpoint is the recognition that all knowledges are strategic and partial (Haraway 1988; Pérez 1999; Sandoval 2000). As Caraway (1991, 193) points out, "Reflexivity is a keyword here, inscribing our feminist theories with the constant imperative to keep looking back over our shoulders to see what and whom we have left out of the identities we present to the world." Self-reflexivity also acknowledges the involvement of political power and privilege, however circumscribed, and the influence these advantages may have in furthering a social justice agenda. Pérez (1991, 173) elaborates: "If I am the world, and I heal myself, then I heal the world. These are personal private revolutions, each member of the collective taking responsibility for her/his contradictions within the collective, willing to grapple with the question, 'Who am I exploiting?'"

This concept is especially important for Latinos traversing feminist paths (Adu-Poku 2001; Anzaldúa and Keating 2002) as they, in many instances, accrue benefits from patriarchal structures. Many respondents exhibited self-reflexivity in claiming a feminist identification. They were aware that their material experience of patriarchy was one of privilege. They were fully aware that men who identified as feminist had to acknowledge that they could not be feminist in the same ways women could; the unearned structural privilege inherent in patriarchy inevitably obstructed their experiencing women's gender subordination. By simultaneously acknowledging male privilege and racial oppression, respondents exhibited something akin to what Anzaldúa calls "mestiza consciousness," which Hurtado (2003b, 18) summarizes as an individual's

> ability to "see" the arbitrary nature of all [social] categories but still take a stand . . . [challenging] Chicana feminists to exclude while including, to reject while accepting, to struggle while negotiating. Chicana feminists variously called this "mestiza consciousness" (Anzaldúa 1987), differential consciousness (Sandoval 1991, 2000), and concientización (Castillo 1994, 171). The basic concept involves the ability to hold multiple social perspectives while simultaneously maintaining a center that revolves around concrete material forms of oppression.

Self-reflexivity recognizes the influence of the individual in the normal course of social interaction and the inherent tension in questioning without rejecting and in critiquing within the "context of common ground" (Dillard 2003, 231).

Our respondents' claims to Intersectional Identities were fraught with complications, not because their definitions of race and gender were based on a false biologicalism, but because they simultaneously understood the feminist concept of positionality on the effects of power relations that conferred privilege on dominant Social Identities. They understood that knowledge did not emerge independent of an individual's particular social positions as situated by gender, race, class, ethnicity, and sexuality (Hurtado 1996, 80). Respondents perceived a fundamental difference in the way that women, as opposed to men, of Color experienced racial and sexist oppression and believed that it was important to reflect on this difference when making claims to certain subject positions. Claiming a politicized identity can be especially troublesome when those claiming the identity do not share in the oppressive experiences that, in many cases, accompany that particular intersection. The problematic lies in the fact that identification with a politicized identity, such as feminist, queer, or Chicano, by someone who does not share in the experiences and consequences associated with that identity has the potential to devalue its significance. Respondents recognized that the link between material experience and politicized identities was important, but they did not view material experience as a uniform category or as the sole criterion for politicized identification as such. Material experience is not *essentially* linked to specific Intersectional Identities in a singular way, nor does it provide the only grounds for claims to that identity.

When a privileged person, either by virtue of gender or race (or both), claims an Intersectional Identity without the accompanying experiences, it can lead to diluting the identity claims and the material experiences of those who are oppressed. Respondents' sensitivity to the precariousness of Intersectional Identity claims is indicative of the decoupling of sex, gender, and sexuality. Rather than simply asserting that men cannot be feminist and falling prey to cultural essentialism and biologicalism, respondents used the concept of positionality and Intersectional understandings of power to complicate their answers.

Respondents readily articulated that certain Social Identities conferred privilege, such as being racially white and male, at the same time that someone could be oppressed by class and sexuality. They gave examples that highlighted Intersectional contradictions. Self-reflexivity therefore led to accountability; that is, each individual member in the community constituted by their Intersectional Identities was accountable to the expectation of personal responsibility. If an individual claimed an Intersectional Identity, say, as a Latino feminist, then he was considered an integral part of that well-defined community, which, in turn, held them accountable for their personal behavior and political choices related to that Intersectional Identity. Each individual's behavior reflected on the community as a whole; therefore, community members had a right to scrutinize that behavior. For accountability to be viable, however, the individual had to internalize that belonging and desire to become better at fulfilling his political commitment with feedback from community members. Accountability therefore was the political aspect of self-reflexivity (Hurtado 1996).

Accountability assumes that the self is not constituted in the individual but, rather, encased in a body that is socially connected; therefore, its subjectivity is constituted through communal relations (Comas-Díaz, Lykes, and Alarcón 1998; Rowe 2005). If one feels whole and happy only through belonging to and identifying with specific communities, then the happiness and well-being of those communities are essential to one's well-being as well. Accountability is not an added burden or restriction, but a compelling reason for political engagement and social existence (Hurtado 2009). Self-reflexivity is about the self; accountability is about the social and political act embedded in the constituencies of political importance to the person. Accountability is intended to ensure that an individual's behavior is in accordance with her or his political commitments and beliefs about transformation and achieving social equity (Hurtado 1996, 2010).

Learning Intersectional Feminisms through Intersectional Relationships: The Importance of Women in Latino Feminist Identifications

The inclusion of men by Chicana feminist writers does not stem from an unbridled commitment to men in their communities. As theorists working in an intellectual field, Chicana feminists have been willing, if necessary, to break with the traditions of their culture and communities to fight for liberation (Blackwell 2011). More than thirty years ago, Anzaldúa (1987, 83–84) asserted,

> Though we "understand" the root causes of male hatred and fear, and the subsequent wounding of women, we do not excuse, we do not condone, and we will no longer put up with it. From the men of our race, we demand the admission/acknowledgment/disclosure/testimony that they wound us, violate us, are afraid of us and of our power. We need them to say they will begin to eliminate their hurtful put-down ways. But more than the words, we demand acts. We say to them: We will develop equal power with you and those who have shamed us.

Chicana feminists have included men in their struggles not out of submission but out of solidarity. Although Chicana and Latina women were willing to work with our respondents by suggesting feminist materials and engaging them in intense debates around gender inequality, those actions should not be construed as submission to patriarchy or to "cultural values." Instead, the very core of Chicana feminisms is collective action. Chicana feminisms assume that consciousness about Intersectional oppression is a relational process that occurs in connection with others.

Chicana feminist mobilization privileges collectivity; the ethos is one of commitment to "bringing along" as Latinos gain critical perspectives on gender relations. Although collective engagement is never without friction (Arredondo et al. 2003), it is nonetheless an absolute cornerstone of Chicana feminisms.[5]

The importance of Latinos having friendships and intimate relationships with feminist women has been demonstrated in research examining feminist men (Vicario 2003; White 2008), and our findings reinforce this point. But exactly what was stimulated in our respondents by their relationships with feminist partners, sisters, and friends? The answer to this question is unexplained in previous studies; a theoretical bridge between these social exchanges and the development of men's feminist consciousness has not been proposed. However, the LMS respondents' answers provide ample evidence of the feminist transformation the men underwent. Without their female relationships, respondents would never have noticed that the barring of women from their workplaces created "geographies of exclusions" (Sibley 1995), where practices reinforcing hegemonic masculinity were allowed to occur unchecked. They would not have understood that such homosocial practices among men are used to maintain inequality between men and women, as well as between different groups of men (Anderson 2005; Connell 1995). Respondents working under these conditions expressed discomfort and also felt excluded. The "marked" difference might not have been based on gender; the exclusion could also have been marked by ethnicity, such as the respondents' last name or their social class. Respondents came to understand that the exclusion could be used as a racialized demarcation of difference. Their feelings of discomfort allowed them to imagine "what it feels like for a girl [woman]" (to return to the earlier quotation by Madonna). They recognized that women would not feel comfortable in such workplaces and that if they were present in these spaces, it would change the gender dynamics. Men's gender consciousness was influenced by "the presence of the absence" (Fine 2002, 21) of women in the workplace. All of this awareness was possible because of the bridging work performed by the women in the respondents' lives. Chicana feminisms explicitly claim "this bridge called my back" (Moraga and Anzaldúa 1983) as an essential component of connecting different social realities. This "work" was named Chicana feminisms not only to make it visible and to acknowledge the toll that it takes on women but to propose it as a political strategy to increase concientización (Castillo 1994) among *all* community members.

Once consciousness was raised, respondents could apply their Intersectional understandings of gender oppressions to men, including fathers and other men in their families. In this instance, the influence came from both positive and negative poles. Many respondents were positively influenced by their fathers' (or father figures') gentleness toward, care of, and love for their spouses and for the other women in their families. They were able to "see" that such positive behaviors were not only individual "personality characteristics" but also counterhegemonic moves against patriarchy. They were able to see masculinity beyond machismo and were open to Anzaldúa's (1987, 83) reminder that the concept of machismo had been perverted to have only negative connotations, which was not always the case: "The modern meaning of the word 'machismo,' as well as the concept, is actually an Anglo invention. For men like my father, being 'macho' meant being strong enough to protect and support my mother and us, yet being able to show love."

On the other hand, the negative behavior exhibited by some men toward women also influenced respondents to become feminists. Instead of excusing abusive and sexist behavior, respondents broke with the gender solidarity often exhibited by men. It did not sit well with them when they saw their sisters and mothers being treated unfairly, and they certainly were mobilized when they saw women experience physical and sexual abuse at the hands of men. They took sides with Anzaldúa's (1987, 83–84) admonishment that "though we 'understand' the root causes of male hatred and fear, and the subsequent wounding of women, we do not excuse, we do not condone, and we will no longer put up with it."

Feminisms and Culture

Like the women cited in *Voicing Chicana Feminisms* (Hurtado 2003b), the respondents in the LMS said they felt tension between the "radical" ideas proposed by Chicana feminists and the desire to respect Chicano/a and Latino/a cultural traditions. Commitment to cultural maintenance can be interpreted as reflecting a way of revaluing a stigmatized heritage that is devalued by the dominant society; in fact, it can be a form of decolonization (Aldama, Sandoval, and García 2012; Hurtado and Gurin 2004). The maintenance of the Spanish language, the rediscovery of the group's history, and the deconstruction of a group's colonization can impale its members from a state of *degrouping*, in which the collectivity is marked as a group only for negative purposes (e.g., stigma, oppression), to a state of *regrouping*, as defined by French social psychologist Erika Apfelbaum (1979, 203):

Whether this rediscovery bears upon a cultural heritage, or whether it is at the start simply a pooling of grievances that raise the community's consciousness of those problems common to the entire (group), this process always serves the function of restructuring the (group), or *regrouping*. "Grievances, problems, and injustices can be expressed and shared by group members, thus developing a 'heritage' of understanding" (Proshansky and Newton 1973, 207). The positive function, sometimes played by art or literature (according to Park 1913/1950), may also be fulfilled by encounters such as consciousness-raising groups. In short, the goal is to re-endow one's own collectivity with its main group support functions, by restoring a cultural heritage (such as literature or music; see Lester 1968), by establishing an historical chronicle, or simply by discovering the commonality of problems.

Or, as the Chicano/a movement has succinctly stated, "La cultura cura (culture heals)." However, Chicana feminisms have never advocated the uncritical consumption of culture; rather, they advocate for a critical lens that values culture at the same time that it reconstitutes it by eradicating its regressive elements.

Cultural negotiation in a racist society demonstrates the way that ethnicity complicates the relationship Latina/os have with feminisms. By modifying aspects of a cultural tradition, respondents addressed the sexism embedded in their own cultural practices. This point echoes Chicana feminist theorizing (Anzaldúa 1987; Anzaldúa and Keating 2002; Hurtado 1996, 2003b) in that it heeds Anzaldúa's (1987, 21–22) call for a critique of culture while simultaneously acknowledging it as a place of safety and nurturance—a home that, although it contains sexist components, provides a degree of insulation from racism:

> Not me sold out my people but they me. So yes, though "home" permeates every sinew and cartilage in my body, I too am afraid of going home. Though I'll defend my race and culture when they are attacked by non-mexicanos, conosco el malestar de mi cultura [I recognize the discontent of my culture]. I abhor some of my culture's ways, how it cripples its women, como burras [like beasts of burden, donkeys], our strengths used against us, lowly burras bearing humility with dignity. The ability to serve, claim the males, is our highest virtue. I abhor how my culture makes macho caricatures of its men. No, I do not buy all the myths of the tribe into which I was born. . . . I will not glorify those aspects of my culture which have injured me and which have injured me in the name of protecting me. . . . So, don't give me your tenets and your laws. Don't

give me your lukewarm gods. What I want is an accounting with all three cultures—white, Mexican, Indian. I want the freedom to carve and chisel my own face, to staunch the bleeding with ashes, to fashion my own gods out of my entrails. And if going home is denied me then I will have to stand and claim my space, making a new culture—una cultura mestiza— with my own lumber, my own bricks and mortar and my own feminist architecture.

As predicted by Intersectionality Theory, these cultural negotiations take place at the intersections of race, ethnicity, class, sexuality, and gender.

Intersectional Chicana Feminisms in Coalition Building and Political Mobilization: Toward a Theory of Liberation

Ultimately, Chicana feminisms are about engaging in political struggle for liberation; as Anzaldúa proclaims (1987, 84), "The struggle of the mestiza is above all a feminist one." Did the feminist-identified respondents from the LMS make the leap from consciousness to commitment to political action? The answer is a resounding yes. Most respondents answered in the affirmative when asked if they would be willing to work in behalf of issues affecting Latino men and women in the future. As a result of their feminist views, many of these respondents also expressed a commitment to political action and personal accountability to decrease sexism because they equated gender hierarchy with other unearned advantages such as class or race privilege. Their commitment to political mobilization stemmed from their intersectional understandings of the interrelatedness of oppressions.

It is important to note that the findings presented in this book have implications for research, feminist theorizing, and coalition building. First, in providing empirical contributions to the literature about feminist-minded Latinos, Chicana feminist thought, and racialized masculinities, this project can aid in the further development of theory seeking to articulate complex and nuanced understandings of the lived experiences of Latino feminist men and the ways in which they develop their racially and class-specific forms of gender consciousness. Second, this research offers practical applications by providing knowledge that can aid in the creation of coalitions across lines of difference for the purpose of political mobilization on behalf of social justice. As Anzaldúa (1987, 80) reminds us, "The answer to the problem between the white race and the colored, between males and females, lies in healing the split that originates in the very foundations of our lives, our culture, our language, our thoughts. A massive uprooting of dualistic thinking in the individual and collective consciousness is the beginning of a long struggle, but one that could, in our best hopes, bring us to the end of rape, of violence, of war."

The respondents' narratives have direct implications for building coalitions across genders because they opened up the possibility of using Intersectional Identities in strategic ways to dismantle oppressive social structures. Respondents' awareness that all oppressions were interconnected made them more likely to engage in what Sandoval (2000, 58) calls a "differential mode of consciousness," whereby people shift from one Intersectional Identity to another (according to the apertures in social structures), creating opportunities to engage in struggles for social justice. Until our study was conducted, it was not clear whether Chicana feminist theory actually applied to Latino men or whether men understood the implications of Intersectionality, especially as it relates to fighting for gender equity. Given the results of the LMS, we now have evidence of at least *our* respondents' awareness of oppressive social structures *and* commitment to social action.

Our respondents, as in the case with Chicana feminists, did not engage in the "ranking of oppressions" (Moraga 1981, 29). Chicana feminisms use relational analyses of power (Hurtado 1996), which approach various oppressions in nonhierarchical ways (Moraga and Anzaldúa 1983). Utilizing Intersectionality as a tool for examining the simultaneity of multiple oppressions lets us take "all claims of oppression seriously in order to dismantle the existing status quo" (Hurtado 2003b, 263). Accordingly, none of the respondents in our sample defined feminism in a way that prioritized one form of oppression over another. Most discussed it as a movement that aimed to dismantle all sources of inequality. The few who did not define feminism as such viewed it as the struggle for women's individual rights. However, these respondents did so in the context of a class struggle; they talked about how women should be paid as much as men, should not be discriminated against in employment, and should not be subjected to sexual harassment at work. The beliefs they expressed about gender inequality in the context of the workplace are indicative of their class consciousness intersecting with their gender consciousness.

Respondents' narratives of the influence of Chicana feminist writings on their views of social inequality validate the power of this intellectual production to begin the serious work of dismantling patriarchy. Respondents related numerous experiences that were reformulated because of their interaction with institutions of higher education, which produced gender consciousness and eventual feminist identification. The Latino feminist men in our study traveled multiple, nonlinear paths to reach a

feminist identification. Their conclusions that oppressive societal structures were interconnected forced an expansion of the definition of shared
interests, such as their ideological position on sexual violence against
women. This issue represents a shared interest that was not necessarily
based on a common Intersectional Identity (e.g., Latina feminist versus
Latino feminist). Davis and Martínez (1994) have indicated that ideological uniformity is not an essential characteristic in creating effective
coalitions; however, the fact that there is a degree of ideological similarity
around the issue of violence against women is particularly hopeful because
it occurs across lines of difference and from members of a social category
(i.e., men) who are most likely to perpetrate such violence.

If systems of racism, sexism, classism, and heterosexism are perceived
as mutually constitutive, then addressing oppression in one domain neces-
sitates dismantling multiple axes of domination. In effect, this creates a
broader definition of shared interests—issues that may appear unrelated
may have underlying connections to other axes of oppression. Making
such connections visible can contribute to the way that shared interests are perceived, which can be instrumental in the creation of effective
coalitions (J. Childs 1990, 2003; Davis and Martínez 1994; Oliver and
Grant 1995). In other words, Intersectionality facilitated our respondents'
ability to see feminisms as being within their purview; becoming feminists
radicalized them to *all* oppressions, thereby achieving the ultimate goal of
Chicana feminisms: to write a theory of liberation for *all*. Chicana feminists' impressive accomplishment was attained through the sheer force of
persisting in building theory that resides "in the flesh" (Moraga and Anzaldúa 1983, 23) and that takes seriously the "lived experience" (Hurtado
2003b, 202) of Chicanas/os as colonized subjects within a historical context of conquest on their native lands.

In writing a liberation theory, early Chicana feminists put all their
eggs in one basket. They had infinite hope that intellectual production
inside and outside the academy would revolutionize ways of thinking and
ultimately generate a differential consciousness that would reconstitute
social reality to gain the traction necessary to change the world. And, indeed, Chicana feminist writers have attained their goal of transformation,
including for men in their communities. They have transfigured higher
education through their writings, even though many of them have written outside the academy. Furthermore, their theory of liberation advocates changing consciousness through education and through nonviolent
political engagement. Our respondents' testimonies verify that the first
part of Chicana feminist writers' liberation theory indeed has succeeded

in creating a critical consciousness about gender relations. The next phase is yet to be tested and will have to answer the question of whether the transformation of consciousness will lead to new forms of social relations that will result in liberation for all.

Final Thoughts

We hope that the exploration of Latino men's experiences reported in this book serves to reduce distortions in the scholarship on Latino men (Noguera, Hurtado, and Fergus 2012) by providing representations that are counter to existing stereotypes (Hurtado and Sinha 2008). The complexities of the respondents' lives also suggest other aspects that remain to be explored. Here we consider two. One is the feminist mothering that produces socially conscious Latino men. Many of the respondents readily acknowledged their mothers as a source of their gender consciousness and their reconsideration of the negative aspects of masculinity. Another is the necessary investigation of male queerness and its connection to feminisms. The Latino Masculinities Study did not pursue either of these topics sufficiently for in-depth analysis. We touch on these topics below and invite our readers to create new areas of study that center on the examination of Latino men through a Chicana feminist lens.

Feminist Mothering of Latino Men

Respondents discussed the importance of their mothers to their definitions of feminisms; this requires a deeper examination of mother-son relationships, particularly how lessons of resistance are transmitted and received by young Latino men and other men of Color. Hurtado (2003b) has demonstrated the way in which this process manifested itself with Chicanas. Similar patterns have been found in African American adolescent girls (Ward 1996). Further studies of feminist-identified Latinos that include this component could potentially shed light on the processes that are implicated in cross-gender familial transmissions of knowledge.

Gay Sexuality and Chicana Feminisms

The core of theorizing about Chicana feminisms has come from the analysis of lesbianism as a challenge to patriarchal norms in Chicano culture (Moraga and Anzaldúa 1983; Pérez 1999; Trujillo 1991). The feminist critique of heteronormativity and developments in Queer Theory have been fully embraced by Chicana Feminisms Theory. Sexuality takes center stage in Chicana feminist production, with its focus on cultural manifestations in gay and transgendered communities across the globe (Cantú 2000; Espín 1996; Ochoa 2006; Schaeffer-Gabriel 2005).

There has also been some pioneering work on sexualities and transnational theorizing of gender for heterosexual Latinos. Zavella and Castañeda (2005) and González-López (2005) illustrate this vein of research with their work on the migration process from Mexico and the rest of Latin America that results in heterosexual women and men undergoing transitions in sexualities. Both studies explore the consequences of coming to the United States, which, in some instances, results in restrictions on enacting sexuality because of a lack of available partners; in other instances, migration increases sexual exploration as local and familial ties are loosened by coming to a new country.

Queer male sexuality, however, has not been as fully incorporated as a topic of research and presents a new area of expansion for Chicana feminisms. We only had 5 out of 105 respondents who identified as gay, limiting our analysis of the relationship between gay sexuality and feminist identification. More attention needs to be paid to the way that sexuality operates as an overarching axis of oppression, particularly for queer Latinos. As Anzaldúa (1987, 84–85) advocated more than thirty years ago,

> *Asombra pensar que hemos, como femenistas y lesbianas, cerrado nuestros cora-zónes a los hombres, a nuestros hermanos los jotos, desheredados y marginales como nosotros* [It is surprising to think that we, as feminists and lesbians, have closed our hearts to the men, our brothers the queer, the disinherited, the marginal like us]. Being the supreme crossers of cultures, homosexuals have strong bonds with the queer white, Black, Asian, Native American, Latino, and with the queer in Italy, Australia and the rest of the planet. We come from all colors, all classes, all races, all time periods. Our role is to link people with each other—the Blacks with Jews with Indians with Asians with whites with extraterrestrials. It is to transfer ideas and information from one culture to another. Colored homosexuals have more knowledge of other cultures; have always been at the forefront (although sometimes in the closet) of all liberation struggles in this country; have suffered more injustices and have survived them despite all odds. Chicanos need to acknowledge the political and artistic contributions of their queer. People, listen to what your *jotería* [queer folk] is saying.

Connell (1995) has described male homosexuality within the hegemonic gender order as the repository of all that is feminine. If we consider the feminization that gay men are often accused of, this process of subordination could illustrate a variation of what Moraga and Anzaldúa call "theory in the flesh" (1981, xix, 211–212) and can be a potential "bridge" (Moraga and Anzaldúa 1981) to empathizing with women that emerges directly from the feminized body. How can this potential experience expand queer Chicana feminist writings? The embodiment of feminization may have an impact on gay Latino men's gender consciousness in profound ways and, when combined with exposure to Chicana feminist writings through higher education, may in fact inform feminist consciousness for gay Latino men.

The existing studies of gay Latino men provide insights into the construction of sexuality in US Latino communities (Almaguer 2004; Cantú 2000, 2004; Roque Ramírez 2003, 2007). However, these studies have not explored the ways in which queer sexuality influences political views toward various oppressions (like sexism, racism, classism, and heterosexism). An area for future exploration is the Intersectional node of race, class, gender, and sexuality in the formation of gender consciousness among young, educated, queer Latinos. Placing sexualities at the center of analysis could also contribute to the technologies of subordination and coalition building around sexual oppression (P. Collins 2004; Hurtado 1998a). The use of sexualities as a tool of oppression represents an area of commonality that can be used in attempts to dismantle existing interlocking systems of oppression in the continued struggle toward social justice.

The last chapter applies Intersectionality to a case study of a Latino man's journey from incarceration to full integration once he was released from prison. As Chicana feminists have claimed, theory should not exist only for academic purposes but should also undergird social change in Chicana/o communities. We hope to illustrate the profound difference that "living Chicana theory" (Trujillo 1998) has made in one man's life.

CHAPTER 7

Intersectionality at Work:
Regression, Redemption, Reconciliation

In 2000 bell hooks wrote that "feminism is for everybody," underscoring that it is a "Living Chicana Theory," as Carla Trujillo (1998) so aptly titled her book. One of the main goals of Chicana feminisms is to help everyone enhance, modify, challenge, fight, and survive their everyday existence (Anzaldúa 1987; Castillo 1994; Saldívar-Hull 2000). Testimonio is one tool used to make Chicana feminisms of use by uncovering life stories that would otherwise remain invisible and using the lessons learned from these stories as a tool for healing (Anzaldúa 1990; Delgado Bernal, Burciaga, and Flores Carmona 2012; Latina Feminist Group 2001). Testimonio is usually a one-person account; however, we present José Hurtado's story as a collaborative testimonio to illustrate the utility of Intersectionality in everyday life. We begin by turning the narrative over to Aída Hurtado, who recounts the collaborative testimonio of how she, her family, and her community applied, without conscious intent, the theoretical underpinnings of Chicana feminisms and Intersectionality to help José, her brother, reintegrate into his family and his newfound community in Northern California. We offer José's story as a feminist example of how context, community, relationships, and a redefinition of masculinity helped one individual overcome the deleterious effects of incarceration and find redemption.

A Collaborative Testimonio: José's Story

"Pepe anda muy mal. Tienen que hablarle. Tenemos miedo de que las cosas no acaben bien [Pepe (José) is on the wrong path. You have to call him.

We are afraid that things will not end well]."[1] This was the content of the long-distance phone call I received from my cousin Sergio in Minnesota, who was worried about my brother. Pepe (to the family) was being tagged by the police for rumored drug sales. He was not a big-time dealer, just one who was trying to survive as well as maintain his habit. I tried reaching him by phone, but we never connected. Then it happened. An undercover Drug Enforcement Administration (DEA) agent set up what seemed like the drug deal of a lifetime for someone not used to the "big time."[2] Pepe took the bait, hoping to score enough to help support his girlfriend and her two children. The drug deal was intentionally set up to require crossing over state lines, making it a federal offense subject to a long mandatory prison sentence. Under federal law, a sentencing judge has almost no discretion to depart from strict sentencing guidelines after someone is convicted of a federal drug offense. Therefore, Pepe was facing a minimum sentence of five years and a maximum of twenty-five.

Our sister Arcelia, who at the time of Pepe's sentencing was a public defender in California and well versed in court proceedings, immediately flew to Iowa, where Pepe's trial was being held. In an imposing federal courthouse, she tearfully testified in his behalf, relating his family background, his character, and the family's love for him. Based on her testimony, proof of his honorable discharge from the US Navy, no criminal history, and a character reference from his high school basketball coach, the judge did something miraculous—he sentenced Pepe to the minimum possible under the law—five years, three months in federal prison. Most individuals convicted of the same offense are likely to receive approximately fifteen years, especially if no one advocates on their behalf. Pepe's fate was signed, sealed, delivered—five years and three months in prison and four years of probation—and his life belonged to the criminal justice system for the next nine years.

In March of 2005, Pepe was released to a halfway house for six months in Salinas, California, thirty-six miles north of Santa Cruz, where I live with my family. For the next five years, Pepe dedicated his life to seeking redemption for all that had happened before and during his incarceration, experiences that had led him to his current status as a parolee living in the care of his family in a new community in a strange region of the country and with few prospects. Statistics show that, on average, former inmates convicted of drug-related crimes remain out of the criminal justice system for only a year before returning to drugs and eventually to prison. Given the challenges Pepe was facing, what were the chances that he could avoid the dominant narrative inscribing his life? And for our purposes here, what could the theoretical aspects of Intersectionality and Chicana feminisms offer to help change the course already expected of him?

Intersectional Identities at Work

At the end of his residency at the halfway house, Pepe was released to live close to me and our two sisters. The three of us identify as feminists and are committed to living by our feminist values.[3] He also joined an extended family of lawyers who have worked as public defenders, as well as my husband, Craig Haney, who is a professor of psychology at the University of California, Santa Cruz and a renowned expert on prison conditions and readjustment after incarceration. However, even with resources as significant as these, formerly incarcerated individuals rarely succeed in "making it" after release from prison.[4] As a family we were committed to helping Pepe succeed, but we were aware of the hurdles ahead of us. We loved him and we hoped for the best as we embarked on our journey to have our brother rejoin the family.

Contextual Factors: *La Red* (The Network) of Caring

Fortunately for our brother, his family happened to live in a community widely known for its liberal politics, feminist leanings, and ethics of caring. Santa Cruz is a progressive college town that supports nontraditional behaviors of all sorts. As part of this ethos, there is a general commitment, including in city government, to destigmatize previous incarceration. There is an assumption that individuals are capable of change and an understanding of the contextual factors that can contribute to negative behaviors. Drug addiction is perceived as not necessarily deviant but as a socially constructed problem. Conviction on drug-related charges is understood as a tool of the state to punish particular populations.

In this community, Pepe did not automatically stand out, by appearance or because of his history. Although Santa Cruz is a predominantly white community,[5] the population is largely dedicated to extending a degree of tolerance toward all its residents. It has a lively street life with many colorful characters walking up and down the outside mall in the downtown area. Our recently released brother found this street life ideologically congruent with his views, as he considered himself an "aging hippie" with a deep love for music, particularly blues and rock and roll. He felt an openness from and fellowship with Santa Cruz residents, especially those who embraced alternative lifestyles. In such a community, he began to heal from past injuries and found camaraderie with "street people" by engaging in pickup games of chess, befriending several homeless (or "non-housed," as they are called in Santa Cruz) individuals, and occasionally treating them to coffee or giving them a few dollars for food. He would often sit with them on one of the many benches lining the main street in downtown Santa Cruz and catch up on what was happening in their lives.

Integral to the spirit of caring in Santa Cruz is the large network of nonprofit organizations that, working in tandem with county agencies, are committed to a philosophy of rehabilitation, recovery, and reentry after incarceration.[6] Crucial to Pepe's reintegration, however, was the nonprofit organization Barrios Unidos, expertly managed by Nane Alejándrez. Of the many factors that led Pepe to redirect his path, Barrios Unidos and the guidance provided by its staff were indeed central to his not returning to prison.

The Role of Barrios Unidos in Pepe's Journey

Barrios Unidos (BU) adheres to four primary strategies to accomplish its mission:[7] (1) leadership and human capital development; (2) civic participation and community mobilization; (3) cultural arts and recreational activities; and (4) coalition building. Over the course of many years, BU has developed a model that seeks to reclaim and restore the lives of struggling Latino youth and men while promoting unity among families and neighbors through community building. According to Acosta (2007), BU aligns itself with the philosophy developed during the Chicano movement and identified in the writing of Chicano activist Corky González, who drew a "straight line of cause and effect between the loss of cultural identity and the frustrations, anger, and breakdown of communal fabric that led to gang and family violence" (Acosta, xli). The leaders of BU committed themselves to

> spiritual expression and indigenous ceremony centerpieces of their theory of change. To them it had become evident that standard conventional interventions alone, emphasizing either constructive alternatives to violence and crime or official criminal sanctions, could not be relied upon to solve the problems of Latino or other youth involved in gang and related antisocial activities. Instead, as they saw it, cultural awakening, awareness, and respect were the essential keys to progress. As a

result, *Cultura es Cura* (Culture is the Cure) came to be known as BU's guiding philosophical tenet, and a wide array of alternative healing and consciousness-raising practices came to anchor the organization's efforts. This was considered groundbreaking, faith-based work aimed at ending the violence in communities across America. Much of BU's development in this direction was inspired by indigenous Native American traditions and influences, including those extending back to the origins of tribal civilizations throughout the Americas. (Acosta 2007, xliv)

From its inception, Barrios Unidos has been in coalition with organizations, progressive women, and other allies who are highly visible in the public arena and who are dedicated to helping men of Color reintegrate after incarceration. Among BU's strong supporters are singer and activist Harry Belafonte, actor and activist Danny Glover, and the cofounder of the United Farm Workers' Union, Dolores Huerta. Connie (Constance) Rice,[8] head of the Los Angeles–based Advancement Project, is another important contributor to the mission of BU (Acosta 2007).[9] Ms. Rice is one of the most widely recognized and effective civil rights attorneys in the country. She views the fate of men of Color as interdependent with the long-term health of the families living in these communities. As she states, "Families are losing an entire generation and community of men to incarceration related to drugs, gang association, and street violence. Even a ferocious feminist like me knows that if you take the men out of the community, the community dies" (Acosta 2007, 177).

When Pepe was released from the halfway house, he needed an organization like BU, where not only the staff but also the founders and supporters understood the connection between drug dealing, economic survival, and the restrictions imposed by masculinity. Everyone involved with BU knew Pepe's story all too well, and their efforts in aligning with BU were designed to prevent Pepe and other formerly incarcerated men from returning to prison.

Barrios Unidos's Philosophy

Formerly incarcerated individuals often need "a safe space" (Fine and Weiss 1998, 243), a haven from the outside world, where the norms and rules of interaction can be confusing and contradictory. The space provided by BU became the saving grace for my brother. At BU, Nane Alejándrez and his team established a norm of nonjudgmental and spiritual acceptance. Upon entering Barrios Unidos, the men are welcomed with an embrace and a greeting that makes reference to "the creator" as the source of guidance and solace. It is a place that does not tolerate drug or alcohol use. In every meeting the philosophy of the organization is reinscribed orally and through ritual. Staff meetings begin with everyone standing in a circle, thanking the creator for another day and for the opportunity to do good in the world. Sage is burned, and the ancestors are summoned to oversee the organization's activities and goals. The safe space created by Barrios Unidos is extended to the small parcel of land the organization owns in the hills of the Santa Cruz Mountains. BU built a sweat lodge as a gathering place for groups of men to come together to detox their bodies as well as their minds. The philosophy developed by Barrios Unidos and the founders of the organization is to aid men of all ages (and, to a lesser extent, girls and young women) who have been institutionalized and need to reenter society by inhabiting the transitional sacred space provided by the organization.

When Pepe left the halfway house, the conditions of his parole required that he obtain a job within a couple of weeks. He was given a list of potential employers—businesses that had volunteered to hire individuals who had been incarcerated. Most of the jobs were entry level, paying low wages, and highly competitive, given the scarcity of opportunities for individuals exiting a halfway house. Pepe suffered several rejections, and there were no clear employment prospects in sight.

Every rejection was painful for my brother. I stopped sleeping and began to worry that he would be returned to prison if he were unable to find a job. The week before the employment deadline set by Pepe's parole officer, I met with Nane and other BU staff for breakfast at a local diner to talk about another matter.[10] As we were leaving, Nane asked me how my brother was doing. I told him that Pepe was having trouble finding a job, and I could not face the prospect of his return to prison. I was obviously upset, and Nane leaned over, put his hand on my shoulder, and said, "We are not going to let that happen." I could hardly believe that his dedication to keeping my brother home was as strong as my own. We made arrangements for my brother to be hired by Barrios Unidos for a temporary part-time job, with enough hours and responsibilities to keep José home.

Nane wisely admonished me as my brother began work, "We'll see how it goes after three months. Sometimes it works out, and sometimes it doesn't." His warning was an honest assessment of the situation. He did not know my brother or his skills, and, most important, he did not know whether Pepe would fit with the philosophy of kindness, gentleness, and acceptance fostered at Barrios Unidos. I felt more grateful than ever to BU because Nane was willing to put himself and his organization on the line for a stranger. I felt the power of acceptance and faith promoted by Barrios Unidos and embodied by Nane Alejándrez. Barrios is indeed an organization of last resort for the many men of all ages who cannot find a path if they want to change their lives away from the streets and back into their communities. I was humbled by Nane's help.

Fortunately, Pepe's part-time employment at BU was extended after three months. In fact, he became a full-time employee and stayed on as a valued member of Nane Alejándrez's team for two years. For Pepe, BU became a source of community and belonging. BU's emphasis on the restitution of Chicano/a culture and the use of indigenous rituals were an essential aspect of his recovery. Whereas he was strongly opposed to twelve-step programs because of their Western, Judeo-Christian religious emphasis, BU's philosophy of "Cultura es cura" resonated with his world-view. Furthermore, BU's dedication to youth reignited Pepe's passion for making a difference in young people's lives. He had been an extraordinary basketball player in high school and had even played briefly for the local college in South Texas after he finished his seven-and-half-year volunteer stint in the navy. His dream job had always been to become a high school English teacher and basketball coach, combining his love of sports with his love of books and interacting with young people. His work at BU re-ignited Pepe's passion of working with youth and propelled his journey of redemption.

The next question that arose was, How could we help Pepe implement his newfound inspiration to work with young people in an educational setting?

Public Education Committed to Rehabilitation

Community College

After Pepe's temporary employment at BU was settled, the subject of college was raised during one of the regular family meetings my two sisters and I had with him. All three sisters hold advanced degrees, and we believe education has been our salvation from the grueling work both of our parents were locked into as farmworkers in the border town of McAllen in South Texas. As an uninsured farmworker, our father died from a heart attack at the age of fifty-nine due to complications from his diabetes. We knew that Pepe's long-term success was highly dependent on obtaining an education. He had always excelled academically, which included graduating with honors from high school and obtaining advanced technological training when he joined the navy shortly after graduation. When he was honorably discharged seven and half years after enlisting, he attempted college several times unsuccessfully until he finally obtained an associate's degree from Worthington Community College a few years before he was arrested in Worthington, Minnesota.[11]

As a professor at the University of California, Santa Cruz (UCSC), I knew many of the faculty and administrators on campus. I contacted a fellow Chicano, Francisco Hernández, vice chancellor for student affairs, to help me find the appropriate channels to guide my brother's academic plan. Vice Chancellor Hernández referred me to Ronaldo Ramírez, who at the time was working in the Office of Development. His wife, Olga Nájera-Ramírez, was a professor in the Department of Anthropology. Both Ronaldo and Olga had helped members of their extended families transfer from community college to four-year universities by engaging the help of Barbara Love, UCSC's articulation officer and liaison for these types of transfers. My brother and I made an appointment with Ms. Love after obtaining all of his transcripts from his various excursions into higher education. Barbara Love was true to her name—a caring, knowledgeable, and nonjudgmental staff member who never made my brother feel embarrassed about attempting to earn a college degree as a reentry student in his late forties. Furthermore, she did not blink when he laid out his educational trajectory during his incarceration. In fact, she thoughtfully proposed ways in which the prison program certifications might earn him additional college credits.

When we left Ms. Love's office, my brother and I hugged each other, feeling hope for his future. She had given him a list of courses to take at the local community college that would allow him to transfer to UCSC, a top-ranked research university. She had demonstrated the open-mindedness prevalent at the university and in the city of Santa Cruz; she had not judged a priori someone's educational potential because of a history of incarceration.

The University

The University of California, Santa Cruz is a liberal institution dedicated to extending the values of the surrounding community. Faculty and administrative units on campus adhere to a philosophy of redemption and of extending resources and kindness to those who have been incarcerated.

The university includes diverse staff in key positions of influence, many of whom have experienced the pain of having relatives incarcerated and the terrible impact that it has on all family members.

When Pepe successfully finished the community college courses necessary to transfer to UCSC, he found yet another network of caring and assistance that was helpful in furthering his goal of obtaining a bachelor's degree. Below I outline several of the crucial units and staff members that were critical in his educational success.

THE CHICANO LATINO ETHNIC RESOURCE CENTER

The Chicano Latino Ethnic Resource Center, or El Centro (The Center), as it is commonly known, is headed by Rosie Cabrera, who had graduated from San Jose State, a university forty-five minutes from the city of Santa Cruz. Rosie, as most undergraduates knew her, was responsible for providing culturally relevant programming and support to undergraduates; a side benefit of her activities was the extensive involvement of Chicano/a Latino/a graduate students in El Centro's endeavors. Rosie received Pepe with open arms. The Center was an important haven for him during his undergraduate years, as he was at least thirty years older than the typical undergraduate on campus. Rosie's inclusion of Pepe in various student activities provided a transitional space for him as he ventured from the now-familiar culture of BU to the student culture prevalent in undergraduate research universities. Rosie and El Centro became a second sacred space for my brother.

THE FACULTY

Pepe attended UCSC for two years, completing a bachelor's degree in community studies. During his entire UCSC tenure, there was not a single faculty member who did not offer to assist Pepe with his educational endeavors. One particular professor who was critical to Pepe's success at the university was Mike Rotkin, a lecturer in the Community Studies Department. Professor Rotkin took Pepe under his wing and supported all of his efforts, including supervising his undergraduate thesis, which was based on his work at BU, where he was counseling youth who had been pushed out of the K-12 school system. In addition to helping him with his thesis, Professor Rotkin became Pepe's greatest advocate, writing him letters of recommendation when, upon graduation from UCSC, Pepe decided to apply to the graduate school in social work at San Jose State University. He wrote the following recommendation for Pepe:

I am very pleased to give you my most positive reference for José Hurtado. . . . I consider him the single, best-prepared student for this professional certification among the scores of thousands of students I have taught over the past forty-two years at the University of California, Santa Cruz. José has received nothing but straight As in our program, and as you will see in his overall transcript, the few grades he has received of less than an A are balanced by several A+ grades, something we do not issue very often here at UCSC. . . . Having been the Mayor of Santa Cruz, California, five times and elected to the City Council six times, I have a very good idea of what any community will expect of a person holding this professional license and I have absolutely no doubt that José is ready to move beyond his past and I know that he is well prepared for work as a LCSW. I also have taught in both men's and women's prisons in California. . . . José has completed his required federal probation without incident, and he is ready and willing to use what he learned. . . . I was the academic supervisor of a full-time, six-month internship/field study that José conducted with Barrios Unidos and Youth Services here in Santa Cruz. José received glowing letters of evaluation from all of his supervisors in the field. His work for me is simply among the best I have ever received from a student working in the area of youth counseling. José is already working at a professional level and was assigned a counseling caseload (under supervision) at Youth Services while he was still an undergraduate student. . . . José has been in a unique position to reach some of the most intractable youth at various levels of gang affiliation and legal trouble. Many of the clients with whom he has been working, are at serious risk for a lifetime in the criminal justice system and José, who is bilingual and quickly able to develop a rapport with the youth and their families, has often been the last hope of diverting some of these young people from a life of crime and incarceration. . . . I have probably recommended a couple of hundred students to social work programs over the past three decades. I have never had a student who was better prepared to be an outstanding practitioner in the field of social work. José has a warm and engaging personality and quickly wins the affection and support of everyone with whom he works. His experience both in life and as a student has prepared him exceptionally well to be an outstanding professional in the field of social work.

I have quoted Professor Rotkin's recommendation letter at length because of its detailed articulation of his views on the reintegration of previously

incarcerated men. Furthermore, his consistent message of hope for someone who has overcome a difficult past is not necessarily the norm, even in
the most prestigious universities, where faculty are highly educated about
criminal justice issues. His position is also illustrative of the relationships
among the city of Santa Cruz, its elected officials (he was both mayor and
city council member multiple times), and the university.

The significance of positive interactions and consistent support of reintegration after incarceration should not be taken for granted, and they
fortified the chances for Pepe's educational success. It is noteworthy that
I did not personally know Professor Rotkin. His interest in Pepe's success was purely as a teacher and a person interested in the well-being of a
male reentry student with a difficult past who was invested in maximizing
his educational opportunities. My brother's performance definitely influenced Professor Rotkin's positive evaluations; my brother had always been
an excellent student, even when in prison, but no one had ever taken the
time and effort to reinforce his positive behaviors in the academy. Most
important, although Professor Rotkin's support was central to Pepe's success, all of the faculty and staff he encountered at UCSC instilled in him
a similar message of hope that he would be capable of forging a new life
through education.

The Family (Extended by Friends)

Of course, the primary responsibility for helping Pepe reintegrate once
he left prison was our immediate family's, including my sisters, my husband, our children, our niece, our sister-in-law, and my elderly mother
(beyond this, our larger extended family of uncles and cousins live in
Mexico, and we have had little or no contact with them over the years).
Not only were the ideas of reintegration and redemption of previously
incarcerated individuals central to our beliefs as a family, but every single
family member worked within, or had a connection with, the criminal
justice system—as lawyers (public defenders and public interest lawyers),
professors (writing about the criminal (in)justice system in the United
States and abroad), and practitioners (social workers). However, it bears
mentioning that our dedication as a family to fight for those mistreated in
prison is not a guarantee that once a family member leaves prison, he or
she will in fact survive the brutal realities of reintegration. We were also
fortunate to have a network of friends whom we considered part of our
extended family, including fellow UCSC professors, graduate students,
and staff members. This network gave Pepe a broader community that at

different times played crucial roles in easing him over the hurdles as he learned to be a free man again.

One of the many obstacles for previously incarcerated individuals is reintegrating into the family left behind and finding a circle of friends. During his five years or so of incarceration, my sisters, mother, and I (several times accompanied by my husband) made yearly pilgrimages to visit him in whichever prison he was assigned to.[12] The task of family reintegration takes time and resources. The fact that everyone in our family was a professional at the time that Pepe was incarcerated made the travel and a regular stipend financially possible. In addition, my retired mother has always been a prodigious letter writer and sent him weekly letters and a small amount of money to help with expenses not covered by the very stringent federal funding for prisoners.

When Pepe was released to the halfway house, he was not given any clothing or toiletries, and not all of his meals were provided. Our family pooled our resources to provide these essentials for him, in addition to driving every weekend to see him, 180 miles for several of us. Once he was permitted day visits away from the halfway house and, eventually, weekend visits, we took turns picking him up and driving him to Santa Cruz to spend time with the family.

Our extended family of friends readily adopted my brother as part of their social circle. Friends like Ronaldo Ramírez, who had helped us locate Barbara Love; Mrinal Sinha, a graduate student in the UCSC Psychology Department; Ciel Benedetto, UCSC's affirmative action officer; and Sophia García, a financial aid officer at UCSC—all found commonalities with my brother and befriended him. No one held him in suspicion because of his previous incarceration. His entry into our extended network of friends and family adhered to the same set of values we observed; everyone was nonjudgmental about Pepe's past and enormously committed to helping him succeed, both in school and in life.

Critical Encounters: The Generosity of the Web of Caring

Two incidents critical to helping Pepe's transition from the halfway house to living with our family are worth noting. While incarcerated, inmates are in close quarters and surrounded by others twenty-four hours a day, seven days a week, making it very difficult upon release for them to be alone. Depression is not uncommon, and social isolation is dreaded until they readjust to life on the outside. Furthermore, total institutions like

Figure 7.1. José Hurtado with his mother

prisons do not allow individual choice—in what inmates wear, when and what they eat, when and how much they sleep, and even when to shower. Recreation and hobbies are rare, and reading (with limited access to the number and variety of books) is one of the very few outlets for inmates who are literate. Television watching is also regulated, as are other sorts of media such as films.

My brother had several advantages: he is an avid reader (science fiction, among other genres),[13] a passionate music listener, and an excellent chess player. Upon his release from the halfway house, Pepe lived with our sister María (a graduate of UCSC and a social worker by training), at the time serving as the deputy director of parks and recreation for the city of San Jose, and my grown daughter Erin (also a UCSC graduate, an investigator for the Santa Cruz Public Defender's Office). The three of us ensured that Pepe spent very little time alone during the first year after his release. On occasion, when family members were not available, my then graduate student and now coauthor, Mrinal Sinha (Ranu to his friends and family), played chess with Pepe in downtown Santa Cruz. Ranu spent hours with him, talking, joking, and generally kibitzing about their chess skills. Ronaldo Ramírez also stepped in and socialized with Pepe by reminiscing about growing up in Texas and sharing the many regional stories South Texans have in common. The importance of this transitional bridge of friendship cannot be overestimated as former inmates adjust to the hustle and bustle of regular life with no guards and wardens monitoring their every move.

As part of the reintegration process, the family decided, with Pepe's agreement, to be open about his incarceration history. We were not ashamed of it because, like so many others, had he received the appropriate treatment for his drug addiction he might have avoided incarceration. He was one of the 60 percent of nonviolent offenders languishing in prisons and jails because of drug offenses when treatment is what is most desperately needed (Schmitt, Warner, and Gupta 2010). Our agreed-upon openness made it easier for our extended networks to help Pepe with his educational endeavors.

Sophia García, one of my oldest friends in Santa Cruz, offered one such opportunity. As a financial aid officer at UCSC she knew of a scholarship for reentry students to get tuition and a modest stipend for school expenses. Pepe applied and wrote the requisite essay explaining his circumstances; Sophia was a formidable advocate on his behalf. He obtained the scholarship, and it ameliorated his financial burden as he obtained one of the best undergraduate educations in the country, if not the world.

Figure 7.2. José Hurtado with his boat

The Boat

Prison restrictions hamper individuals from developing healthy engagements and interests. Once released from prison, it is not uncommon for
many former inmates to return to their old habits of drinking and drug
use. My brother has a deep love of the ocean. He had been a "navy man"
and had traveled the world on board a guided missile cruiser. One of his
favorite activities in Santa Cruz was to take long walks along beautiful
West Cliff Drive. Fortuitously, our friends and colleagues Dr. Heather
Bullock and Dr. Julian Fernald were seeking to discard a sailboat they no
longer used. In one of our family gatherings, Pepe mentioned his deep
connection to the ocean, and they spontaneously offered him the sailboat
as a gift. My brother was dumbfounded by their generosity. For the next
three years, sailing in the Monterey Bay became his salvation. Whenever
he felt anxious, depressed, overwhelmed by the number of changes he was
undergoing, sailing became his release. He invited friends and acquain-
tances, including young people from BU, to experience sailing in the bay,
his form of renewal. The boat became the gift that allowed him to heal
spiritually by communing with nature and feeling the generosity of spirit
of two of our closest friends.

Media to the Rescue

Pepe rejoined a family of extremely busy professionals. By the time he was released from prison, all of our careers were in full swing. My husband and I were professors; our three children were grown, two were about to enter law school and another one was already a professor at a prestigious university on the East Coast; my youngest sister and her partner were lawyers in the San Francisco Public Defender's Office; and my other sister was a high-level city administrator in San Jose, and her daughter was attending community college in San Francisco.

Under these circumstances, Pepe could have quickly become alienated within a family that, no matter how well intentioned, had very little time to spend with him on a daily basis. Our family, fortunately, lived within a relatively close geographical area in Northern California — Santa Cruz County and the cities of San Jose and San Francisco. We made a commitment to spend all holidays together at our home in Santa Cruz. As the eldest, I was the closest in age to Pepe and in many ways the most familiar with his upbringing, given our shared childhood. Our sisters are sixteen (Arcelia) and nine (María) years younger than Pepe. I also lived in the same city as Pepe and had the most flexibility because of my senior academic appointment.

During the first year after Pepe left the halfway house, I became the closest I have ever been to him. However, despite all the resources I have just listed, daily interactions were not always feasible, especially when I was required to travel for professional purposes. Fortunately, I came up with a solution that at first I thought would never work. Pepe has always been technically inclined and enjoys working with gadgets. Yet, in the five years he had been incarcerated, the world had undergone a technological revolution — cell phones, the Internet, personal computers, digital cameras, among many other developments. Prisons, for the most part, do not allow access to technology in any broad sense. In fact, we rarely talked by phone to my brother during his incarceration. We relied mostly on handwritten notes and annual visits. Pepe was religious about sending us birthday cards, handmade when he could not purchase them, and long, detailed letters.

When he was released from prison on March 3, 2005, he was driven to Denver from Florence, Colorado, a rural town 110 miles away, and dropped off downtown to catch the Greyhound bus for the ten-hour ride to Salinas, California, where he was admitted to the halfway house.[14] Pepe had to wait twelve hours for the bus. To pass the time, he walked up and down

Denver's outdoor mall and was startled because many people seemed to be talking to themselves. At first, he thought they were addressing him, but he quickly realized that passersby were wearing earphones and talking on their cell phones. This was only the beginning of the surprises he encountered heralding the technological advances during his incarceration.

Given his ability and interest in technology, I immediately introduced my brother to e-mail and iTunes—two technologies that figuratively saved his life and mine. Soon after he left the halfway house, I gave him my aging computer on which I had downloaded over a thousand songs. I knew his love of music and I recalled how he had bought a small radio while he was in prison with money our mother had sent him. He listened to National Public Radio, but his favorite was listening to blues stations. I gave him a brief lesson on operating iTunes, showed him how to download songs, build playlists, and burn CDs. He learned quickly, and iTunes became his new passion (one that he still holds dear—one Christmas, as a stocking stuffer, we all received CDs of his favorite songs specifically tailored to each family member's musical taste). I also taught him how to do Google searches, including locating song lyrics and biographies of his favorite artists. We opened an e-mail account for him and created a family e-mail alias for group communication.

For the next two years, I received daily e-mails from my brother, giving me an overview of his day, his feelings, and his dreams. I responded to all of his e-mails, and our relationship deepened as we reconnected as siblings and as family members. The family alias allowed us to communicate each other's milestones (Pepe's grades, my new publications, my husband's honors, and many more family achievements). Pepe developed an e-mail relationship with various colleagues and friends, including his professors, fellow students, and our extended family/friends network.

During his first Christmas at home, we gave him a digital camera, and he became the official family photographer. Pepe has taken thousands of family pictures celebrating a variety of events, building an archive that has become precious to all of us. Technological developments helped save him and us by keeping us connected and informed about each other's lives.

Individual Identity: Agentic Tools for Survival and Crucial Points of Transition

Conocimiento: Affirmation and Consciousness Raising (CR)

As feminists, my sisters and I were committed to the full integration of our brother into the family. We used Gloria Anzaldúa's process of cono-cimiento,[15] our cultural translation of CR groups in the '70s, an activity feminists engaged in during the height of the white feminist movement. White feminists used CR groups to help women articulate their vulnerabilities but also to provide a feedback loop to raise consciousness about possible blind spots about their own oppression. Gloria Anzaldúa (2002) developed conocimiento as a culturally specific method for individuals to overcome and heal from trauma. Conocimiento is situated within indigenous beliefs about the connection between the spirit and consciousness.

As noted by several scholars, prison can be one of the most racist environments systematically created by institutional policies. Prisoners are assigned living quarters based on race, and racialized groups like the Aryan Brotherhood, Black Guerilla Family, and Nuestra Familia reside in designated areas of prisons. Racial segregation in prison allows interracial animosities to ferment, develop, and be acted on through open displays of aggression and even murder. Adding further dysfunction, prisons are gender segregated, and in high-security prisons, inmates do not have intimate contact with members of the opposite sex for years. If serving life sentences, inmates may not have contact with the opposite sex ever again.

Ideologies that promote race difference and misogyny are so deeply engrained that they become naturalized.[16] Formerly incarcerated men are required to learn a new discourse in which racialization, homophobia, and misogyny are not as freely accepted in everyday communication or banter. As feminists, my sisters and I had to confront our brother's use of expressions and attitudes that violated his otherwise easygoing and loving ways with everyone around him. We had excruciating conversations about whether we were being overly sensitive and politically demanding in criticizing his vocabulary, attitudes, and humor, or was our "calling him out" a feminist act that would ultimately raise his consciousness and make him aware that there was such a thing as "words that wound" (Matsuda et al. 1993). However, we were also concerned about sending our brother into a state of shock—un arrebato, in Anzaldúan terms—if we pointed out his biased behavior. Would he feel attacked? Unloved? Alone? Thrown back into a dungeon of despair, the way he felt while he was in prison? After much trepidation, we decided to hold family meetings with the four of us (the three sisters and Pepe) and begin the process of conocimiento.

Anzaldúa (2002) describes conocimiento as a seven-stage spiral process without a start or end point. It moves forward continually and nonchronologically. Conocimiento begins with an arrebato—a jolt of awareness, a crash of emotional or physical sensation—igniting the second stage, nepantla—a liminal space of openness to new perspectives. The Coatlicue state (named for a dark Mexican goddess) designates the third stage, which is one of turmoil that new perspectives can often provoke. Growth is not easy or neat, and one of Anzaldúa's central insights is that experiencing pain is critical to the process of coming to awareness. On the other side of the pain caused by the arrebato, individuals often find a path for action. Awareness can lead them to act productively in the world. The inner work may lead to public acts and to the creation of "a new narrative articulating" a "personal reality" (Anzaldúa 2002, 545) that integrates the new awareness.

The process of conocimiento also requires that the new personal narrative be in dialogue with others, a potentially dangerous process because of the risks of rejection and conflict that could cause an individual to revert to the Coatlicue state. If individuals work through each of the first six stages, they can proceed to the seventh stage, enabling them to make holistic alliances with other individuals and groups to collaborate in producing positive engagements with the world.

Conocimiento is a continuous process; all seven stages can be reached in a matter of hours, or the process can take years. Conocimiento can influence one of the individual's Social Identities (which are part of the overall Intersectional Identities)—race awareness, for example—and yet leave others untouched, so that, say, the individual will still be completely unaware of oppression based on gender. As individuals explore every aspect of their Intersectional Identities, conocimiento can facilitate insights that lead from awareness to public and, many times, political actions.

From the beginning, the process of conocimiento worked well; our family meetings were full of insights and growth. The meetings gave us an opportunity to express our concerns but also to show our love and support while Pepe listened. He, in turn, voiced his impressions and motivations for expressing himself the way he did. After almost two years of these monthly meetings, we had all changed. The sisters understood the trauma and isolation Pepe had been subjected to and the context in which denigration of others was a way to survive. I, especially, came to understand the vulnerabilities that result from a socialization into masculinities that do not allow men to connect, talk, and explore personal issues with men or with women.

Social Psychological Reframing: The Dance of Survival through Mestiza Consciousness

In his memoir (2001, 253–254), Jimmy Santiago Baca discusses the years he spent in prison and his will to survive and become a writer after his release. After five years in prison, Baca anxiously awaits his release on what he believes is the designated day of completion of his sentence:

> April 17, my release date, finally arrived. I had my boxes packed, and I sat in my cell the whole day waiting for someone to come and get me, but nobody did. Then, toward the end of the day, a guard came to escort me to the Parole Board room. They had finally figured it out. But when I got to the door, the warden met me. Before I could walk in, he said it was the wrong day and ordered Mad Dog Madril [a guard] to return me to my cell. Where the Parole Board usually sat, the seats were empty. The warden was fucking with me. For days I said nothing, did nothing. I went to eat and then back to my cell. I was trying to hold myself together. I got another slip to appear before the Board for the following morning. All night I tossed, eyes wide open, staring into the cavernous cell-block space and wondering if I was ever going to get out.

In one of the most poignant moments in the memoir, after repeated delays, Baca narrates the point that almost resulted in his giving up hope of ever being a free man (2001, 254):

> I was falling deeper and deeper into melancholy. The warden has finally won, I thought; he has finally broken my spirit. I was thinking of things I wouldn't ordinarily entertain. There was a certain convict who had taken a baseball bat and beaten a Chicano over the head. I had been playing handball when I saw it happen at the far end of the field. After finishing the game with Macaron, I walked over to the convict and told him that if I didn't get out, I was coming for him.

In addition to considering committing violence that was unthinkable for him before, Baca was also rethinking his long-term adaptation to a warped environment where there was little room for affection and long-term physical comfort. In his words (2001, 254–255):

> About this time a beautiful boy by the name of Chiquita had come to my cell and asked if I would be her sugar daddy. I had never messed around with a guy, fearing that it might ruin the pleasure I found in being with women. But now, thinking I might never get out, I told her that if I didn't make my Board, we'd talk, and in the meantime, I'd keep her under my wing and make sure nobody raped her. I'd never talked to fags in prison. But as Chiquita began to sit at my table in the chow hall, and as I listened to her talk, for the first time in my life I realized that some men really had female spirits. When I spoke to her, I was speaking to a woman.

The continued delays and lack of information drove Baca closer to his breaking point: "By the beginning of June, I was cracking up. I had lost a lot of weight and I had sleeplessness circles under my eyes. I was belligerent and surly because I was supposed to be free but was still sitting in prison. I was already beginning to think that I might have to stay indefinitely or do my sentence over" (2001, 256). Then without warning, Baca was let out of prison at four in the morning in June, two months after he was supposed to have been released.

To those who have not been incarcerated, a two-month delay might seem trivial after so many years in prison. For many inmates who are denied freedom in all realms of their existence, however, any delay feels like death, a death they experience daily by being constantly monitored and by not being able to exert their human agency. Because of this loss of control, what seems like a trivial postponement can result in an inmate's throwing away accumulated "credits" and reverting to or even venturing into more destructive behaviors than before. Baca prepared himself to adopt the mentality of the incarcerated, including sexual practices that were not enticing before, as a way to survive the hellish environment from which he saw no escape.

These choques (collisions), in Anzaldúan terms, come unexpectedly; even inmates are unaware of what will trigger an arrebato. In Pepe's case, he had been on probation for four years.[17] As part of the conditions for the first six months of his probation, he had mandatory monthly visits to his probation officer in San Jose, California.[18] I always accompanied Pepe to the probation office, and we had lunch afterward to alleviate the stress.

In addition to the monthly visits to San Jose, other probation officers came to Pepe's home to inspect his living quarters. For the first six months, he was required to call in every night from his home phone at 8 pm. If we had a family gathering, we rushed to get back so he could make the call. As the scheduled end of his probation approached, Pepe was beyond excited. He felt absolute freedom within reach. Like Jimmy Santiago Baca, who packed his belongings and waited in his cell expectantly, Pepe gleefully called me on the day officially marking the end of his probation. We went out for a celebratory dinner, and I commemorated the occasion by taking his first photo as a newly free man.

However, during the evening, he learned that the end of his probation had been delayed. In my eyes the delay seemed like a minor matter, given his progress—he was thriving at the university, he had a great job at BU, he was receiving internship credit from his BU job toward his undergraduate degree, and he was fully integrated into our family. None of these successes prevented him from becoming depressed upon hearing that the probation was still in place. It was the first time I felt scared that he might regress and do something unpredictable. I knew from reading my husband's work on reintegration that Pepe's feelings were real and there was no talking him out of them. Yet I could not risk his possibly undoing all that he had accomplished.

Fortuitously, at that time I was writing a chapter on Gloria Anzaldúa's work and her influence on my work (Hurtado 2011). As I reread her sections on mestiza consciousness (Anzaldúa 1987, 79),[19] I came across the following passage: "The new mestiza copes by developing a tolerance for contradictions, a tolerance for ambiguity. She learns to be an Indian in Mexican culture, to be Mexican from an Anglo point of view. She learns to juggle cultures." Suddenly I knew what to do.

As Anzaldúa proposes, a mestiza consciousness can examine multiple sides of an issue acknowledging both the pain *and* the possibility, and takes a stand on the side of hope to survive "un choque," which can send an individual into a stupor of fear and inaction. I did not tell my brother about Anzaldúa; I simply became the bridge between the concept and the action necessary to reframe the delay in ending his probation. As Edwina Barvosa (2011, 126), in analyzing Anzaldúa, indicates,

> From her earliest writings to her last, Anzaldúa insists that the ideal role of the person with mestiza consciousness is as a social bridge who works to unite divided peoples. The mestiza-as-social-bridge uses the various knowledges and perspectives that she has gained through living her multiple identities at the margins of many different social locations to help link people who are otherwise divided. In so doing, she helps others gain

perspectives that they have not gleaned from whatever configuration of identities they have so far obtained.

To serve the bridging function for my brother, I relied on the notion of "reframing," a social psychological mechanism that examines a problem from the perspective of what it offers toward positive change rather than focusing on the hurdles to overcome. Pepe and I had the following e-mail exchange shortly after we discovered the reasons for the delay in ending his probation:

On Mar 5, 2009, at 7:35 pm, jose13hurtado@_____ wrote:

It was too good, the thought that after four years of probation they would just let me go. I spoke with [probation officer] today and [she/he] let me know that I was released early from Florence due to good behavior, but that my sentence runs until September 1st of this year. Basically another six months. So, bummer that it is, and I am bummed, it is business as usual until September. Anyway, thanks for all the great thoughts and wishes, I have a little longer to go!!
  Love you all,
PEPE
&&&&&&&&&&&&&&&&&&&&&&&&&&&&&

On 3/5/09, Aída Hurtado <aida@___> wrote:

Mijo, this is NOT bad news. How can it be—we got you here earlier than we expected and we have been enjoying you longer than if you had not come home. This is a teensy weensy little blip on the road to a wonderful life. Consider it a pre-party to the big party. You still get an iPhone on Wed after you see [probation officer]. We love you very much and are immensely proud of you.
  PS I made hamburgers for dinner so you'll have your lunch by the door tomorrow and don't forget the 3 bags. Also, I'll write you a check for Costco and for taking the Xmas stuff to the carriage house. xox, me
&&&&&&&&&&&&&&&&&&&&&&&&&&&&&

From: jose13hurtado@_____
Subject: Re: Bad news...
Date: March 5, 2009 9:07:20 PM PST
To: Aida Hurtado <aida@___>

You are indeed the coolest carnala [sister], you are right about what happened, it is all in how you see it. I don't have to see [probation officer] now, so we can meet earlier on Wednesday in San Jose, I get out of class at 2:45 pm so we can probably meet somewhere soon thereafter.[20] I will stop by early in the morning for the stuff, OK? Have a good night, I love you much!

PEPE

To people who are not aware of the difficulties of reintegration after incarceration, the exchange above may seem somewhat mundane. However, for those who have experienced prison, the nuance of the pain and the magnitude of the disappointment when predicted events fall through cannot be overstated. Denying them the right to choose the smallest of personal behaviors violates inmates' sense of humanhood. This level of control is designed to "break" them, as Jimmy Santiago Baca so pointedly relates. I intuitively felt (guided by the reading I had done in my husband's area of work) that a delay in freedom was not a simple disappointment for Pepe. I knew he felt defeated and put back in "the cage," as he often referred to his cell in prison. I knew it was urgent that I respond to his e-mail quickly with an alternative "reframing," one that would come naturally to most folks who had not experienced incarceration or those who have the facultad (gift) to trigger a mestiza consciousness that rescues one's value. This is not to say that a mestiza consciousness necessarily averts the initial anger when one's agency is blocked; rather, the facultad permits a reframing to avoid sinking into the dark place of depression and reactance that can lead to destructive behavior. It is normal for individuals when confronted with failure to initially feel disappointment, followed by anger, and then, hopefully, to find a way to reframe the events in order to pull out of their funk. Furthermore, most individuals have multiple sources of support to help them reframe: a partner, friends, parents, colleagues. When the failure is constant, unpredictable, and out of one's control, it can lead to a cycle of reactance that can be followed by destructive behavior. My brother was relying on me to help him recalibrate his feelings, to help him feel his feet on firm ground, and to avoid hopelessness.

I also intuitively knew that I had to reinforce the aspect of Pepe's life that he was most proud of: reintegration into our family. Through my readings in the literature on incarceration, I had learned that, while one is in prison, small material possessions—a radio, writing paper, cigarettes—have great significance. These small accouterments are ways of reconstituting the self in order to feel worthy. I had promised my brother an iPhone because he loved the technology and the new features the iPhone promised—iTunes, texting, digital camera, and e-mail—the technological features that kept my brother connected on a daily basis to all of us regardless of where we were geographically. True to his "hippie" philosophy, Pepe has never has been a materialistic person. His interest has always been in the relationships that material things can facilitate. The gift of an iPhone was a reminder of our family's accessibility.

Reframing through mestiza consciousness avoided the abyss of despair and provided alternative activities so that my brother could avoid thinking solely about the disappointment. We had worked out an arrangement where he would pick up at my house the lunch I prepared. He truly appreciated this small gesture on my part. In addition, he helped with small errands for which he earned the equivalent of a graduate assistant's pay. He enjoyed exploring different stores, parts of the city, and services he had never been exposed to. By shifting the content of my e-mail message to the more enjoyable and mundane aspects of our interactions, I made it easier for Pepe to snap out of it and feel joy again. His e-mail response to my message assured me that despite the longer-than-expected probation we had averted a potential setback. He had regained his psychological and emotional balance after what might appear to most people to be a very minor and temporary setback.

Tying It All Together

In this chapter, we have returned to the origins of Intersectionality by providing an analysis of social interventions that may succeed in reconstructing masculinities away from patriarchal definitions. Figure 7.3 represents the application of Intersectionality through Social Identity, which may aid in understanding José's successful reintegration. We began the analysis by describing the context José had to function within: a feminist, progressive community with an ethos of redemption and rehabilitation that was systematically manifested through nonprofits in the community and people elected to city positions and embodied in the faculty, staff, and students at the local university. The context of the community is reinforced in José's family structure, with three strong feminist sisters at the helm of his reintegration, all of whom have committed resources, time, friendship, and love. The larger family context is composed of individuals actively involved in the criminal justice system and dedicated to reforms that would help individuals like José, who happen to be members of the

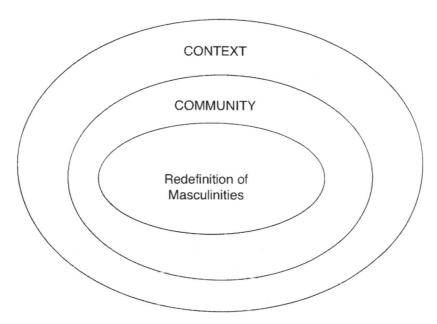

Figure 7.3. Different levels of intervention

family but also represent the larger constituencies of concern to all members of the family. This context is represented in the larger of the circles in figure 7.3.

Second, José had to enter a life space (Lewin 1948) and engage in developing and fortifying social relations based on his Intersectional Identities—that is, working-class man, previously incarcerated individual, racially mestizo, of Mexican culture and language, heterosexual, and engaged with various individuals based on these categorical memberships or Social Identities. Different social outlets provided different solutions. Barrios Unidos helped José as a man who is Latino, culturally Mexican, Spanish/English bilingual, and working class. The women mentioned in this chapter identified as feminist and were crucial in José's building relationships that helped with his transitions. These women—his sisters, UCSC staff and faculty, and BU female employees—perceived José's Intersectional Identities as important in understanding his incarceration around a nonviolent offense arising out of drug addiction. They understood that incarceration rates are higher among men of Color who are working class and who grow up in poverty.

Furthermore, as proposed by Chicana feminisms, José's experiences with the criminal justice system are not independent of the feminist concerns in Chicana/o communities. All of the Chicanas mentioned in José's narrative have male relatives (sometimes more than one) affected by the criminal justice system in the form of incarceration, arrest, juvenile detention, or unwarranted police harassment. To some extent, the Chicanas in this narrative felt that José was like one of the family because of their experiences with their own male family members. It is noteworthy that the Chicanas mentioned in José's narrative, although originating in working-class families (many times from farmworker backgrounds), were successful professionals now, yet the men in their lives had not escaped being touched by the criminal justice system. The relationships José was developing in his new context were with individuals who understood his experiences and who were willing to undergird his commitment to reintegration after incarceration.

Intersectionality based on Social Identity theory also takes into account personal identity; that is, regardless of the context and social relationships, people have individual will and agency. However, unlike Western theories of self in which individual will trumps social identifications, individual identity within Intersectionality is relationally constituted so that individuals gain agency because of the context and relationships in which they are embedded. In José's case, the acceptance and instrumental help he received fortified him to listen to feedback on his individual behaviors because he knew he was loved unconditionally and the feedback was relationally communicated—it was not only his needs but the needs of the people around him that he cared about. When he was asked by his sisters to be more aware of his racialized language because his family was multiracial, including his two nephews, who are of African American and Latino ancestry, he understood immediately that it was not only a personal criticism but a relational one that affected his standing in the family. He was reassured that his individual behavior was not a matter of pass/no pass for familial belonging. In true feminist practice dedicated to social transformation and not moralistic judgments, his family proposed alternative behaviors as another adaptation to familial belonging. José embraced many of the opportunities for personal growth through his relational networks and his reward was to become a better family member and a better counselor to youth.

The New Mestizo: Redefinition of Masculinity

An important part of José's growth was his very personal redefinition of masculinity. Like most men, he had very few venues in which to talk intimately about many of the matters discussed in this narrative. He was taught to be jovial, easygoing, and kind. Whenever he was hurt or something was troubling him, he learned to withdraw and deal with it alone. Through the process of social and psychological reintegration, José was better able to express a wider range of emotions; for instance, many times he used e-mail (or card writing) to express his love for his family. This e-mail sent to his sister on her birthday is not atypical:

Good morning Chatoski!

I hope that when you receive this you are well in both health and spirits. . . . I woke up this morning feeling grateful for having you in my life. . . . I think about it and it is probably the most important thing that has happened to me since prison . . . to re-integrate with you, Craig and the rest of my family would not have been possible without your forgiveness and understanding. My life as it is right now would never have happened if you did not offer me a place next to you as I was released from the cage. That being said, it goes much further than that. You have been my inspiration, my foundation, my guidance and my example. When I get into an overwhelming situation I ask myself "what would Chata do?" "What would Craig do?" Some people ask themselves what would Jesus do, I ask myself what would my sister and brother do? Ha, it works for me! You are an amazing person; I am in awe of you and your life. You manage to be so good to all those that you love, every one whose life you touch is the better for it. I am blessed that you were born my sister. Not only do you do for us, you also have the best sense of humor of all of us, you make life fun and your wit makes me laugh, even when laughing is the last thing on my mind! Your home is a haven for me, a place that I find peace and the joy of feeling like I belong, the warmth of family that has so eluded me in the past and has sent me in tailspins of self-destruction. As I ponder my life in my bear cave over here in San Leandro, I may be alone but I know that I am not lonely, you walk this earth and I walk right next to you in spirit! To have that is one of the best things in my life! To have your affection and your cariño [affection] is to me one of the biggest blessings that I have in life. . . . I know that I am not a perfect brother, I could have done so many things different and avoided throwing much of my life away, but that was not my fate. I am what I am, and chose what I chose, and I have put it all to rest in the past, burying my broken bones and all the pain that comes with them . . . But one thing I know for sure, in the now, I love you more than my words can express! It is your birthday, and I for one am celebrating that you were born my sister!!!!!!!!!!!!!!!!!!!!!

Te quiero chingos carnala!

PEPE

As the e-mail illustrates, a central development in his redefinition of masculinity is his admiration of and respect for women—feminist women at that. He has come to pride himself on being a man who works well with women, including those in supervisory positions at work. He acknowledges learning from the women (many of whom are self-identified feminists) who have contributed to his recovery and reintegration after incarceration.

We want to emphasize that José's story is not meant to be a "Cinderello" narrative of unbridled triumph over adversity, a Chicana/o version of *Les Misérables*, or a psychological Horatio Alger story. Now and then we are reminded that he carries a deep sorrow that his experiences in prison gave him, a perspective that the rest of the family does not have. For example, he sent the following e-mail after Aída's husband obtained life in prison (instead of the death sentence) in one of his cases:

There is a man in a cell right now feeling unimaginable gratefulness for the fact that Craig Haney is alive and doing what he does. . . . I am grateful too Craig, you are awesome! I am so blessed to be a part of this family!

JOSÉ

In 2010 José completed the master's program in social work at San Jose State and is currently working as a social worker in Alameda County in the Bay Area. He has twenty-nine foster young people under his charge. He has become a specialist in transitioning his clients who are about to age out from foster care to becoming self-sufficient, productive adults. José, in conjunction with a team of specialists, teaches young people the life skills that are ordinarily learned within families, for example, opening a bank account, applying to the local community college, planning for an educational future. He helps them to get off the streets and to find housing. He also makes court appearances and writes briefs advocating for foster youth. Not a month goes by when he fails to write an e-mail to

Figure 7.4. José Hurtado with the tres hermanas

the family expressing his profound happiness at having such a meaningful job (figure 7.4).

As a practicing social worker, José has become known in his office as an expert on helping the foster youths who are the most difficult to reach—both young men and women. He fights hard when these youths fail to respond to opportunities and his supervisor directs him to dismiss the case. Dismissal means that someone as young as fifteen can have all resources withdrawn and be let out on the street to fend for herself or himself. José knows to try harder, to invent new tactics to reach these young people. Most important, he tries to see their gifts rather than their vulnerabilities. His nonjudgmental manner, nascent mestiza consciousness, and deepening respect for women have resulted in a heightened sensitivity toward young women and men. He has convinced a young woman to forgo prostitution, found her an apartment, and successfully enrolled her in community college; he has reunited a foster adolescent with his out-of-state grandmother instead of assigning him to yet another foster family; and he placed a fifteen-year-old who was in over ten foster homes in one year in a foster home near her siblings, realizing she is more likely to stay there because her siblings are the only family she knows.

As Chicana feminists proclaim, we are not individuals only; we are relationally constituted in such a way that if our brother or sister hurts, so do we. Chicana feminists are dedicated to the goal of social justice, which includes the welfare of families and communities and all causes that create more just human arrangements (Fregoso 2003).

All José ever wanted (like many men in his situation) was a shot at a family life with people who loved and supported him and, in his words, "had his back." José is striving to use his talents to help others like him and to live the mundane details of life without fear, turmoil, violence, loneliness, and isolation. He is a human being with foibles, as we all are. For most of his life, however, José's shortcomings and history were used as indicative of his "criminal nature" and his inability to live productively. His amazing intellectual and social talents remained unrecognized before his arrival in Santa Cruz and his reintegration with his family and extended network of caring family and friends. Intersectional understandings allowed everyone involved to help José become the full human being he always aspired to be.

José received the following card from the estranged mother of one of the foster youths he helped leave the streets:

Jose, where do I begin? What words could I possibly find that would describe my feelings? Twenty years I have been involved in the system three reunifications for Emma alone. Every new worker initiating the standard items, counseling, therapy, psychological evaluations, parenting classes, anger management, etc., etc. . . . and I have honored them all! However, in this last involvement to do what I have done over and over again almost sent me over the edge. To have my daughter missing and to be admitted 8 times to the hospital last year I was ready to die . . . literally. Then you came on board. Yet I thought after 20 years of dealing with social workers the to-do list was going to appear! I couldn't have done it yet you were the kindest, most attentive, problem solving oriented person I have ever met. Even after I verbally attacked you on our first phone conversation because of the Prozac that I took for work. I finally have been able to stabilize and achieve some clarity. You are my final angel, my answers to my prayers to the universe, they were heard and you were sent upon us! You are amazing and I can tell you that there are days I cry because you believed in my daughter and have helped her to move forward. Why couldn't they have found you for us earlier? As you can see I have an amazing incredible daughter in this world. To have found her and to see the change in her was the last thing I could have imagined. You are wise beyond the master's degree you hold. You are gifted with a special empathy and objectivity not of this world. Thank you, thank you and thank you from the core of my being and God bless you on your journey. A huge hug, handshake and my deepest wishes of peace and happiness. Thank you from the bottom of my heart.

The sentiments expressed in this card are for José but also for every single person who helped him on his journey to happiness. The circle is complete.

APPENDIX

Seven Stages of Conocimiento

GLORIA ANZALDÚA

Éste arrebato [the first stage], the earthquake, jerks you from the familiar and safe terrain and catapults you into nepantla, the second stage. In this liminal, transitional space, suspended between shifts, you're two people, split between before and after. Nepantla, where the outer boundaries of the mind's inner life meet the outer world of reality, is a zone of possibility. You experience reality as fluid, expanding and contracting. In nepantla you are exposed, open to other perspectives, more readily able to access knowledge derived from inner feelings, imaginal states, and outer events, and to "see through" them with a mindful, holistic awareness. Seeing through human acts both individual and collective allows you to examine the ways you construct knowledge, identity, and reality, and explore how some of your/others' constructions violate other people's ways of knowing and living.

When overwhelmed by the chaos caused by living between stories, you break down, descend into the third space, the Coatlicue depths of despair, self-loathing, and hopelessness. Dysfunctional for weeks, the refusal to move paralyzes you. In the fourth space a call to action pulls you out of your depression. You break free from your habitual coping strategies of escaping from realities you're reluctant to face, reconnect with spirit, and undergo a conversion.

In the fifth space your desire for order and meaning prompts you to track the ongoing circumstances of your life, to sift, sort, and symbolize your experiences and try to arrange them into a pattern and story that speak to your reality. You scan your inner landscape, books, movies, philosophies, mythologies, and the modern sciences for bits of lore you can patch together to create a new narrative articulating your personal reality. You scrutinize and question dominant and ethnic ideologies and the mind-sets their cultures induce in others. And, putting all the pieces together, you reenvision the map of the known world, creating a new description of reality and scripting a new story.

In the sixth space you take your story out into the world, testing it. When you or the world fail to live up to your ideals, your edifice collapses like a house of cards, casting you into conflict with self and others in a war between realities. Disappointed with self and others, angry and then terrified at the depth of your anger, you swallow your emotions, hold them in. Blocked from your own power, you're unable to activate the inner resources that could mobilize you. In the seventh, the critical turning point of transformation, you shift realities, develop an ethical, compassionate strategy with which to negotiate conflict and difference within self and between others, and find common ground by forming holistic alliances. You include these practices in your daily life, act on your vision—enacting spiritual activism.

Notes

Preface

1. We have chosen to use the term *masculinities* to make visible the diversity that exists within the category of "man" and how forms of masculinity vary across lines of race, social class, culture, sexuality, geography, and historical context. In doing so, we also wish to highlight the relational nature of practices associated with these gender-based identities as well as the consequences of these practices within and across groups. As Connell (1995, 37) writes: "To recognize diversity in masculinities is not enough. We must also recognize the *relations* between the different kinds of masculinity: relations of alliance, dominance, and subordination. These relationships are constructed through practices that exclude and include, that intimidate, exploit and so on. There is a gender politics within masculinity."

2. We have chosen to use the term *feminisms* to emphasize the diverse range of perspectives present in academic feminist discourse. According to Hurtado and Roa (2005, 815): "There are many definitions of feminism, and many scholars now assert that the word should be used in its plural form to encompass women's various social locations. As such, Chicana feminisms address the specific historical, economic, and social experiences of women of Mexican descent in the United States. The field of Chicana feminisms developed within the context of feminist movements in the United States, including the feminist writings of African-American, Asian-American, Native-American, and white scholars."

3. The dedication was designed by Eric Almanza. His artwork can be found at http://www.ericalmanza.com.

Introduction

1. In 1976, after much lobbying, the US Congress passed Public Law 94-311, sponsored by Rep. Edward Roybal (D) of California, titled "Joint resolution relating to the publication of economic and social statistics for Americans of Spanish origin or descent." This law mandated the collection of information about US

residents of Mexican, Cuban, Puerto Rican, Central American, South American, and other Spanish-speaking-country descent (Pub. L. No. 94-311, 1976). In 1997, the Office of Management and Budget issued a second directive that added the term *Latino* to the law (Portes and Rumbaut 2006). According to the Pew Research Center, "The use of the terms 'Hispanic' and 'Latino' to describe Americans of Spanish origin or descent is unique to the U.S. and their meaning[s] continue to change and evolve. Outside of the U.S., these terms are not widely used . . . and may also have different meanings." The Pew Research Center concludes: after "nearly four decades since the United States government mandated the use by federal agencies of the terms 'Hispanic' or 'Latino' to categorize Americans who trace their roots to Spanish-speaking countries, . . . the labels still haven't been fully embraced by the group to which they have been affixed" (http://www .pewhispanic.org/2012/04/04/when-labels-dont-fit-hispanics-and-their-views -of-identity/).

Chapter 1: Beyond Machismo

1. Other sociodemographic characteristics of CFS and LMS respondents will be reviewed in the chapters that follow.

2. Seventy-one of the Latino respondents who answered the BWMS questionnaire were selected for in-depth interviews that became part of the LMS. Only a few men who completed the questionnaire did not identify as Latino or white. Several identified as Asian American and several as African American. These men were excluded from the BWMS because their number was too small to broaden the study.

Chapter 2: Chicana Intersectional Understandings

This chapter includes material that originally appeared in Aída Hurtado and Karina Cervántez, "A View from Within and from Without: The Development of Latina Feminist Psychology," in *The Handbook of U.S. Latino Psychology: Developmental and Community-based Perspectives*, ed. Francisco A. Villarruel, Gustavo Carlo, Josefina M. Contreras Grau, Margarita Azmitia, Natasha J. Cabrera, and T. Jaime Chahin, 171–190 (Thousand Oaks, CA: Sage, 2009).

1. According to the Chicano Art website (www.chicanoart.org/nepantla .html), "The term, *Nepantla* is a Nahuatl (Aztec language) term connoting *in between* or a reference to the space of *the middle*. . . . Most often the term is referencing endangered peoples, cultures, and/or gender, who due to invasion/conquest/ marginalization or forced acculturation, engage in resistance strategies of survival. In this sense, this larger, cultural space of *Nepantla* becomes a postmodern paradigm or consciousness rooted in the creation of a *new middle*. Anzaldua calls this *La Nueva Mestizaje* [*sic*], the intent of which is to heal from the open wound of colonial occupation. Sometimes, it is a reference to living in the *borderlands* or *crossroads*, and the process of creating alternative spaces in which to live, function or create. In other words, it is the process of developing political, cultural or

psychological consciousness as a means of survival. For populations impacted by the historical trauma of colonialism and what some have termed *spiritual conquest*, one strategy of cultural survival, or decolonization is the process of *transcultura-tion*, which in many ways is resisting the mainstream, while, reinterpreting and redefining cultural difference as a place of power."

2. One dimension of diversity of special interest to feminists reflects inequalities in power and privilege. Feminist psychologists have a basic commitment to social action (Russo and Vaz 2001, 280). However, the added issue of power when considering diversity is not universally used or theoretically integrated as directly as the paradigm we propose in this chapter.

3. Kurt Lewin, a social psychologist, developed the concept of life space (1948), which is defined as the psychological environment existing in an individual's (or in the collective group's) mind at a certain point in time. The life space is dynamic, changing with time and experience.

4. Castillo is expanding Paulo Freire's notion of concientización (consciousness awareness) to include gender. The intrinsic connectedness of the individual's experience and the sociopolitical structure in which the individual exists is a fundamental tenet of liberation psychology and is referred to as "concientización." The idea is that an individual's behavior is not a result of intrapsychic processes, as proposed by traditional psychologists; behavior is the result of individuals operating within oppressive and alienating social structures. Martín-Baró argues that the awareness of concientización brings with it the understanding that individual psychology cannot be understood without addressing the social structures which contribute to a psychologically distressing environment for oppressed communities.

Chapter 3: Toward New Masculinities

This chapter includes material that originally appeared in Aída Hurtado and Mrinal Sinha, "More Than Men: Latino Feminist Masculinities and Intersectionality," *Sex Roles* 59, nos. 5-6 (2008): 337-349. Reprinted with the kind permission of Springer Science + Business Media.

1. A theme is defined as a common thread that continually emerges in the data, although the form of the theme is not always identical (Morse and Richards 2002). We conducted the thematic analysis using a combination of inductive and deductive coding techniques (Fereday and Muir-Cochrane 2006; Fink 2003).

2. Sinha coded the thirty-six interviews. A graduate student was trained in the coding protocol and coded the interviews independently a second time to determine intercoder reliability. The second coder was not aware of the research questions being addressed in the study.

3. All disagreements were reconciled by a third coder, also a graduate student, who was trained in the coding protocol (and who was also unaware of the research questions being addressed).

4. We obtained written permission from respondents to use their real names in published findings.

5. Ironically, Ricky Martin eventually acknowledged that he was gay.

Chapter 4: The Latino/a Gendered Educational Pipeline

This chapter includes material that originally appeared in the following two sources: Aída Hurtado and Mrinal Sinha, "Differences and Similarities: Latina and Latino Doctoral Students Navigating the Gender Divide," in *Journey to the Ph.D.: The Latina/o Experience in Higher Education* (Sterling, VA: Stylus Publishing, 2006); Aída Hurtado, Craig W. Haney, and José G. Hurtado, "Where the Boys Are: Macro and Micro Considerations for the Study of Young Latino Men's Educational Achievement," in *Invisible No More: Understanding the Disenfranchisement of Latino Men and Boys*," ed. Pedro Noguera, Aída Hurtado, and Edward Fergus, 101–115 (New York: Routledge, 2012), © 2011 by Noguera, Hurtado, and Fergus, reproduced by permission of Taylor and Francis Group, LLC, a division of Informa plc.

1. On February 26, 2012, around 7:00 pm in Sanford, Florida, seventeen-year-old Trayvon Martin was fatally shot by twenty-eight-year-old George Zimmerman. Martin was walking through a gated community to the home of his father's fiancée. He was returning from a local convenience store after purchasing a can of iced tea and a bag of Skittles. Zimmerman, a neighborhood watch volunteer, claimed he was threatened by the presence of the unarmed African American high school student, who was wearing a hooded sweatshirt, because of what he described as an unnaturally slow and meandering gait. A confrontation ensued, Zimmerman shot Martin, and six weeks later, Zimmerman was arrested and charged with second-degree murder. Against the backdrop of Florida's "Stand Your Ground" law, Zimmerman claimed he had shot Martin in self-defense after being attacked by the teen. The trial, televised nationally on cable networks and streamed live across the Internet, kept the country captivated awaiting a verdict. Following four weeks of testimony, more than a dozen witnesses, and a host of controversy, Zimmerman was acquitted of all charges, unleashing impassioned statements by President Barack Obama coupled with protests across the country (www.huffingtonpost.com/2013/07/13/george-zimmerman-not-guilty_n_358 8743.html?view=print&comm_ref=false).

2. www.whitehouse.gov/the-press-office/2013/07/19/remarks-president-trayvon-martin.

3. www.huffingtonpost.com/2013/07/13/george-zimmerman-not-guilty_n_35 88743.html?view=print&comm_ref=false.

4. Although there were some class variations among the respondents in both studies, there were too few middle-class Latinos and Latinas to analyze the Intersectional node of class (see table 4.2).

5. For purposes of clarity, we use the ethnic labels used in the reports we cite. Otherwise, we use the ethnic label *Latina/os*, which refers to individuals with Latin American ancestry.

6. Quinceañeras are celebrated in many Latin American countries when a young woman turns fifteen. The tradition originated to announce a young woman's coming of age and presentation to society as available for marriage. The quinceañera celebration entails an elaborate party, many times with hundreds of guests, a Catholic mass, formal attire, a dinner, and a dance. The cost can run into the thousands of dollars and can pose a financial burden for many families, espe-

cially when they are working class and have several daughters. Boys do not typically have this type of celebration.

7. In 2008, 72 percent of African American babies were born to unmarried mothers in comparison to 17 percent to Asians, 29 percent to whites, 53 percent to Latinas/os, and 66 percent to Native Americans. The rate for the overall US population was 41 percent (Washington, 2010).

Chapter 5: Relating to Feminisms

1. See chapter 1 for a full description of the study.

2. The book became such a cultural phenomenon that it led to a major film directed by Hall Barlett and starring Anthony Quinn as Jesús Sánchez, the patriarch of the family. Quinn's character is an alcoholic and abusive womanizer in conflict with his daughter, Consuelo (played by Mexican actress Lupita Ferrer), as she attempts to break from being a submissive daughter. Her grandmother advises Consuelo to marry as the way to escape her abusive father. Among those in attendance at the film's US premiere on November 17, 1978, were President Jimmy Carter and Rosalyn Carter. All proceeds from the premiere went to the Mexican American Legal Defense and Educational Fund, a progressive legal organization dedicated to fighting discrimination against Latinos; see www.jimmycarterlibrary .gov/documents/diary/1978/d111678t.pdf.

3. The term "subculture of poverty" (later shortened to "culture of poverty") first appeared in Oscar Lewis's other famous ethnography, *Five Families: Mexican Case Studies in the Culture of Poverty* (1959). He argues there that although the burdens of poverty are systemic, they nonetheless lead to the formation of an autonomous subculture as children are socialized into behaviors and attitudes that perpetuate their inability to escape the underclass.

4. *The Negro Family: The Case for National Action* (Moynihan 1965), commonly known as the Moynihan Report, was written by assistant secretary of labor Daniel Patrick Moynihan, a sociologist and later a US senator. The report attributes poverty in African American communities to the relative absence of two-parent families, which Moynihan claims hinders progress toward economic and political equality.

5. Seventy-one of the Latino respondents in the BWMS also participated in the LMS.

6. Scales were derived from the Sex Role Attitude Items and Scales from US Sample Surveys (Mason 1975, as cited in Renzetti 1987; Mason and Lu 1988), the Liberal Feminist Attitude and Ideology Scale (LFAIS) (Morgan 1996), and the British version of the Attitudes towards Women Scale (AWS-B) (Parry 1983). We elected to use the British version of the AWS because it was developed explicitly for respondents from working-class backgrounds.

7. The specific yes-no questions asked the following: (1) Have you ever felt as though you were harassed by the police? (2) Has anyone in your family or extended family ever been in prison or jail? (3) When you were growing up were there gangs in your neighborhood? (4) Has anyone in your family or extended family ever belonged to a gang? In addition, respondents were asked the follow-

ing: (1) The approximate ethnic composition of your high school was (a) Mostly people of Color (e.g., Latinos, Asians, African Americans), (b) About an even mixture of people of Color and Anglos/whites, (c) Mostly Anglo/white, (d) Almost all Anglo/white, (e) Other (Specify: _____); (2) The approximate ethnic composition of your neighborhood was (same response categories as the prior question).

8. The central purpose of parametric inferential statistics is to draw inferences about populations of people based on a sample taken from a specific population (Cronk 2010).

9. Although there are various types of t-tests, in this chapter we utilize only the independent samples t-test, which determines whether the mean (average) score on a variable (in our case, parental income and parental education level) is reliably different between two independent groups, here, Latino and white respondents.

10. The p value is a statement on the probability of a specific result occurring purely by chance.

11. There are various types of chi-square tests; the one used here is called a chi-square test of independence. This statistical technique tests whether two variables are independent of each other, or if there is some interaction between them in relationship to an outcome variable (in our case, is there an interaction between belonging to a particular racial and ethnic group and being harassed by the police?). Similar to t-tests, p values are also calculated when conducting these tests and provide the same information (i.e., the probability of statistically reliable interactions occurring as a function of chance).

12. Factor analysis techniques provide only correlations and cannot be used to determine causation; that is, we are presenting an exploratory study of the interaction between respondents' race, ethnicity, and class and their gender attitudes and views on feminisms. We cannot determine through EFA whether the resulting differences in attitudinal structures are caused by the differences in the respondents' backgrounds. The analysis presented in this chapter is purely correlational.

13. The process of finding underlying dimensions to the data through groupings of variables (i.e., emerging factors) renders factor analysis an ideal data reduction tool, which is also an important function of this technique. For example, if four questions provide as much information as ten questions on the same topic, an EFA allows the researcher to eliminate six questions and still obtain substantive, statistically reliable information.

14. Mathematically, a single question used to measure a concept is never as good as several questions (with the same options to answer). For example, if a researcher aims to measure (or assess) respondents' views on sexism, it is better to ask several questions on the topic rather than only one. An EFA helps a researcher determine how many questions and which ones are ideal, statistically speaking, for measuring a particular concept (or construct).

15. We used EFA instead of confirmatory factor analysis because we were not testing a specific hypothesis. Our aim was to explore the constructs, which drove responses to the questionnaire items. We were looking specifically for commonalities and differences between Latino and white respondents. Because confirmatory factor analysis is used primarily to test theory and specific hypotheses, we opted not to use this technique.

16. Generally, factor loadings of .3 (Kline 1994) or .32 (Tabachnik and Fidell 1996) have been described as acceptable. Kline points out that .3 is a somewhat "arbitrary and conservative criterion" and one that has been demonstrated to be quite useful (54). Tabachnik and Fidell argue that "as a rule of thumb, only variables with a loading of .32 and above are interpreted" (677). They specify that loadings larger than .71 are considered excellent, loadings of .63 are considered very good, loadings of .55 are considered good, .45, fair, and .32, poor (Tabachnik and Fidell, 1996, 677).

17. Factor loadings are central to the interpretation of factors; larger factor loadings provide "clues" to the identification and naming of specific factors (Kline 1994). That is, a simple way to interpret the relationship between variable loadings and a factor is to think of the relative strength of indicators of a concept: the stronger the indicators of a concept, the more likely it is that we have a good measurement.

18. We conducted varimax rotation of the factor matrix to minimize shared variance. We used orthogonal extraction to treat each emerging factor as independent, or uncorrelated with each other.

19. Eigenvalues are statistical values that refer to the amount of variance explained by each factor; the scree plot is a visual representation of those eigenvalues.

20. Many researchers extract components that have eigenvalues greater than 1; this decision has been criticized on the grounds that it underestimates the number of factors to extract (Humphreys 1964, as cited in Henson and Roberts 2006). The scree plot has been cited as more accurate, but it tends to overestimate the number of factors to extract (Henson and Roberts 2006). By using these in combination, we heed the call of researchers to "use both multiple criteria and reasoned reflection" (Henson and Roberts 2006, 399) in order to offset the weaknesses associated with each and extract the most accurate number of factors.

21. The five factors had eigenvalues greater than 2, with the scree test suggesting no additional interpretability of components below this value.

22. Fifteen items were dropped because they did not load highly on any one factor or loaded substantially on more than one factor. Low factor loadings and items that "cross-load" (i.e., that are associated with more than one factor) add "noise," which can hinder the researcher in interpreting the factor structure while adding little to the analysis. Inclusion of these items would have inhibited the interpretability of the factor structure, a central issue identified by Tabachnik and Fidell (1996) when conducting principal components factor analysis.

23. Cronbach's alpha, an index of reliability that is also known as internal consistency (how well the items hang together), was .657, with values greater than .70 considered acceptable (Cronbach 1951).

24. Although the coefficient alpha was relatively low, this factor was retained and evaluated as interpretable because it had ten items with factor loadings of .4 or higher with a sample size that was equal to 150 respondents (Stevens 2002).

25. Initially, four factors were extracted (all of which had eigenvalues greater than 2), but the fourth factor was rejected due to lack of statistical reliability. The four factors had eigenvalues greater than 2, with the scree test suggesting no additional interpretability of components below this value. A total of thirteen attitudinal statements were dropped from the initial fifty: four statements loading on

factor 4, which was itself dropped, and nine other statements because they did not load highly on one factor or loaded highly on multiple factors.

26. Nine items were dropped because they did not load highly on any one factor or loaded substantially on more than one factor.

27. The remaining two items in the Latinos' traditional gender roles factor did not load on any factor for white respondents: "Women should have completely equal opportunities in getting jobs and promotions as men"; and "If a woman goes out to work, her husband should share the housework, such as washing dishes, cleaning, and cooking."

28. The two items in the whites' feminist consciousness factor did not load on any factor for Latino respondents: "Even though some things have changed, women are still treated unfairly in today's society"; and "If women want to get ahead, there is little to stop them."

29. Fifteen percent of Latinos, in comparison to only 7 percent of white respondents, had read Gloria Steinem or heard her speak.

30. *The House on Mango Street* is a novel that is widely assigned in California public high schools, which may explain its readership across race, ethnic, and class lines.

Chapter 6: Relating to Oppression

1. The 19 respondents gave a variety of reasons for their reservations in fully identifying as feminists. The most common reason, given by 6 respondents, was that they still exhibited behaviors and gender beliefs that were not completely without sexist prejudice; that is, although they identified with feminisms, they felt they did not live up to feminist ideals. Other reasons given were not being competent enough to assess women's experiences, not fully understanding the issues entailing a feminist position, and not actively participating in feminist political action. A few respondents said that they had feminist beliefs and values, but they were hesitant to identify with the label "feminist" per se. Two respondents indicated that they had reservations because they supported only certain feminist-related issues, such as helping their communities with medical care, and were not informed about broader feminist issues. Regardless of their stated reservations, all of these 19 respondents discussed feminist issues and elaborated on their affinity with feminisms, hence their inclusion here.

2. There were only five gay respondents in the LMS, and, therefore, we were unable to conduct a thorough analysis at the Intersectional node of sexuality, ethnicity, and race in the development of a feminist identification. All five gay respondents identified as feminist.

3. In *The Color of Privilege: Three Blasphemies on Race and Feminism*, Hurtado (1996) proposes that white women derive a degree of structural and emotional privilege from their familial relationships to white patriarchy, as daughters, mothers, sisters, spouses, cousins, and aunts of white men. White women inherit a relational power dynamic that informs their perspective and thus their feminisms.

4. Of the 105 respondents in the Latino Masculinities Study, 66 also answered

the Brown and White Masculinities questionnaire (see chapter 5 for a description of the topics covered). Fifty respondents identified as feminist (16 did not). Of those, 25 had taken an undergraduate or graduate course in Chicana/o studies; 14 had taken one in women's studies; 26 had read, heard of, or had heard Gloria Anzaldúa speak; 46 had read, heard of, or had heard Sandra Cisneros speak; 34 had read or heard of *Borderlands/La Frontera*; and 42 had read or heard of *The House on Mango Street*.

5. White hegemonic feminisms are based on individual freedom, the goal is to gain full rights as *individuals* unhampered by the restrictions of sex, gender, and sexuality. Chicana feminisms is about a theory of liberation for *all*, utilizing the Chicana experience as the basis for theorizing.

Chapter 7: Intersectionality at Work

1. Pepe stands for José in Spanish, as Bill does for William in English.

2. DEA agents work for the US Department of Justice as part of the Drug Enforcement Administration. According to the website, "DEA Special Agents are a select group of men and women from diverse backgrounds whose experience and commitment make them the premier federal drug law enforcement agents in the world" (http://www.justice.gov/dea/careers/agent/faqs.html#question001).

3. Arcelia Hurtado, the youngest in the family, is an attorney and currently deputy director of the National Center for Lesbian Rights, a nonprofit legal organization in San Francisco, California, dedicated to "advancing the civil and human rights of lesbian, gay, bisexual, and transgendered people and their families through litigation, public policy advocacy, and public education" (www.nclrights .org/site/PageServer?pagename=about_overview). María Hurtado, the second-youngest in the family, holds a master's degree in social work and is currently assistant city manager for the city of Tracy, California. Formerly she was a practicing social worker running two nonprofits dedicated to helping individuals with substance abuse problems. One of them, Hermanas (Sisters) Recovery Program, is a residential treatment program specializing in providing Latinas substance abuse treatment services (http://directory.intherooms.com/Treatment-Centers /Hermanas-Recovery-Program/1866). Aída Hurtado is professor and chair of the Chicana and Chicano Studies Department, University of California, Santa Barbara, and has written extensively on Chicana feminisms.

4. Notice the sad trajectories of many members of the Kennedy family who were never able to overcome their addictions.

5. In 2005, the city of Santa Cruz had a population of 58,982, 56 percent white and 34.8 percent Hispanic (www.santacruzchamber.org/cwt/external/wcpages /facts/demographics.aspx).

6. For example, Barrios Unidos, Defensa de Mujeres, Hermanas, Fenix, Friends Outside, GEMMA, Pajaro Valley Prevention and Student Service, RISE, SI SE PUEDE (Yes You Can), Santa Cruz Youth Services, and Santa Cruz Probation Services.

7. Barrios Unidos (BU) started in 1977 as a community-based movement

dedicated to ending urban violence in California. In 1993, Santa Cruz Barrios Unidos became a nonprofit organization dedicated to the prevention and curtailment of "violence amongst youth within Santa Cruz County by providing them with life enhancing alternatives" (www.barriosunidos.net/about.html).

8. Connie Rice obtained her undergraduate degree from Harvard University and her law degree from New York University. In 2006, prior to cofounding the Advancement Project, she was codirector of the Los Angeles office of the NAACP Legal Defense and Educational Fund. She "has led multi-racial coalitions of lawyers and clients to win more than $10 billion in damages and policy changes, through traditional class action civil rights cases redressing police misconduct, race and sex discrimination and unfair public policy in transportation, probation and public housing" (www.advancementprojectca.org/?q=node/305).

9. The Advancement Project is dedicated to engineering "large-scale systems change to remedy inequality, expand opportunity and open paths to upward mobility. Our goal is that members of all communities have the safety, opportunity and health they need to thrive" (www.advancementprojectca.org/?q=What-we -do). The Advancement Project focuses on four areas: educational equity, equity in public funds, healthy city, and urban peace. Connie Rice's allegiance to BU is particularly aligned with the last area of focus—urban peace—which entails a commitment to "reduce and prevent community violence, making poor neighborhoods safer so that children can learn, families can thrive and communities can prosper" (www.advancementprojectca.org/?q=What-we-do).

10. At the time I was a member of the BU board.

11. The community college has since been renamed Minnesota West Community College.

12. Pepe was incarcerated in Worthington, Minnesota, until his trial, which was held in Iowa. My youngest sister, Arcelia, and her partner, Niki, both of whom at the time were public defenders in San Francisco, attended Pepe's trial and testified, pleading with the presiding judge for a lesser sentence. After his trial, Pepe was transferred to a prison outside Minneapolis, where my mother, my husband, and I visited him. Then he was transferred to the prison in Florence, Colorado, and my sisters, my niece, and I visited him every year until his release in 2005.

13. See Jimmy Santiago Baca's powerful prison memoir on the role of reading and writing in aiding his survival in prison and eventual rehabilitation (2001).

14. Prison rules prevented the family from buying him an airline ticket to California or accompanying him on the bus ride. Needless to say, we were extremely worried about his traveling alone after so many years in prison and possible exposure to alcohol and drugs while on his own with no support.

15. Conocimiento can be thought of as the process of "coming to a spiritual and political awareness that moves from . . . inner work to public acts" of accountability, personal growth, and contributions to social justice. See the appendix for a summary of the seven stages of conocimiento (http://womenscrossroads.blogspot .com/2006/01/gloria-anzaldua-personal-is-political.html).

16. Women's prisons do not generate man hating to the same degree that misogyny is created in men's prisons.

17. The four-year probation requirements included attendance at an outpatient

drug treatment program for six months and drug testing four times a month for the first three months, then twice a month for the next three months.

18. San Jose is a forty-five-minute drive from Santa Cruz. This requirement alone would trip up most parolees, who normally do not have access to a car and are required to use unreliable public transportation, thereby risking delays. While on probation, formerly incarcerated individuals are not given much leeway if they are late or miss appointments with their probation officers.

19. According to Delgado Bernal (2001, 626), "A mestiza is literally a woman of mixed ancestry, especially of Native American, European, and African backgrounds. However, the term mestiza has come to mean a new Chicana consciousness that straddles cultures, races, languages, nations, sexualities, and spiritualities — that is, living with ambivalence while balancing opposing powers."

20. At this time, Pepe was attending San Jose State for his master's in social work. As mentioned earlier, I usually drove from Santa Cruz to San Jose to meet him on the days he had appointments with his probation officer.

Works Cited

Acosta, Frank De Jesús. 2007. *The History of Barrios Unidos: Healing Community Violence*. Houston: Arte Público Press.

Adu-Poku, Samuel. 2001. "Envisioning (Black) Male Feminism: A Cross Cultural Perspective." *Journal of Gender Studies* 10 (2): 157–167.

Alarcón, Norma. 1990. "The Theoretical Subject(s) of *This Bridge Called My Back* and Anglo-American Feminism." In *Making Face, Making Soul: Haciendo Caras*, edited by Gloria Anzaldúa, 356–369. San Francisco: Aunt Lute Books.

Aldama, Arturo J., Chela Sandoval, and Peter J. García. 2012. *Performing the U.S. Latina and Latino Borderlands*. Bloomington: Indiana University Press.

Alexander, Bryant Keith, ed. 2013. "From Emmett Till to Trayvon Martin." Special issue, *Cultural Studies↔Critical Methodologies* 13.

Alexander, Michelle. 2010. *The New Jim Crow: Mass Incarceration in the Age of Color Blindness*. New York: New Press.

Almaguer, Tomás. 2004. "Chicano Men: A Cartography of Homosexual Identity and Behavior." In *Men's Lives*, 6th ed., edited by Michael S. Kimmel and Michael A. Messner, 433–446. Boston: Allyn and Bacon.

Alvarez, Rodolfo. 1973. "The Psycho-Historical and Socioeconomic Development of the Chicano Community in the United States." *Social Science Quarterly* 53 (4): 920–942.

Anderson, Eric. 2005. *In the Game: Gay Athletes and the Cult of Masculinity*. Albany: State University of New York Press.

Anzaldúa, Gloria E. 1987. *Borderlands/La Frontera: The New Mestiza*. San Francisco: Spinsters/Aunt Lute.

———, ed. 1990. *Making Face, Making Soul: Haciendo Caras: Creative and Critical Perspectives by Feminists of Color*. San Francisco: Aunt Lute Books.

———. 2002. "Now Let Us Shift . . . The Path of Conocimiento . . . Inner Work, Public Acts." In *This Bridge We Call Home: Radical Visions for Transformation*, edited by Gloria E. Anzaldúa and AnaLouise Keating, 540–578. New York: Routledge.

Anzaldúa, Gloria E., and AnaLouise Keating, eds. 2002. *This Bridge We Call Home: Radical Visions for Transformation*. New York: Routledge.

Apfelbaum, Erika. 1979. "Relations of Domination and Movements for Libera-
tion: An Analysis of Power between Groups." In *The Social Psychology of Inter-
group Relations*, edited by William G. Austin and Stephan Worchel, 188–204.
Monterey, CA: Brooks/Cole.
———. 1999. "Relations of Domination and Movements for Liberation: An
Analysis of Power between Groups." *Feminisms and Psychology* 9 (3): 267–272.
Apple, Michael W. 1978. "Ideology, Reproduction, and Educational Reform."
Comparative Educational Review 22:367–387.
Archer, Louise, Simon D. Pratt, and David Phillips. 2001. "Working Class Men's
Constructions of Masculinity and Negotiations of (Non)Participation in
Higher Education." *Gender and Education* 13:431–449.
Arredondo, Gabriela, Aída Hurtado, Norma Klahn, Olga Nájera-Ramírez, and
Patricia Zavella, eds. 2003. *Chicana Feminisms: A Critical Reader*. Durham, NC:
Duke University Press.
Ashe, Fidelma. 2004. "Deconstructing the Experiential Bar: Male Experience and
Feminist Resistance." *Men & Masculinities* 7 (2): 187–204.
Baca, Jimmy Santiago. 2001. *A Place to Stand*. New York: Grove Press.
Baca Zinn, Maxine. 1975. "Chicanas: Power and Control in the Domestic Sphere."
De Colores 2:19–31.
———. 1982. "Chicano Men and Masculinity." *Journal of Ethnic Studies* 10:29–44.
———. 1994. "Adaptation and Continuity in Mexican-origin Families." In *Mi-
nority Families in the United States: A Multicultural Perspective*, edited by Ronald
Lewis Taylor, 226–235. Englewood Cliffs, NJ: Prentice Hall.
Baca Zinn, Maxine, and Bonnie Thornton Dill, eds. 1994. *Women of Color in U.S.
Society*. Philadelphia: Temple University Press.
———. 1996. "Theorizing Difference from Multiracial Feminism." *Feminist
Studies* 22 (2): 321–331.
Barvosa, Edwina. 2008. *Wealth of Selves: Multiple Identities, Mestiza Consciousness,
and the Subject of Politics*. College Station: Texas A&M University Press.
———. 2011. "Mestiza Consciousness in Relation to Sustained Political Soli-
darity: A Chicana Feminist Interpretation of the Farmworker Movement."
Aztlán 36 (2): 121–154.
Barvosa-Carter, Edwina. 2007. "Mestiza Autonomy as Relational Autonomy: Am-
bivalence and the Social Character of Free Will." *Journal of Political Philosophy*
15 (1): 1–21.
Baumeister, Roy F. 1998. "The Self." In *The Handbook of Social Psychology*, vol. 1,
edited by Daniel T. Gilbert, Susan T. Fiske, and Gardner Lindzey, 680–740.
New York: Oxford University Press.
Beauvoir, Simone de. 1989 (1952). *The Second Sex*. New York: Vintage Books Print.
Bilmes, Murray. 1992. "Macho and Shame." *International Forum of Psychoanalysis*
1:163–168.
Blackwell, Maylei. 2011. *Chicana Power! Contested Histories of Feminism in the Chi-
cano Movement*. Austin: University of Texas Press.
Bost, Suzanne. 2005. "Gloria Anzaldúa's Mestiza Pain: Mexican Sacrifice, Chicana
Embodiment, and Feminist Politics." *Aztlán* 30:5–36.
Browne, Irene, and Misra Joya. 2003. "The Intersection of Gender and Race in
the Labor Market." *Annual Review of Sociology* 29:487–513.

Canada, Geoffrey. 1995. *Fist Stick Knife Gun: A Personal History of Violence in America*. Boston: Beacon.

Cantú, Lionel. 2000. "Entre Hombres/Between Men: Latino Masculinities and Homosexualities." In *Gay Masculinities*, edited by Peter M. Nardi, 224–246. Thousand Oaks, CA: Sage.

———. 2004. "A Place Called Home: A Queer Political Economy: Mexican Immigrant Men's Family Experiences." In *Men's Lives*, 6th ed., edited by Michael S. Kimmel and Michael A. Messner, 484–496. Boston: Allyn and Bacon.

Cantú, Norma E., ed. 2008. *Paths to Discovery: Autobiographies from Chicanas with Careers in Science, Mathematics, and Engineering*. Los Angeles: UCLA Chicano Research Center Publications.

Caraway, Nancie. 1991. *Segregated Sisterhood: Racism and the Politics of American Feminism*. Knoxville: University of Tennessee Press.

Casillas, Dolores Inés. 2011. "Sounds of Surveillance: U.S. Spanish-language Radio Patrols La Migra." *American Quarterly* 63 (3): 807–829.

———. 2014. *Sounds of Belonging: U.S. Spanish-language Radio and Public Advocacy*. New York: New York University Press.

Castillo, Ana. 1994. *Massacre of the Dreamers: Essays on Xicanisma*. Albuquerque: University of New Mexico Press.

Child, Dennis. 2006. *The Essentials of Factor Analysis*. 3rd ed. New York: Continuum International.

Childs, John Brown. 1990. "Coalitions and the Spirit of Mutuality." In *Building Bridges: The Emerging Grassroots Coalition of Labor and Community*, edited by Jeremy Brecher and Tim Costello, 234–242. New York: Monthly Review Press.

———. 2003. *Transcommunality: From the Politics of Conversion to the Ethics of Respect*. Philadelphia: Temple University Press.

Christian, Barbara. 1985. *Black Feminist Criticism: Perspectives on Black Women Writers*. New York: Teachers College Press.

Christian, Harry. 1994. *The Making of Anti-sexist Men*. London: Routledge.

Cisneros, Sandra. 1984. *The House on Mango Street*. New York: Vintage Books.

Collins, Gail. 2013. "At a Time When Women Can Be Free, Finally, to Move On to Something More." *New York Times Sunday Magazine*, January 27.

Collins, Patricia Hill. 1991. "On Our Own Terms: Self-defined Standpoints and Curriculum Transformation." *NWSA Journal* 3 (3): 367–381.

———. 1999. "Moving beyond Gender: Intersectionality and Scientific Knowledge." In *Revisioning Gender*, edited by Myra Marx Farree, Judith Lorber, and Beth B. Hess, 261–284. Thousand Oaks, CA: Sage.

———. 2000. *Black Feminist Thought: Knowledge, Consciousness, and the Politics of Empowerment*. 2nd ed. New York: Routledge.

———. 2004. *Black Sexual Politics: African Americans, Gender, and the New Racism*. New York: Routledge.

Colón, Alice E. Warren. 2003. "Puerto Rico: Feminism and Feminist Studies." *Gender & Society* 17 (5): 664–690.

Coltrane, Scott. 1994. "Theorizing Masculinities in Contemporary Social Science." In *Theorizing Masculinities*, edited by Harry Brod and Michael Kaufman, 39–60. Thousand Oaks, CA: Sage.

Comas-Díaz, Lillian. 2000. "An Ethnopolitical Approach to Working with People of Color." *American Psychologist* 55 (11): 1319–1325.

Comas-Díaz, Lillian, M. Brinton Lykes, and Renato D. Alarcón. 1998. "Ethnic Conflict and the Psychology of Liberation in Guatemala, Peru, and Puerto Rico." *American Psychologist* 53 (7): 778–792.

Connell, Raewyn W. 1987. *Gender and Power: Society, the Person, and Sexual Politics*. Stanford, CA: Stanford University Press.

———. 1995. *Masculinities*. Oxford: Polity Press.

Corbett, Christianne, Catherine Hill, and Andresse St. Rose. 2008. *Where the Girls Are: The Facts about Gender Equity in Education*. Washington, DC: American Association of University Women.

Crenshaw, Kimberlé. 1989. "Demarginalizing the Intersection of Race and Sex: A Black Feminist Critique of Anti-discrimination Doctrine, Feminist Theory, and Anti-racist Politics." In *Feminist Legal Theory: Foundations*, edited by D. Kelly Weisberg, 383–395. Philadelphia: Temple University Press.

———. 1995. "Mapping the Margins: Intersectionality, Identity Politics, and Violence against Women of Color." In *Critical Race Theory: The Key Writings That Formed the Movement*, edited by Kimberlé W. Crenshaw, Neil Gotanda, Gary Peller, and Kendall Thomas, 357–383. New York: New Press.

Cronbach, Lee J. 1951. "Coefficient Alpha and the Internal Structure of Tests." *Psychometrika* 16:297–334.

Cronk, Brian C. 2010. *How to Use PASW Statistics: A Step-by-Step Guide to Analysis and Interpretation*. 6th ed. Glendale, CA: Pyrczak Publishing.

Davis, Angela Y. 1983. *Women, Race, and Class*. New York: Vintage Books.

Davis, Angela Y., and Elizabeth Martínez. 1994. "Coalition Building among People of Color." *Inscriptions* 7:1–7.

Delgado Bernal, Dolores. 1998. "Grassroots Leadership Reconceptualized: Chicana Oral Histories and the 1968 East Los Angeles School Blowouts." *Frontiers* 19 (2): 113–142.

———. 2001. "Learning and Living Pedagogies of the Home: The Mestiza Consciousness of Chicana Students." *Qualitative Studies in Education* 14 (5): 623–639.

Delgado Bernal, Dolores, Rebeca Burciaga, and Judith Flores Carmona. 2012. "Chicana/Latina Testimonios: Mapping the Methodological, Pedagogical, and Political." *Equity & Excellence in Education* 45 (3): 363–372, DOI:10.1080/1066 5684.2012.698149.

Dillard, Cynthia B. 2000. "The Substance of Things Hoped for, the Evidence of Things Not Seen: Examining an Endarkened Feminist Epistemology in Educational Research and Leadership." *Qualitative Studies in Education* 13 (6): 661–681.

———. 2003. "Cut to Heal, Not to Bleed: A Response to Handel Wright's 'An Endarkened Feminist Epistemology?' Identity, Difference and the Politics of Representation in Educational Research." *International Journal of Qualitative Studies in Education* 16 (2): 227–232.

Domínguez, Virginia R. 1992. "Invoking Culture: The Messy Side of 'Cultural Politics.'" *South Atlantic Quarterly* 91 (1): 19–42.

Du Bois, W. E. B. 1903. *The Souls of Black Folk*. Chicago: A. C. McClurg.

Ennis, Sharon R., Merarys Ríos-Vargas, and Nora G. Albert. 2011. "The Hispanic Population: 2010." Washington, DC: US Department of Commerce, Economics and Statistics Administration, US Census Bureau.

Espín, Oliva M. 1996. "Leaving the Nation and Joining the Tribe: Lesbian Immigrants Crossing Geographical and Identity Borders." *Women & Therapy* 19 (4): 99–107.

Fenstermaker, Sarah, and Candace West, eds. 2002. *Doing Gender, Doing Difference: Inequality, Power, and Institutional Change*. New York: Routledge.

Fereday, Jennifer, and Eimear Muir-Cochrane. 2006. "Demonstrating Rigor Using Thematic Analysis: A Hybrid Approach of Inductive and Deductive Coding and Theme Development." *International Journal of Qualitative Methods* 5: article 7. http://www.ualberta.ca/~iiqm/backissues/5_1/html/fereday.htm.

Ferguson, Ann Arnett. 2000. *Bad Boys: Public Schools in the Making of Black Masculinity*. Ann Arbor: University of Michigan Press.

Figueroa, Julie L. 2002. "Out of the Neighborhood and Into the Ivory Tower: Understanding the Schooling Experiences of Latino Male Undergraduates as Process of Negotiation and Navigation." PhD diss., University of California, Berkeley. *Dissertation Abstracts International* 63:9.

Figueroa, Julie L., and Eugene Garcia. 2006. "Tracing Institutional Racism in Higher Education: Academic Practices of Latino Male Undergraduates." In *Addressing Racism: Facilitating Cultural Competence in Mental Health and Educational Settings*, edited by Madonna G. Constantine and Daral W. Sue, 195–212. Hoboken, NJ: John Wiley & Sons.

Fine, Michelle. 2002. "The Presence of an Absence." *Psychology of Women Quarterly* 26 (1): 9–24.

Fine, Michelle, and Lois Weis. 1998. *The Unknown City: The Lives of Poor and Working-class Young Adults*. Boston: Beacon Press.

Fine, Michelle, Lois Weis, Judi Addelston, and Julia Marusza. 1997. "(In)Secure Times: Constructing White Working-Class Masculinities in the Late 20th Century." *Gender and Society* 11 (1): 52–68.

Fine, Michelle, Lois Weis, Linda Powell Pruitt, and April Burns, eds. 2004. *Off White: Readings on Power, Privilege, and Resistance*. New York: Routledge.

Fink, Arlene G. 2003. *How to Manage, Analyze, and Interpret Survey Data*. 2nd ed. Thousand Oaks, CA: Sage Publications.

Flores, María T. 2000. "La Familia Latina." In *Family Therapy with Hispanics*, edited by María T. Flores and Gabrielle Carey, 3–28. Needham Heights, MA: Allyn and Bacon.

Flores-Ortiz, Yvette G. 2004. "Domestic Violence in Chicana/o Families." In *The Handbook of Chicana/o Psychology and Mental Health*, edited by Roberto J. Velásquez, Leticia M. Arellano, and Brian W. McNeill, 267–284. Mahwah, NJ: Lawrence Erlbaum.

Franklin, Clyde W., II. 1987. "Surviving the Institutional Decimation of Black Males: Causes, Consequences and Intervention." In *The Making of Masculinities: The New Men's Studies*, edited by Harry Brod, 155–169. New York: Routledge.

Fregoso, Rosa-Linda. 2003. *Mexicana Encounters: The Making of Social Identities on the Borderlands*. Berkeley: University of California Press.

Friedan, Betty. 1963. *The Feminine Mystique*. New York: W. W. Norton.

Gamboa, Suzanne. 2001. "Diploma Deficit: Fewer Caps, Gowns for Hispanic Girls." *Monitor*, January: 1A, 8A.

Ginorio, Angela, and Michelle Huston. 2001. *Si, Se Puede, Yes We Can: Latinas in School*. Washington, DC: American Association of University Women.

González-López, Gloria. 2005. *Erotic Journeys: Mexican Immigrants and Their Sex Lives*. Berkeley: University of California Press.

Greene, Susan, Craig Haney, and Aída Hurtado. 2000. "Cycles of Pain: Risk Factors in the Lives of Incarcerated Mothers and Their Children." *The Prison Journal* 80 (1): 3–23.

Griffin, Christine. 1989 "'I'm Not a Women's Libber, but . . .': Feminism, Consciousness and Identity." In *The Social Identity of Women*, edited by Suzanne Skevington and Deborah Baker, 173–193. London: Sage Publications.

Gurin, Patricia, Aída Hurtado, and Timothy Peng. 1994. "Group Contacts and Ethnicity in the Social Identities of Mexicanos and Chicanos." *Personality and Social Psychology Bulletin* 20:521–532.

Gurin, Patricia, Arthur H. Miller, and Gerald Gurin. 1980. "Stratum Identification and Consciousness." *Social Psychology Quarterly* 43:30–47.

Gurin, Patricia, Biren (Ratnesh) A. Nagda, and Ximena Zúñiga. 2013. *Dialogue across Difference: Practice, Theory, and Research on Intergroup Dialogue*. New York: Russell Sage Foundation.

Gutiérrez, Ramón A. 1991. *When Jesus Came, the Corn Mothers Went Away: Marriage, Sexuality, and Power in New Mexico, 1500–1846*. Stanford, CA: Stanford University Press.

Gutmann, Matthew C., ed. 2003. *Changing Men and Masculinities in Latin America*. Durham, NC: Duke University Press.

Hammond, Wizdom Powell, and Jacqueline S. Mattis. 2005. "Being a Man about It: Manhood Meaning among African-American Men." *Psychology of Men & Masculinity* 6:114–126.

Haney, Craig W. 1982. "Criminal Justice and the Nineteenth-Century Paradigm: The Triumph of Psychological Individualism in the 'Formative Era.'" *Law and Human Behavior* 6 (3–4): 191–209.

———. 2003. "The Psychological Impact of Incarceration: Implications for Post-Prison Adjustment." In *Prisoners Once Removed: The Impact of Incarceration and Reentry on Children, Families, and Communities*, edited by Jeremy Travis and Michelle Waul, 33–66. Washington, DC: Urban Institute.

———. 2005. *Death by Design: Capital Punishment as a Social Psychological System*. Oxford: Oxford University Press.

———. 2006. *Reforming Punishment: Psychological Limits to the Pains of Imprisonment*. Washington, DC: American Psychological Association.

———. 2008. "Counting Casualties in the War on Prisoners." *University of San Francisco Law Review* 43:87–138.

Haney, Craig, and Aída Hurtado. 1994. "The Jurisprudence of Race and Meritocracy: Standardized Testing and 'Race-Neutral' Racism in the Workplace." *Law and Human Behavior* 18 (3): 223–247.

Haney, Craig W., and Philip G. Zimbardo. 2009. "Persistent Dispositionalism in Interactionist Clothing: Fundamental Attribution Error in Explaining Prison Abuse." *Personality and Social Psychology Bulletin* 35:807–814.

Haney-López, Ian. 2003. *Racism on Trial: The Chicano Fight for Justice.* Cambridge, MA: Belknap.

Haraway, Donna. 1988. "Situated Knowledges: The Science Question in Feminism and the Privilege of Partial Perspective." *Feminist Studies* 14 (3): 575–599.

Hartsock, Nancy. 1983. *Money, Sex, and Power: Toward a Feminist Historical Materialism.* Boston: Northeastern University Press.

Henson, Robin K., and J. Kyle Roberts. 2006. "Use of Exploratory Factor Analysis in Published Research: Common Errors and Some Comment on Improved Practice." *Educational and Psychological Measurement* 66 (3): 393–416.

Hochschild, Arlie Russell. 1989. *The Second Shift.* New York: Penguin Books.

Hogg, Michael A., and Scott A. Reid. 2006. "Social Identity, Self-Categorization, and the Communication of Group Norms." *Communication Theory* 16:7–30.

hooks, bell. 1984. *Feminist Theory: From Margin to Center.* Boston: South End Press.

———. 2000. *Feminism Is for Everybody: Passionate Politics.* Cambridge, MA: South End.

Hoynes, Hilary W., Marianne E. Page, and Ann H. Stevens. 2005. *Poverty in America: Trends and Explanations.* Cambridge, MA: National Bureau of Economic Research.

Hughes, Everett C. 1945. "Dilemmas." *American Journal of Sociology* 50 (5): 353–359.

Hurtado, Aída. 1996. *The Color of Privilege: Three Blasphemies on Race and Feminism.* Ann Arbor: University of Michigan Press.

———. 1997. "Understanding Multiple Group Identities: Inserting Women into Cultural Transformations." *Journal of Social Issues* 53:299–328.

———. 1998a. "The Politics of Sexuality in the Gender Subordination of Chicanas." In *Living Chicana Theory*, edited by Carla Trujillo, 383–428. Berkeley, CA: Third Woman.

———. 1998b. "Sitios y Lenguas: Chicanas Theorize Feminisms." *Hypatia* 13 (2): 134–159.

———. 1999. "A Crossborder Existence: One Woman's Migration Story." In *Women's Untold Stories: Breaking Silence, Talking Back, Voicing Complexity*, edited by Abigail Stewart and Mary Romero, 83–101. New York: Routledge.

———. 2003a. "Theory in the Flesh: Toward an Endarkened Epistemology." *International Journal of Qualitative Studies in Education* 16:215–225.

———. 2003b. *Voicing Chicana Feminisms: Young Women Speak Out on Sexuality and Identity.* New York: New York University Press.

———. 2003c. "Underground Feminisms: Inocencia's Story." In *Chicana Feminisms: A Critical Reader*, edited by Gabriela F. Arredondo, Aída Hurtado, Norma Klahn, Olga Nájera-Ramírez, and Patricia Zavella, 260–290. Durham, NC: Duke University Press.

———. 2005. "The Transformative Power of Chicana/o Studies: Social Justice and Education." *International Journal of Qualitative Studies in Education* 18 (2): 185–197.

———. 2009. "'Lifting As We Climb': Educated Chicanas' Social Identities and Commitment to Social Action." In *Mexicans in California: Transformations and Challenges*, edited by Ramón Gutiérrez and Patricia Zavella, 111–129. Berkeley: University of California Press.

———. 2010. "Multiple Lenses: Multicultural Feminist Theory." In *Handbook of Diversity in Feminist Psychology*, edited by Hope Landrine and Nancy Russo, 29–54. New York: Springer Publishing.

———. 2011. "Making Face, Rompiendo Barreras (Breaking Barriers): The Activist Legacy of Gloria E. Anzaldúa." In *Bridging: How and Why Gloria Evangelina Anzaldúa's Life and Work Transformed Our Own*, edited by AnaLouise Keating and Gloria González-López, 49–62. Austin: University of Texas Press.

Hurtado, Aída, and Carlos H. Arce. 1987. "Mexicans, Chicanos, Mexican Americans, or Pochos . . . Qué Somos? The Impact of Language and Nativity on Ethnic Labeling." *Aztlan* 17 (1): 103–130.

Hurtado, Aída, and Karina Cervántez. 2009. "A View from Within and from Without: The Development of Latina Feminist Psychology." In *The Handbook of U.S. Latino Psychology: Developmental and Community-based Perspectives*, edited by Francisco A. Villarruel, Gustavo Carlo, Josefina M. Grau, Margarita Azmitia, Natasha J. Cabrera, and T. Jaime Chahin, 171–190. Thousand Oaks, CA: Sage.

Hurtado, Aída, Karina Cervántez, and Michael Eccleston. 2009. "Infinite Possibilities, Many Remaining Obstacles: Language, Culture, and Identity in Latino/a Educational Achievement." In *The Handbook of Latinos and Education: Theory, Research and Practice*, edited by Enrique G. Murillo, Sofía A. Villenas, Ruth Trinidad Galván, Juan Sánchez Muñoz, Corinne Martínez, and Margarita Machado-Casas, 284–299. New York: Routledge.

Hurtado, Aída, and Patricia Gurin. 1987. "Ethnic Identity and Bilingualism Attitudes." *Hispanic Journal of Behavioral Sciences* 9 (1): 1–18.

———. 2004. *¿Quién Soy? ¿Quienes Somos? (Who Am I? Who Are We?): Chicana/o Identity in a Changing U.S. Society*. Tucson: University of Arizona Press.

Hurtado, Aída, Craig W. Haney, and José G. Hurtado. 2012. "Where the Boys Are: Macro and Micro Considerations for the Study of Young Latino Men's Educational Achievement." In *Invisible No More: Understanding the Disenfranchisement of Latino Men and Boys*, edited by Pedro Noguera, Aída Hurtado, and Edward Fergus, 101–115. New York: Routledge.

Hurtado, Aída, María A. Hurtado, and Arcelia L. Hurtado. 2007. "Tres Hermanas (Three Sisters): A Model of Relational Achievement." In *Doing the Public Good: Latina/o Scholars Engage Civic Participation*, edited by Kenneth P. González and Raymond V. Padilla, 39–58. Sterling, VA: Stylus.

Hurtado, Aída, and Jessica M. Roa. 2005. "Chicana Feminisms." In *New Dictionary of the History of Ideas*, edited by M. Cline Horowitz, 815–817. Charles Scribner's Sons.

Hurtado, Aída, and J. M. Silva. 2008. "Creating New Social Identities in Children through Critical Multicultural Media: The Case of *Little Bill*." *New Directions for Child and Adolescent Development* 120:17–30.

Hurtado, Aída, and Mrinal Sinha. 2005. "Restriction and Freedom in the Construction of Sexuality: Young Chicanas and Chicanos Speak Out." *Feminism & Psychology* 15:33–38.

———. 2006a. "Differences and Similarities: Latina and Latino Doctoral Students Navigating the Gender Divide." In *The Latina/o Pathway to the Ph.D.:*

Abriendo Caminos, edited by Jeanett Castellanos, Alberta M. Gloria, and Mark Kamimura, 149–168. Sterling, VA: Stylus.

———. 2006b. "Social Identity and Gender Consciousness with Latinos." Paper presented at the meeting of the National Association for Chicana and Chicano Studies, Guadalajara, Mexico, June–July.

———. 2008. "More Than Men: Latino Feminist Masculinities and Intersectionality." *Sex Roles* 59 (5–6): 337–349.

Hurtado, Aída, and Abigail J. Stewart. 2004. "Through the Looking Glass: Implications of Studying Whiteness for Feminist Methods." In *Off White: Readings on Power, Privilege, and Resistance*, edited by Michelle Fine, Lois Weis, Linda Powell Pruitt, and April Burns, 315–330. New York: Routledge.

Hurtado, Aída, and Luis Vega. 2004. "Shift Happens: Spanish and English Transmission between Parents and Their Children." *Journal of Social Issues* 60 (1): 137–156.

Jaggar, Allison M. 1983. *Feminist Politics and Human Nature*. Totowa, NJ: Rowman and Allanheld.

Johnson, Allan G. 2005. *The Gender Knot: Unraveling our Patriarchal Legacy*. Philadelphia: Temple University Press.

Kline, Paul. 1994. *An Easy Guide to Factor Analysis*. New York: Routledge.

Kosambi, Meera. 1995. "An Uneasy Intersection: Gender, Ethnicity, and Crosscutting Identities in India." *Social Politics* 2:181–194.

Kranzler, Gerald. 2007. *Statistics for the Terrified*. 4th ed. Upper Saddle River, NJ: Prentice Hall.

Latina Feminist Group. 2001. *Telling to Live: Latina Feminist Testimonios*. Durham, NC: Duke University Press.

Lester, Julius. 1968. *Look Out, Whitey! Black Power's Gon' Get Your Mama*. New York: Grove Press.

Lewin, Kurt. 1948. *Resolving Social Conflicts: Selected Papers on Group Dynamics*. Oxford: Harper.

Lewis, Oscar. 1959. *Five Families: Mexican Case Studies in the Culture of Poverty*. New York: Basic Books.

———. 1961. *The Children of Sanchez: Autobiography of a Mexican Family*. New York: Vintage Books.

Lorde, Audre. 1984. *Sister Outsider: Essays and Speeches*. Trumansburg, NY: Crossing Press.

Lugones, María. 2003. *Pilgrimages/Peregrinajes: Theorizing Coalition against Multiple Oppressions*. New York: Rowman and Littlefield.

MacKinnon, Catherine A. 1982. "Feminism, Marxism, Method, and the State: An Agenda for Theory." *Signs* 7 (3): 515–544.

Madsen, William. 1964. *Mexican-Americans of South Texas*. New York: Holt, Rinehart and Winston.

Majors, Richard, and Janet Mancini Billson. 1992. *Cool Pose: The Dilemmas of Black Manhood in America*. New York: Lexington Books.

Martín-Baró, Ignacio. 1994. *Writings for a Liberation Psychology*. Translated by Adrianne Aron. Cambridge: Harvard University Press.

Martinez, Teresa A. 2005. "Making Oppositional Culture, Making Standpoint: A Journey into Gloria Anzaldúa's Borderlands." *Sociological Spectrum* 25:539–570.

Mason, Karen Oppenheim, and Yu-Hsia Lu. 1988. "Attitudes towards Women's Familial Roles: Changes in the United States, 1977–1985." *Gender and Society* 2 (1): 39–57.

Matsuda, Mari, Charles R. Lawrence III, Richard Delgado, and Kimberlé W. Crenshaw. 1993. *Words That Wound: Critical Race Theory, Assaultive Speech, and the First Amendment.* Boulder, CO: Westview.

Mauer, Marc. 2011. "Addressing Racial Disparities in Incarceration." *The Prison Journal* 91 (3): 87s–101s.

McCall, Leslie. 2005. "The Complexity of Intersectionality." *Signs: Journal of Women and Culture in Society* 30 (3): 1771–1800.

McIntosh, Peggy. 1989. "White Privilege: Unpacking the Invisible Knapsack." *Peace and Freedom* (July–August): 9–10.

Minority Rights Group International. 2005. World Directory of Minorities and Indigenous Peoples: Puerto Rico: Overview. http://www.minorityrights.org /5258/puerto-rico/puerto-rico-overview.html#peoples (accessed July 4, 2015).

Mirandé, Alfredo. 1997. *Hombres y Machos: Masculinity and Latino Culture.* Boulder, CO: Westview.

Moraga, Cherríe. 1981. "La Güera." In *This Bridge Called My Back: Writings by Radical Women of Color,* edited by Cherríe Moraga and Gloria Anzaldúa, 27–34. Watertown, MA: Persephone Press.

———. 2011. *A Xicana Codex of Changing Consciousness: Writings, 2000–2010.* Durham, NC: Duke University Press.

Moraga, Cherríe, and Gloria E. Anzaldúa, eds. 1981. *This Bridge Called My Back: Writings by Radical Women of Color.* Berkeley: Third Woman Press.

———. 1983. 2nd ed. *This Bridge Called My Back: Writings by Radical Women of Color.* New York: Kitchen Table: Women of Color Press.

Morgan, Betsy Levonian. 1996. "Putting the Feminism into Feminism Scales: Introduction of a Liberal Feminist Attitude and Ideology Scale (LFAIS)." *Sex Roles* 34 (5–6): 359–390.

Morse, Janice M., and Lyn Richards. 2002. *README FIRST for a User's Guide to Qualitative Methods.* Thousand Oaks, CA: Sage.

Moynihan, Daniel Patrick. 1965. *The Negro Family: The Case for National Action.* Washington, DC: Office of Policy Planning and Research, US Department of Labor.

Nardi, Peter M., ed. 2000. *Gay Masculinities.* Thousand Oaks, CA: Sage.

Nesiah, Vasuki. 2000. "Toward a Feminist Internationality. A Critique of U.S. Feminist Legal Scholarship." In *Global Critical Race Feminism: An International Reader,* edited by Adrien Katherine Wing, 42–54. New York: New York University Press.

Noguera, Pedro, Aída Hurtado, and Edward Fergus, eds. 2012. *Invisible No More: Understanding the Disenfranchisement of Latino Men and Boys.* New York: Routledge.

Oakes, Jeannie. 1985. *Keeping Track.* New Haven: Yale University Press.

Ochoa, M. 2006. "Queen for a Day: Transformistas, Misses and Mass Media in Venezuela." PhD diss., Stanford University. *Dissertation Abstracts International* 66:11.

Ogletree, Charles. 2012. *The Presumption of Guilt: The Arrest of Henry Louis Gates, Jr. and Race, Class and Crime in America*. New York: Palgrave Macmillan.

Oliver, Melvin L., and David M. Grant. 1995. "Making Space for Multiethnic Coalitions: The Prospects for Coalition Politics in Los Angeles." In *Multiethnic Coalition Building in Los Angeles: A Two-Day Symposium, November 19-29, 1993*, edited by Eui-Young Yu and Edward T. Chang. Claremont, CA: Regina Books for Institute for Asian American and Pacific Asian Studies, California State University.

Ostrander, Susan A. 1984. *Women of the Upper Class*. Philadelphia: Temple University Press.

Panitz, Daniel R., Richard D. McConchie, Richard S. Sauber, and Julio A. Fonseca. 1983. "The Role of Machismo and the Hispanic Family in the Etiology and Treatment of Alcoholism in Hispanic American Males." *American Journal of Family Therapy* 11 (1): 31-44.

Paredes, Américo. 1977. "On Ethnography Work among Minority Groups: A Folklorist's Perspective." *New Scholar* 6:1-32.

Park, Robert Ezra. 1950 (1913). *Race and Culture*. Glencoe, IL: Free Press.

Parry, Glenys. 1983. "A British Version of the Attitudes towards Women Scale (AWS-B)." *British Journal of Social Psychology* 22:261-263.

Payne, Yasser A. 2006. "'A Gangster and a Gentleman': How Street Life-oriented, U.S.-born African Men Negotiate Issues of Survival in Relation to Their Masculinity." *Men and Masculinity* 8 (3): 288-297.

Paz, Octavio. 1961. *The Labyrinth of Solitude: Life and Thought in Mexico*. Translated by Lysander Kemp. New York: Grove.

Pérez, Emma. 1991. "Sexuality and Discourse: Notes from a Chicana Survivor." In *Chicana Lesbians: The Girls Our Mothers Warned Us About*, edited by Carla Trujillo, 159-184. Berkley, CA: Third Woman Press.

———. 1999. *The Decolonial Imaginary: Writing Chicanas into History*. Bloomington: Indiana University Press.

Pesquera, Beatriz M., and Denise A. Segura. 1993. "There Is No Going Back: Chicanas and Feminism." In *Chicana Critical Issues*, edited by Norma Alarcón, Rafaela Castro, Emma Pérez, Beatriz Pesquera, Adaljiza Sosa Riddell, and Patricia Zavella, 95-115. Berkeley, CA: Third Woman Press.

Phinney, Jean S. 1996. "When We Talk about American Ethnic Groups, What Do We Mean?" *American Psychologist* 51:918-927.

Portes, Alejandro, and Raúl Rumbaut. 2006. *Immigrant America: A Portrait*. Berkeley: University of California Press.

Proshansky, Harold, and Peggy Newton. 1973. "Colour: The Nature and Meaning of Negro Self-identity." In *Psychology and Race*, edited by Peter Watson, 176-212. Chicago: Aldine.

Pyke, Karen D. 1996. "Class-based Masculinities: The Interdependence of Gender, Class, and Interpersonal Power." *Gender and Society* 10 (5): 527-549.

Pyke, Karen D., and Denise L. Johnson. 2003. "Asian American Women and Racialized Femininities: 'Doing' Gender across Cultural Worlds." *Gender & Society* 17 (1): 33-53.

Rastogi, Sonya, Tallese D. Johnson, Elizabeth M. Hoeffel, and Malcolm P. Drewery. 2011. *The Black Population: 2010.* Washington, DC: US Department of Commerce, Economics and Statistics Administration, US Census Bureau.

Reicher, Stephen. 1996. "Social Identity and Social Change: Rethinking the Context of Social Psychology." In *Social Groups and Identities: Developing the Legacy of Henri Tajfel,* edited by W. Peter Robinson, 317–336. Oxford: Butterworth-Heinemann.

———. 2004. "The Context of Social Identity: Domination, Resistance, and Change." *Political Psychology* 25 (6): 921–945.

Reicher, Stephen, and Nick Hopkins. 2001. "Psychology and the End of History: A Critique and a Proposal for the Psychology of Social Categorization." *Political Psychology* 22 (2): 383–407.

Rendón, Laura I. 1992. "Eyes on the Prize: Students of Color and the Bachelor's Degree." *Transfer: The National Center for Academic Achievement and Transfer Working Papers* 3 (2): 1–20.

———. 2008. *Sensipensante (Sensing/Thinking) Pedagogy: Educating for Wholeness, Social Justice and Liberation.* Sterling, VA: Stylus.

Renzetti, Claire M. 1987. "New Wave or Second Stage? Attitudes of College Women toward Feminism." *Sex Roles* 16 (5–6): 265–277.

Ríos, Victor M. 2011. *Punished: Policing the Lives of Black and Latino Boys.* New York: New York University Press.

Roa, Jessica. 2003. "Multicultural Feminisms: Coalitions between Young Chicana and White Women." Paper presented at the meetings of the National Association of Chicana/Chicano Studies, Los Angeles, April 2–6.

Roberts, Rosemarie A. 2005. "Radical Movements: Katherine Dunham and Ronald K. Brown Teaching toward Critical Consciousness." PhD diss., City University of New York. *Dissertation Abstracts International* 65.12-B: 6710.

Roque Ramírez, Horacio N. 2003. "That's *My* Place! Negotiating Racial, Sexual, and Gender Politics in San Francisco's Gay Latino Alliance, 1975–1983." *Journal of History of Sexuality* 12 (2): 224–258.

———. 2007. "'Mira Yo Soy Boricua y Estoy Aquí!' Rafa Negrón's Pan Dulce and the Queer Sonic Latinaje of San Francisco." *CENTRO: Journal for the Center of Puerto Rican Studies* 19 (1): 274–313.

Rowe, Aimee Carrillo. 2005. "Be Longing: Toward a Feminist Politics of Relation." *NWSA Journal* 17 (2): 15–46.

Rubin, Lisa R., Carol J. Nemeroff, and Nancy F. Russo. 2004. "Exploring Feminist Women's Body Consciousness." *Psychology of Women Quarterly* 28:27–37.

Russo, Nancy Felipe, and Kim Vaz. 2001. "Addressing Diversity in the Decade of Behavior: Focus on Women of Color." *Psychology of Women Quarterly* 25 (4): 280–294.

Sáenz, Victor B., and Luis Ponjuan. 2009. "The Vanishing Latino Male in Higher Education." *Journal of Hispanic Higher Education* 8 (1): 54–89.

Saldívar-Hull, Sonia. 2000. *Feminism on the Border: Chicana Gender Politics and Literature.* Berkeley: University of California Press.

Sandoval, Chela. 1991. "U.S. Third World Feminism: The Theory and Method of Oppositional Consciousness in the Postmodern World." *Genders* 10:1–24.

———. 2000. *Methodology of the Oppressed.* Minneapolis: University of Minnesota Press.

Schaeffer-Gabriel, Felicity. 2005. "Planet-Love.com: Cyberbrides in the Americas and the Transnational Routes of U.S. Masculinity." *Signs: Journal of Women in Culture and Society* 32 (2): 331–356.

Schmitt, John, Kris Warner, and Sarika Gupta. 2010. "The High Budgetary Cost of Incarceration." Washington, DC: Center for Economic and Policy Research.

Schott Foundation. 2012. "The Urgency of Now: The Schott 50 State Report on Black Males and Public Education." http://www.schottfoundation.org/publi cations-reports.

Sibley, David. 1995. *Geographies of Exclusion: Society and Difference in the West.* New York: Routledge.

Sinha, Mrinal. 2003. "Chicano Masculinities: Young Men and Feminism." Paper presented at the meeting of the National Association of Chicana/Chicano Studies, Los Angeles, April 2–6.

———. 2007. "Intersecting Social Identities: The (Feminist) Standpoint(s) of Latino Men." PhD diss., University of California, Santa Cruz. *Dissertation Abstracts International* 68:8.

Skemp, Richard R. 1978. "Relational Understanding and Instrumental Understanding." *Arithmetic Teacher* 26 (3): 9–15.

Small, Mario Luis, David J. Harding, and Michele Lamont. 2010. "Reconsidering Culture and Poverty." *Annals of the American Academy of Political and Social Science* 629:6–27.

Stanton, Elizabeth Cady, Susan B. Anthony, and Matilda Joslyn Gage, eds. 1889. *History of Woman Suffrage.* 2nd ed. Rochester, NY: Charles Mann.

Stevens, James P. 2002. *Applied Multivariate Statistics for the Social Sciences.* 4th ed. Mahwah, NJ: Lawrence Erlbaum.

Stewart, Abigail J., and Christa McDermott. 2004. "Gender in Psychology." *Annual Review of Psychology* 55:519–544.

Stewart, Abigail, and Mary Romero, eds. 1999. *Women's Untold Stories: Breaking Silence, Talking Back, Voicing Complexity.* New York: Routledge.

Stoetzler, Marcel, and Nira Yuval-Davis. 2002. "Standpoint Theory, Situated Knowledge and the Situated Imagination." *Feminist Theory* 3 (3): 315–333.

Strong, W. F., Jeffrey S. McQuillen, and James D. Hughey. 1994. "*En el Laberinto de Machismo*: A Comparative Analysis of Macho Attitudes among Hispanic and Anglo College Students." *Howard Journal of Communications* 5 (1–2): 18–35.

Tabachnik, Barbara G., and Linda S. Fidell. 1996. *Using Multivariate Statistics.* 3rd ed. New York: HarperCollins College.

Tajfel, Henri. 1972. "Social Categorization." Translation of "La Catégorisation Sociale." In *Introduction à la Psychologie Sociale*, vol. 1, edited by S. Moscovici, 272–302. Paris: Larousse.

———. 1981. *Human Groups and Social Categories: Studies in Social Psychology.* New York: Cambridge University Press.

Tanesini, Alessandra. 1999. *An Introduction to Feminist Epistemologies.* Malden, MA: Blackwell.

Tombs, David. 2002. "Honor, Shame, and Conquest: Male Identity, Sexual Violence, and the Body Politic." *Journal of Hispanic/Latino Theology* 9 (4): 21–40.

Torres, Mellie. 2009. "From the Bricks to the Hall." *Harvard Educational Review* 79 (4): 594–601.

Trujillo, Carla M., ed. 1991. *Chicana Lesbians: The Girls Our Mothers Warned Us About*. Berkeley, CA: Third Woman.

——, ed. 1998. *Living Chicana Theory*. Berkeley, CA: Third Woman.

Turner, John C., and Rina S. Onorato. 1999. "Social Identity, Personality, and the Self-Concept: A Self-Categorization Perspective." In *The Psychology of the Social Self*, edited by Tom R. Tyler, Roderick M. Kramer, and Oliver P. John, 11–46. Mahwah, NJ: Lawrence Erlbaum.

Twenge, Jean M. 1997. "Attitudes toward Women, 1970–1995: A Meta-Analysis." *Psychology of Women Quarterly* 21 (1): 35–51.

Valenzuela, Angela. 1999. "'Checking Up on My Guy': High School Chicanas, Social Capital, and the Culture of Romance." Special issue, "Educated Latinas Leading America," *Frontiers: A Journal of Women Studies*, 20 (1): 60–79.

Vásquez, Melba J. 2002. "Complexities of the Latina Experience: A Tribute to Martha Bernal." *American Psychologist* 57:880–888.

——. 2003. "*Troxel v. Granville*: Impact on Ethnic Minority Families." *Family Court Review* 41 (1): 54–59.

——. 2006. "Counseling Men: Perspectives and Experiences of a Woman of Color." In *In the Room with Men: A Casebook of Therapeutic Change*, edited by Matt Englar-Carlson and Mark A. Stevens, 241–255. Washington, DC: American Psychological Association.

Vicario, Brett Anthony. 2003. "A Qualitative Study of Profeminist Men." PhD diss., Auburn University. *Dissertation Abstracts International* 64:11.

Wacquant, Loïc. 2001. "Deadly Symbiosis: When Ghetto and Prison Meet and Mesh." *Punishment and Society* 3 (1): 95–134.

Ward, Janie Victoria. 1996. "Raising Resisters: The Role of Truth Telling in the Psychological Development of African-American Girls." In *Urban Girls: Resisting Stereotypes, Creating Identities*, edited by Bonnie J. Ross Leadbeater and Niobe Way, 85–99. New York: New York University Press.

Washington, Jesse. 2010. "Blacks Struggle with 72 Percent Unwed Mothers Rate: Debate Growing in and Outside the Black Community on How to Address the Rising Issue." NBCNews.com. November 7. http://www.nbcnews.com/id/39993685/ns/#.UnPK2xY2_zI.

Weis, Lois, Craig Centrie, Juan Valentín-Juarbe, and Michelle Fine. 2002. "Puerto Rican Men and the Struggle for Place in the United States: An Exploration of Cultural Citizenship, Gender, and Violence." *Men and Masculinities* 4:286–302.

West, Heather C., William J. Sabol, and Sarah J. Greenman. 2010. *Bureau of Justice Statistics: Prisoners in 2009*. Washington, DC: US Department of Justice, NCJ231675.

White, Aaronette M. 2007. "All the Men Are Fighting for Freedom, All the Women Are Mourning Their Men, but Some of Us Carried Guns: A Raced-gendered Analysis of Fanon's Psychological Perspectives on War." *Signs* 32 (4): 857–884.

——. 2008. *Ain't I a Feminist? African American Men Speak Out on Fatherhood, Friendship, Forgiveness, and Freedom*. Albany: State University of New York Press.

Wilson, Julee. 2013. "Black College Student Arrested for Buying a Designer Belt, Barneys & NYPD Slapped with Lawsuit." *Huffington Post*, October 23. http://www.huffingtonpost.com/2013/10/23/trayon-christian-lawsuit-barneys-new-york-nypd_n_4148490.html.

Yosso, Tara, William Smith, Miguel Ceja, and Daniel Solórzano. 2009. "Critical Race Theory, Racial Microaggressions, and Campus Racial Climate for Latina/o Undergraduates." *Harvard Educational Review* 79 (4): 659–690.

Zambrana, Ruth E. 2011. *Latinos in American Society: Families and Communities in Transition*. Ithaca, NY: Cornell University Press.

Zavella, Patricia. 2003. "Talk'n Sex: Chicanas and Mexicanas Theorize about Silences and Sexual Pleasures." In *Chicana Feminisms: A Critical Reader*, edited by Gabriela Arredondo, Aída Hurtado, Norma Klahn, Olga Nájera-Ramírez, and Patricia Zavella, 228–253. Durham, NC: Duke University Press.

———. 2011. *I'm Neither Here nor There: Mexicans' Quotidian Struggles with Migration and Poverty*. Durham, NC: Duke University Press.

Zavella, Patricia, and Xóchitl Castañeda. 2005. "Sexuality and Risks: Gendered Discourses about Virginity and Disease among Young Women of Mexican Origin." *Journal of Latino Studies* 3 (2): 226–245.

Index